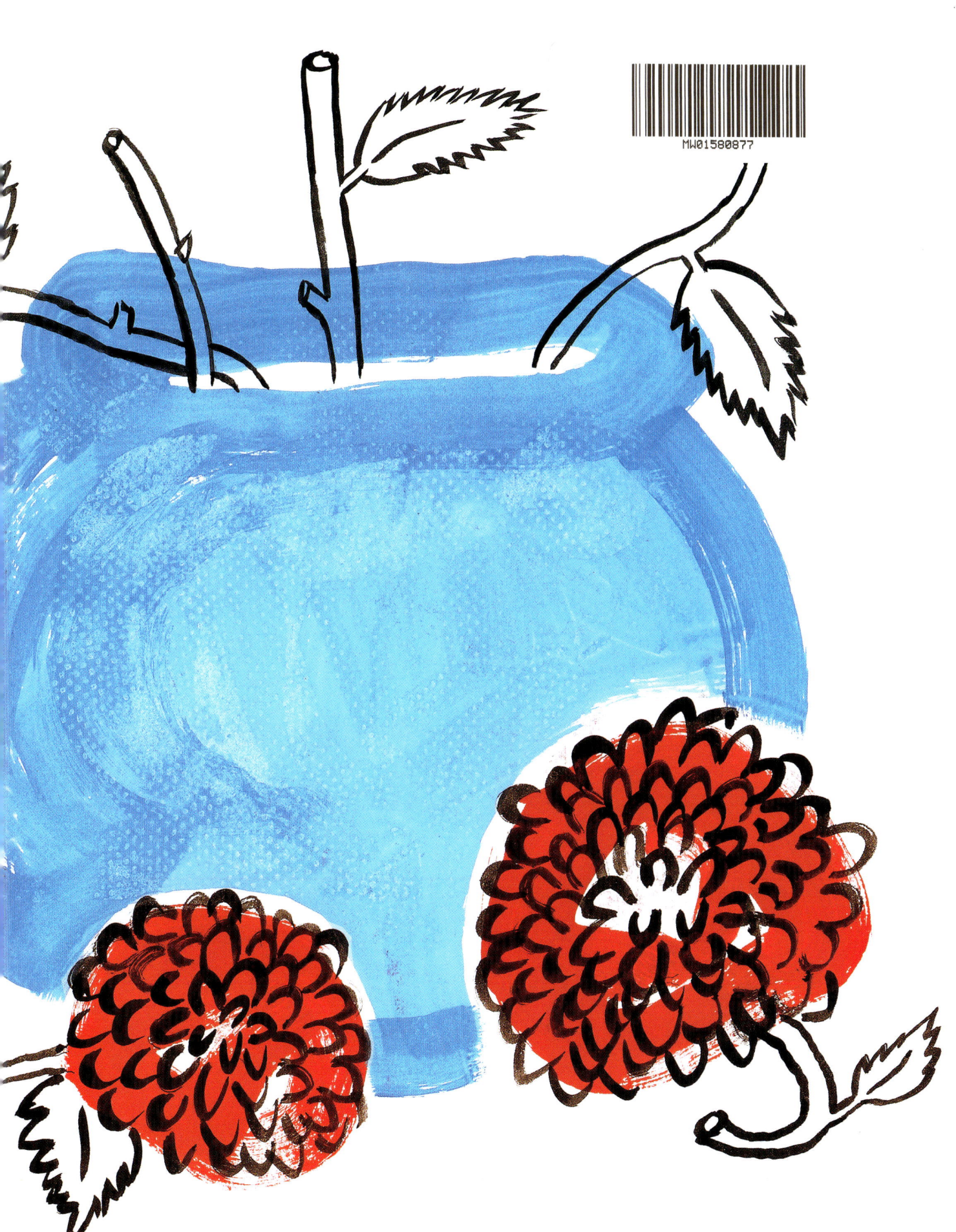

Signature*Flowers*

Victoria Leacock

Signature

BROADWAY BOOKS | MELCHER MEDIA
NEW YORK

Flowers

a Revealing Collection *of* Celebrity Drawings

foreword by Molly Ringwald
introduction by George Plimpton
text by Victoria Leacock
with Justin Bond

This book was produced by Melcher Media, Inc.
131 Varick Street, Suite 913, New York, NY 10013
Under the editorial direction of Charles Melcher.

Editor: Gillian Casey Sowell
Production Director: Andrea Hirsh
Designer: Pentagram Design, Inc.
Artwork photographer: Oi-Cheong Lee

Special thanks to: Joel Avirom, Tracy Behar, Duncan Bock, Angela Casey, Esther Chak, Sha-Mayne Chan, Elaine Chang, Roberto de Vicq de Cumptich, Tony Davis, Emily Donaldson, Avital Fryman, Kate Giel, Rebecca Holland, Wendy Kagan, Jang Kim, Orville Kiser, John Klotnia, Philomena Mariani, Matthew Martin, Rachel Rusch, Trigg Robinson, Abie Safdie, Hyewon Shin, Bill Shinker, Greg Simpson, Debbie Stier, and Megan Worman.

Thirty percent of the author's proceeds from the sale of this book will be donated to Love Heals, the Alison Gertz Foundation for AIDS Education, and to the American Foundation for AIDS Research (AmFAR).

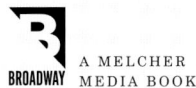 A MELCHER MEDIA BOOK

SIGNATURE FLOWERS. Compilation copyright © 1998 by Melcher Media, Inc., and Victoria Leacock. Foreword copyright © 1998 by Molly Ringwald. Introduction copyright © 1998 by George Plimpton. All other text copyright © 1998 by Victoria Leacock. Artwork on front endpaper copyright © 1988 by The Estate of Keith Haring. Artwork on page 30 copyright © 1982 by David Hockney. Artwork on page 55 copyright © 1998 by Shawn Colvin. Artwork on page 59 copyright © 1984 by The Estate of Keith Haring. Copyright in the individual artworks remains with the artists. All rights reserved. Printed in Hong Kong by Midas Printing Ltd. No part of this book may be reproduced or transmitted in any form or by any means, electronic or mechanical, including photocopying, recording, or by any information storage and retrieval system, without written permission from the publisher. For information, address Broadway Books, a division of Bantam Doubleday Dell Publishing Group, Inc., 1540 Broadway, New York, NY 10036.

Artwork on page 57 appears courtesy of the heirs of Ginger Rogers, represented by The Roger Richman Agency, Inc., Beverly Hills, CA. Photographs on page 13: Victoria Leacock and Andy Warhol courtesy Victoria Leacock; Richard Leacock courtesy Robert Haller; Marilyn West courtesy David Vestal. Photographs on page 23 courtesy Eric Bogosian. Author photograph on page 128 courtesy Douglas Levere.

Broadway Books titles may be purchased for business or promotional use or for special sales. For information, please write to: Special Markets Department, Bantam Doubleday Dell Publishing Group, Inc., 1540 Broadway, New York, NY 10036.

BROADWAY BOOKS and its logo, a letter B bisected on the diagonal, are trademarks of Broadway Books, a division of Bantam Doubleday Dell Publishing Group, Inc.

Library of Congress Cataloging-in-Publication Data is available.

ISBN 0-7679-0293-9

FIRST EDITION

98 99 00 01 02 10 9 8 7 6 5 4 3 2 1

Front endpaper: Keith Haring, 1988
Back endpaper: Francesco Clemente, 1990

THIS BOOK IS DEDICATED with love and affection to the memory of Andy Warhol and my mom, who planted the seeds that made this book blossom, and in tribute to Alison Gertz, Jonathan Larson, Gordon Rogers, and Pamela Shaw, who will remain in my heart forever.

CONTENTS

8 Foreword *by* Molly Ringwald

15 Andy Warhol	32 Barbara Walters	49 Angela Lansbury
16 John Shea	33 Gus Van Sant	49 Tatum O'Neal
17 Dennis Hopper	34 Rex Smith	50 Ross Bleckner
18 Robert De Niro	35 *Flower Story:* Tony Awards	51 Diane Keaton
19 Cindy Sherman	36 Francis Ford Coppola	52 Peter Greenaway
20 Alexander S. C. Rower	37 Stephen Sprouse	54 Paul Shaffer
21 Robert Altman	38 Mark Kostabi	55 Shawn Colvin
22 Cynthia Gibb	39 Elizabeth Taylor	56 RuPaul
23 Eric Bogosian	40 Sarah McLachlan	57 Ginger Rogers
24 Ramones	41 Molly Ringwald	58 *Flower Story:* Keith Haring
25 *Flower Story:* Ramones	42 Richard Leacock	59 Keith Haring
26 Jann Wenner	43 *Flower Story:* Richard Leacock	60 John Huston
27 Richard Gere	44 Justin Bond	61 Anjelica Huston
28 Peter Riegert	45 Mike Newell	62 Leslie Caron
29 Mary McCormack	46 Danny DeVito	63 Madonna
30 David Hockney	47 Bette Midler	64 Martin Charnin
31 Richard Linklater	48 James Haygood	65 Celine Dion
32 Dick Clark	49 Lauren Bacall	66 Spalding Gray
32 Walter Cronkite	49 Deborah Harry	68 Lili Taylor
32 Rex Reed		69 Patrick Stewart

10 Introduction *by George Plimpton* **12** The First Flower

70 Susan Saint James	88 Roland Topor	105 Joseph Papp
71 Alex Tavoularis	89 Steve Rubell	105 Liz Smith
72 Jon Robin Baitz	90 Milos Forman	106 Cindy Crawford
72 Joan Didion	91 *Flower Story:* Milos Forman	107 Betty Buckley
72 Bret Easton Ellis	92 Jules Fisher	108 *Flower Story:*
72 Jay McInerney	93 Richard Avedon	Leonardo DiCaprio
73 Norman Mailer	94 Paul Newman	109 Leonardo DiCaprio
74 George Plimpton	95 Liza Minnelli	110 John Cage
76 Martin Scorsese	96 Campbell Scott	111 Merce Cunningham
77 *Flower Story:*	97 Geraldine Page	112 Gina Gershon
Martin Scorsese	98 *Flower Story:*	113 Princess Grace of Monaco
78 Martin Scorsese	Jonathan Larson	114 Alison Gertz
80 Elliott Gould	99 Jonathan Larson	115 *Flower Story:* Alison Gertz
81 Mark Romanek	100 Penelope Ann Miller	116 Andy Warhol
82 Hilary Knight	101 Michael Bay	117 Victoria Leacock
83 Lena Horne	102 Viva	118 Biographies
84 Maxene Andrews	103 Richard E. Grant	128 Acknowledgments
85 Bill Plympton	104 Rufus Sewell	*Endpapers:*
86 Jean Pierre Jeunet	105 Bill Boggs	Front Keith Haring
87 Ben Stiller	105 Connie Chung	Back Francesco Clemente

MOLLY RINGWALD | *Foreword*

It's been said that we all have two families: the one we're born with and the one we choose. With relatives, you're either lucky or you're not. With friends, you can only hope that you've been prepared to choose well; of course, there's an element of fate, too. Not everyone can boast of having a friend like Victoria Leacock in their life, but I can. She is my second family. It was in New York City in 1991. I had just portrayed Alison Gertz in a movie based on her life and her courageous fight against AIDS, and Ali and I were promoting the film together. After all the press was done, we went back to her apartment so I could meet her closest female friends, including Victoria, for lunch. It was very chatty, gossipy, and hilarious—and difficult to believe that one day Ali might not be there.

VICTORIA AND I got along instantly—"I love your headband!" "Oh, thanks! Where'd you get that lipstick?"—but it wasn't until months later that we really got to know each other. I was back in New York for an AIDS benefit that Victoria had helped arrange, and we went to see Ali together. The disease had clearly taken its toll; Ali had retreated into a fantasy world. She was calling herself the Queen of America, her friend Dini, her lady-in-waiting, and Victoria, a saint. We were trying to follow her train of thought and to stay upbeat when Ali made an announcement: She wanted to read us her last will and testament. We did as the good queen ordered—we sat and listened. I believe Victoria and I held hands.

ON THAT SAD day our friendship was cemented, and a tacit agreement made—we would be there for each other no matter what. And we have been. Victoria was there to comfort me after I broke up with my boyfriend (false alarm), and I was there to take her to the memorial of another close friend, Jonathan Larson. We've had glorious times, too. In Paris, eating third helpings of her father Ricky

Leacock's famous osso buco (okay, that was me, not Victoria); and in Barbados, flirting with all the boys at New Year's (Victoria, not me). I acted in her first short film, and she willingly offered to be an extra in one of mine. Picture the scene: a border-town location, sweltering heat. In take after take, a bus pulls away from the dusty roadhouse. On it are ten Mexican farmworkers and one city girl with a flower book tucked under her arm—Victoria. Her sense of adventure is unparalleled.

SHE REALLY IS Eloise—the effusive girl who lives in the Plaza Hotel, from the book by Kay Thompson and illustrator Hilary Knight—with a pinch of Holly Golightly thrown in for good measure. Who else but Eloise could possibly collect all of these signature flowers, or even have the whimsy to think of it? Victoria had the idea when she was a girl, and more impressively, the dedication to follow through with it over the years. Like Eloise, she has been in the right place at the right time, or she's been in the wrong place and just made it right. Her powers of persuasion are not to be believed, and there is no place she hasn't considered to be splendid for flower hunting.

VICTORIA'S JOY AT acquiring new flowers is infectious. It was cause for major celebration when Hilary Knight presented her with an Eloise flower, and again when Milos Forman finally sent his drawing, after having held on to the book for three months. What's particularly amazing is everything that Victoria sees in the flowers. Each flower to her is special and steeped with meaning. This is really her garden that she has carefully tended, cultivated, and loved. Happily for the rest of the world, she's letting us in on her secret.

I AM GLAD and eternally grateful to be able to count her as a friend—and as family.

—Molly Ringwald, *New York City, 1998*

GEORGE PLIMPTON | *Introduction*

I wish I'd thought of this as a boy writing away for autographs—asking for something more than a mere scribble. I'm not sure what would have come back if I'd asked for a flower. Probably nothing, since I was writing to baseball players. I'm not sure I would have had the courage to ask for such a thing: "Dear Lou Gehrig, You're my favorite player. I've always wanted to play first base for the New York Yankees. Could you please draw me a flower?" Doesn't sound right. On the other hand, perhaps they would have jumped at the chance to do something more with the pen than what they'd done thousands of times before. Imagine the value of a flower, say, wrought by Babe Ruth, or Joe DiMaggio—surely the prize of one's collection. Indeed I know of athletes' autographs that suggest they are trying to break out of the mold—in particular Lynn Swann's autograph . . . a great whorl of lines by the great Pittsburgh Steelers' receiver from which, miraculously, the outlines emerge not only of his name but a swan. A true work of art!

SOME YEARS AGO, eons since those boyhood enthusiasms about autographs, I became interested in the actual act of writing one's name on a piece of paper, how long it took to do, and how fortunate celebrities were who had short names. Mel Ott, for example, from my era of baseball fanaticism. Or more recently, Pete Rose. Or from other fields, Cher or Madonna. Compare the ease with which these fortunates can get through a line of fans at autograph tables—a slight flourish of the pen! Imagine, in a similar situation, Arnold Schwarzenegger, and how he must envy Oscar Robertson, the Hall of Fame basketball player known as the "Big O" and who signed his name exactly that way: "O."

I ONCE WROTE Sudahuru Oh, the Japanese Babe Ruth, for his autograph, thinking that perhaps the character for Oh would be even shorter than "O" or at least a close second. I was startled on receipt of his autograph to discover that it ran down the length of the page. Apparently Oh is uncommonly common and has to be qualified by a given name—much as one would be disappointed if Chipper Jones, the Atlanta Braves' baseball star, didn't write Chipper at the autograph table and left the collector to stare moodily at "Jones."

ARTISTS, AS ONE would expect, often add a sketch alongside their names, at least if they're of the old school and can draw. Some years ago the *Paris Review* published a portfolio of drawings from the Livres d'Or, large leather-bound books kept by many Paris restaurants and bar owners in which their guests, especially if well known, are asked to inscribe their names and if possible a sentiment or two in praise of the food and drink. The portfolio included sketches by Picasso, Matisse, Derain, Steinberg, Vertès, Cocteau, Dufy, and an extraordinary sketch of a pair of horses by Toulouse-Lautrec. Nonartists also did sketches for the Livres d'Or—Charlie Chaplin (an apt drawing of Charlot with cane) and Jacques Tati (also a self-portrait) among them.

AS FOR LETTER writers who append what the autograph profession refers to as a "device" to their signature, the list is long. Francis Poulenc, one of "Les Six" group of composers, often drew a little "pin" sketch of himself at the piano. Ezra Pound occasionally drew the "Ez" letters of his given name in the form of a face. Beatrix Potter drew sketches above her signature—rabbits from her Peter Rabbit classics. Jean Cocteau added stars to his. Caruso did self-portraits. Perhaps the most famous of "device" signatures is that of James McNeill Whistler, who often signed his letters (and invariably his paintings) with a butterfly.

VICTORIA IS NOT the first to put together a collection of autographs based on a single theme. Often what is asked for is rather quirky: at the turn of the century a curious fad was to ask friends and celebrated people for drawings of pigs, which they were asked to sketch while blindfolded. More recently, Brigid Berlin of Andy Warhol's Factory put together a book of the outlines of as many male genitalia as their various owners would permit to be traced. Hardly a coffee-table book! How fortuitous that Andy Warhol drew a flower to get Victoria started on her splendid enterprise.

—George Plimpton, *New York City, 1998*

THE FIRST FLOWER

As a present for my thirteenth birthday, my mother gave me a ticket to the premiere screening of Martin Scorsese's *New York, New York* at Lincoln Center. There I was, dressed in one of my mom's most beautiful party dresses, feeling grown-up for the first time in my life, when in walked Robert De Niro and Liza Minnelli. I was overwhelmed by the glamour, the beauty, and the excitement. I've been starstruck ever since.

SOME PEOPLE ARE raised in a family of doctors or lawyers and, in due course, find themselves in the family business. My father, Richard Leacock, is a filmmaker and my mother, Marilyn West, was a fashion model, writer, and painter, so my fascination with writers, artists, and directors seems almost preordained. I was born to it.

IN CHICAGO IN 1942, at the age of fourteen, my mother sat through six consecutive performances of the Andrews Sisters. She sat in the same seat in the front row every night. When a messenger was sent to ask if the sisters could do anything for her, Mom said that she'd love to meet them backstage—a wink during the show would let her know it was okay. Maxene Andrews winked, Mom went backstage, and a great friendship was begun. Maxene brought my mother to California and arranged for her to meet the right people to begin a modeling career. Years later Maxene became my godmother.

BY THE TIME I was twelve my mother was bedridden with rheumatoid arthritis. I became her only connection to the outside world. After *New York, New York* I began going to more and more parties and special events, always returning home to regale my mother with tales of that evening's adventures.

IN 1977 I was back at Lincoln Center for a tribute to director George Cukor. At the party afterward, I was on line for the buffet when a young reporter mistook me for Bianca Jagger. I was amazed. The wife of Mick Jagger was dark and exotic looking. I was a fourteen-year-old with freckles and a ponytail. An older man with pale skin and a shock of silver hair standing next to me intervened, explaining that I was not Bianca. As the reporter walked away, the older man

(opposite top) Andy Warhol and Victoria Leacock, 1980.
(opposite bottom) Victoria's parents, Richard Leacock, 1973, and Marilyn West, 1954.

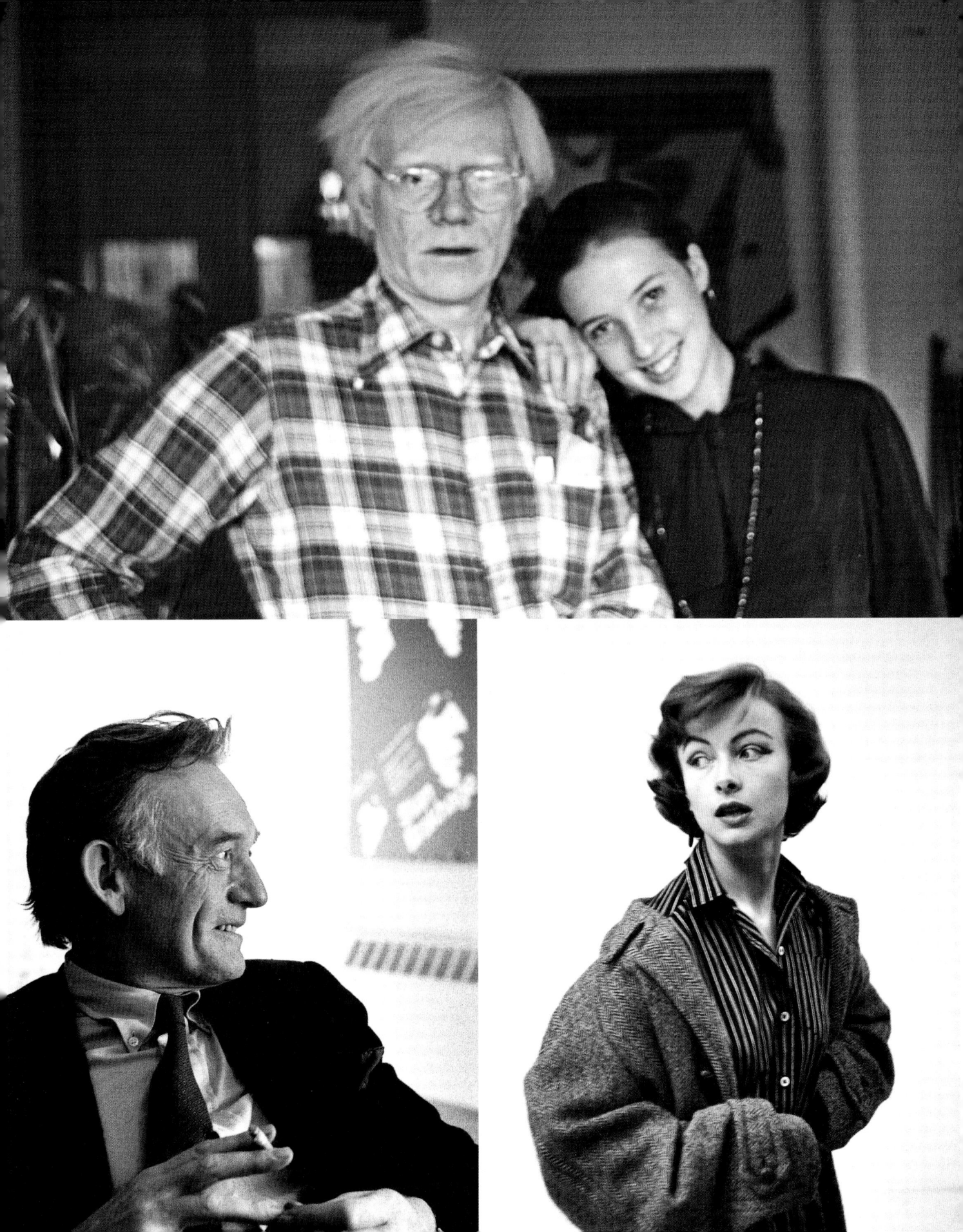

looked me over and we both started laughing. It was Andy Warhol. We chatted, and as we reached the desserts, he invited me to visit him at his studio, the Factory.

BEGINNING THAT WEEK, I went to see Andy every Friday after school. As he signed hundreds of silkscreens or arranged images on the floor, I would share my worries about an impending math test or gush about the boy I liked in English class. If I got there early enough I would be invited for lunch. Andy gave me sound advice about fashion, including the timeless, "Never wear a shoelace as a headband." He listened with interest to my adventures and even set me up on a blind date. And then there was that stark summer day when I came to tell him that my mother had died and he held me in his arms.

MY MOTHER HAD encouraged my friendship with Andy, and it was she who suggested I ask him to draw a picture for me. Now, I felt awkward about this. Andy was a famous artist and asking him to draw a picture was asking for something of value. But I did like the idea of having a drawing from him. In July 1979 I asked Andy if he would make the first entry in my Flower Autograph Book. He drew a simple black rose on the first page of a brown, hardcover sketchbook. Andy loved the idea and made me promise to show him the flowers as I gathered them. With each new drawing I brought the book to show Andy. When the first book was full, he inaugurated the second book, then the third, and finally the fourth. The last time I saw Andy we were at a screening. He invited me to join him on line at the concession stand and bought me popcorn. While we waited he had me tell his friend about the flower books. I kissed him goodbye and told him that I loved him. He died three weeks later.

SO MUCH HAS changed since that first night at Lincoln Center. Many of the people in this book are gone. Some have become friends. As I've grown older, I've put less and less time into collecting these flowers and placed more energy into my own career as a filmmaker and writer. I'm so proud and honored that all of the contributors were generous and gracious enough to share their time and talents with me. Like any garden, this one has been well tended with hard work, some disappointment, and a lot of love. It holds many memories for me. One thing, though, is certain: These flowers are perennials—they will live forever.

—Victoria Leacock, *New York City, 1998*

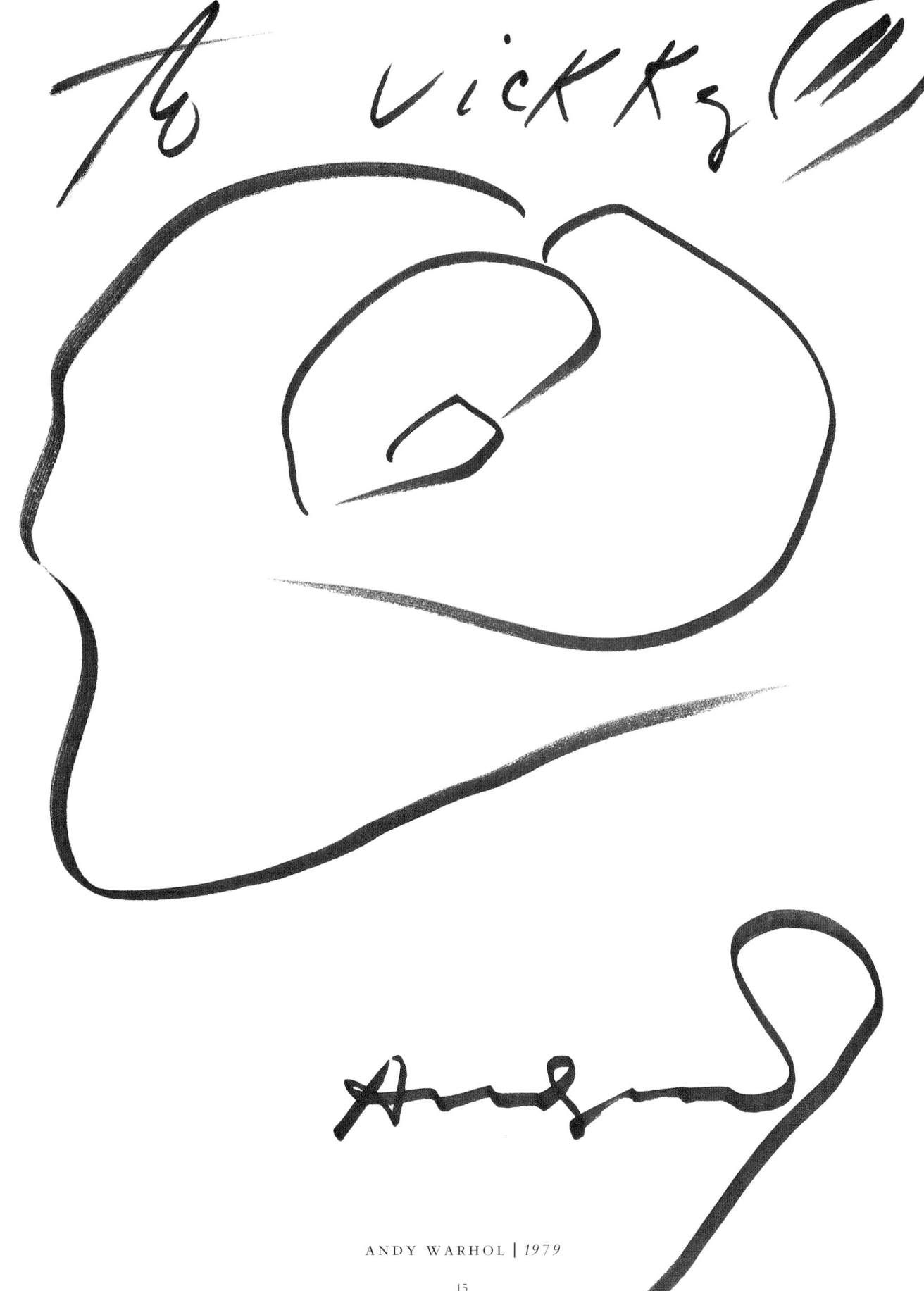

ANDY WARHOL | *1979*

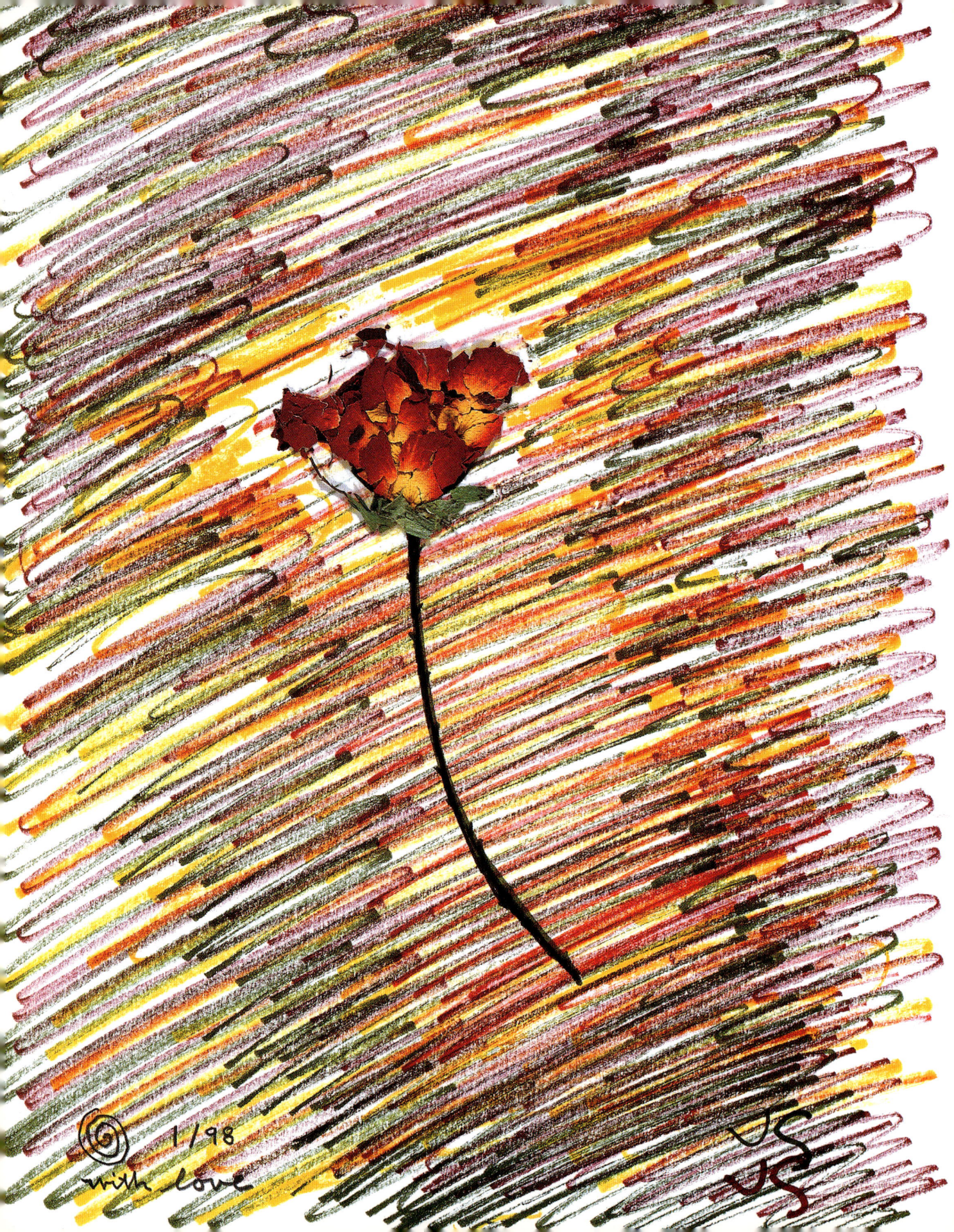

DENNIS HOPPER | *1988*
JOHN SHEA | *1998 (facing)*

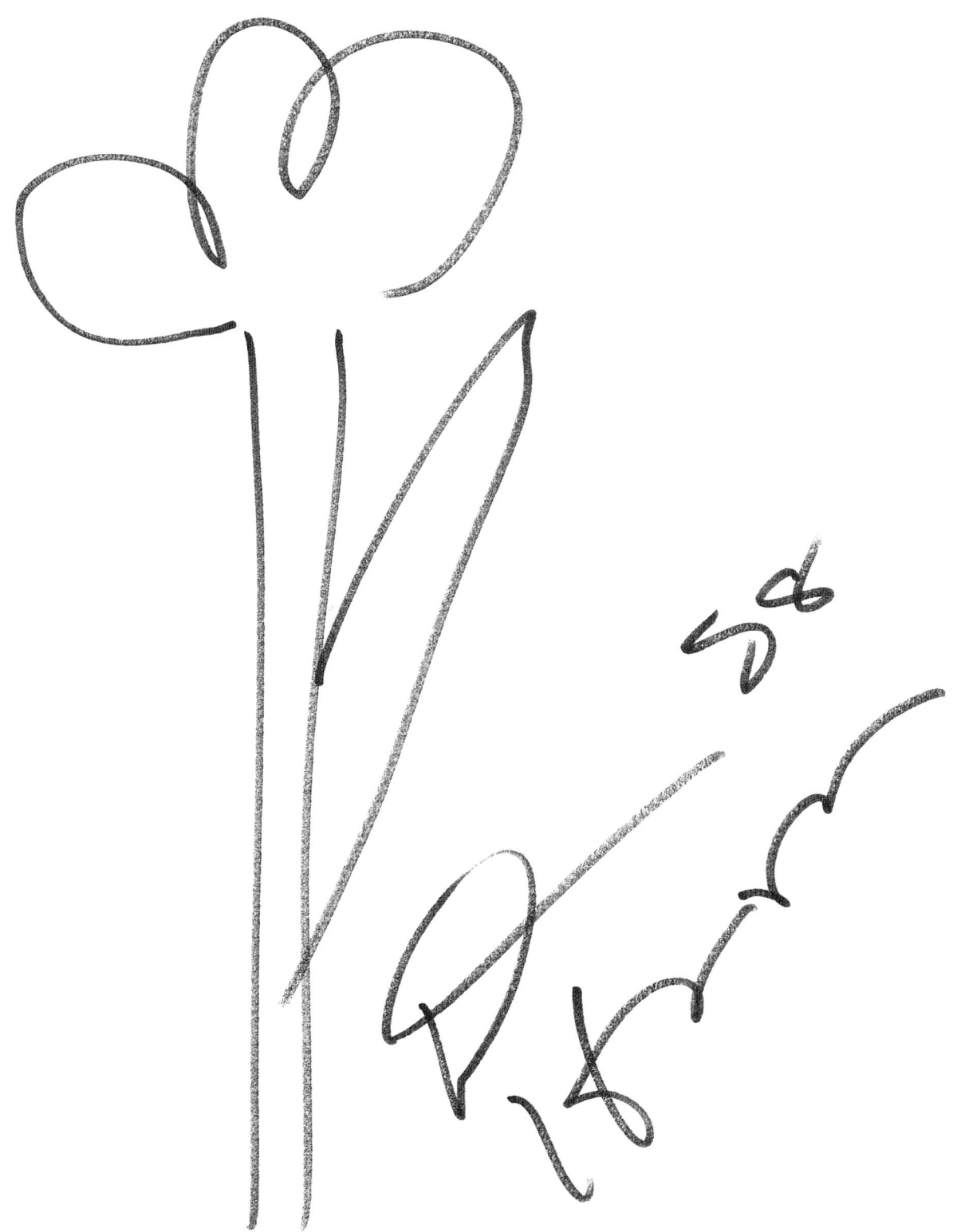

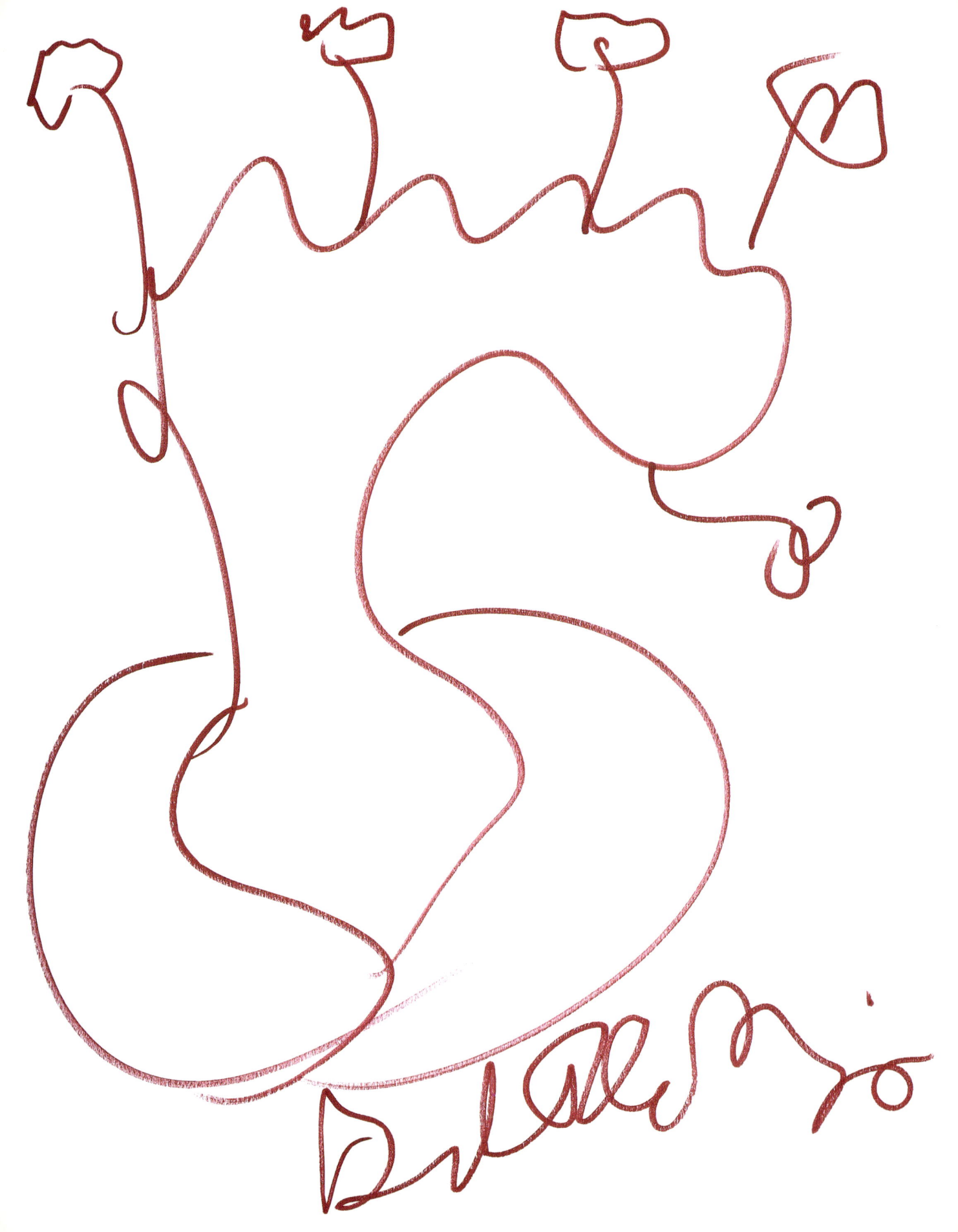

CINDY SHERMAN | *1996*
ROBERT DE NIRO | *1989 (facing)*

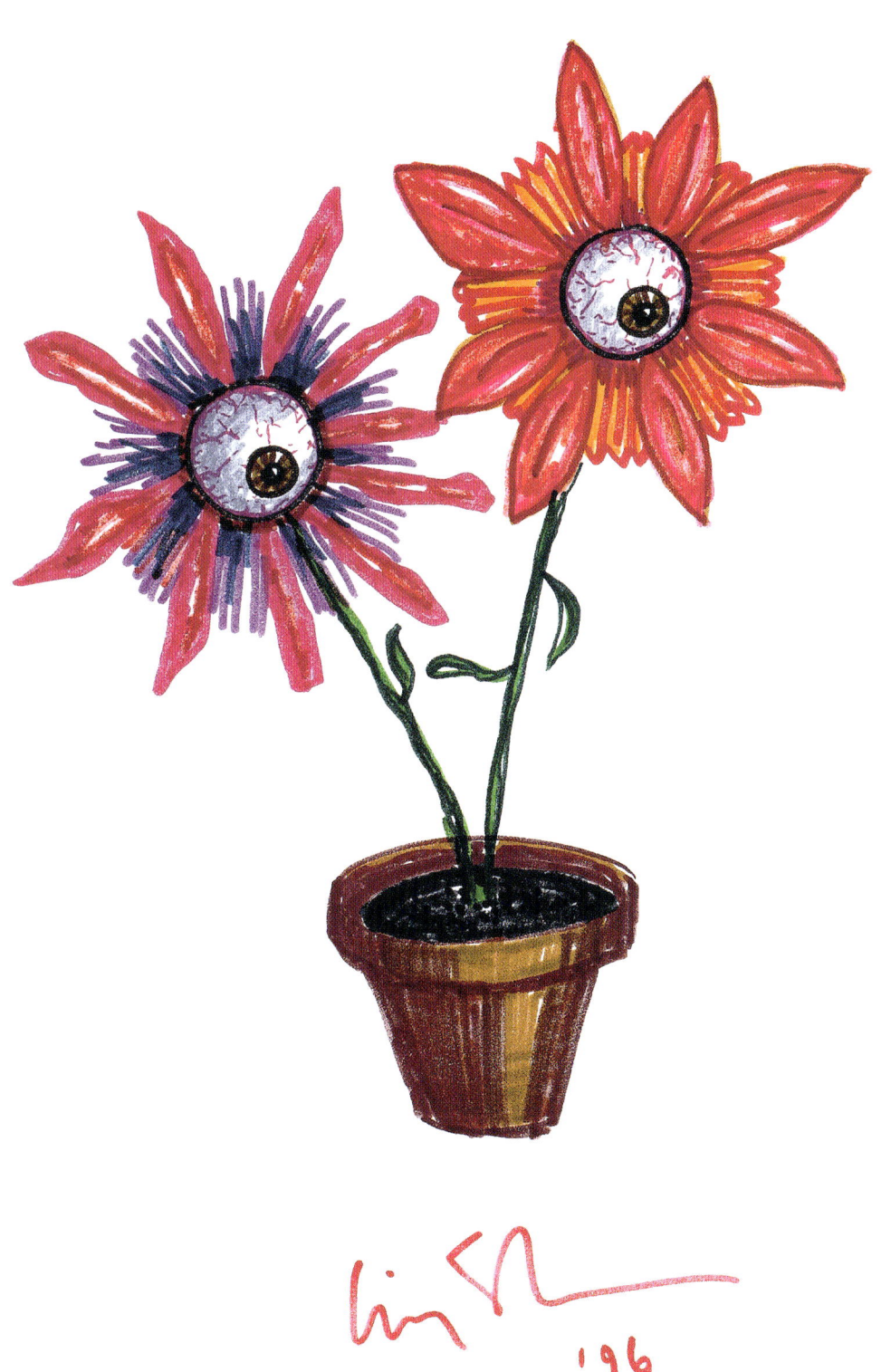

ALEXANDER STERLING CALDER ROWER | *1987*

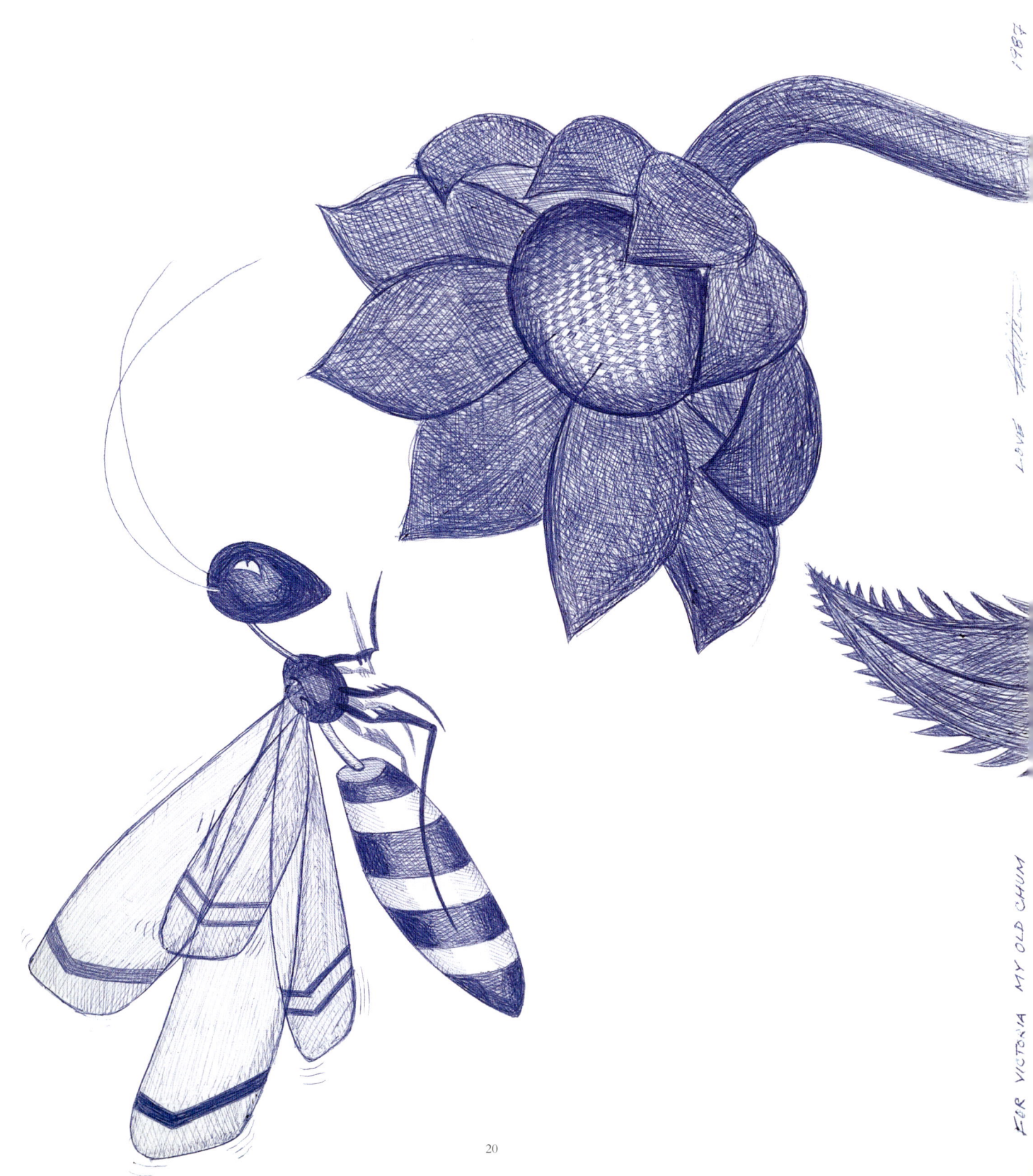

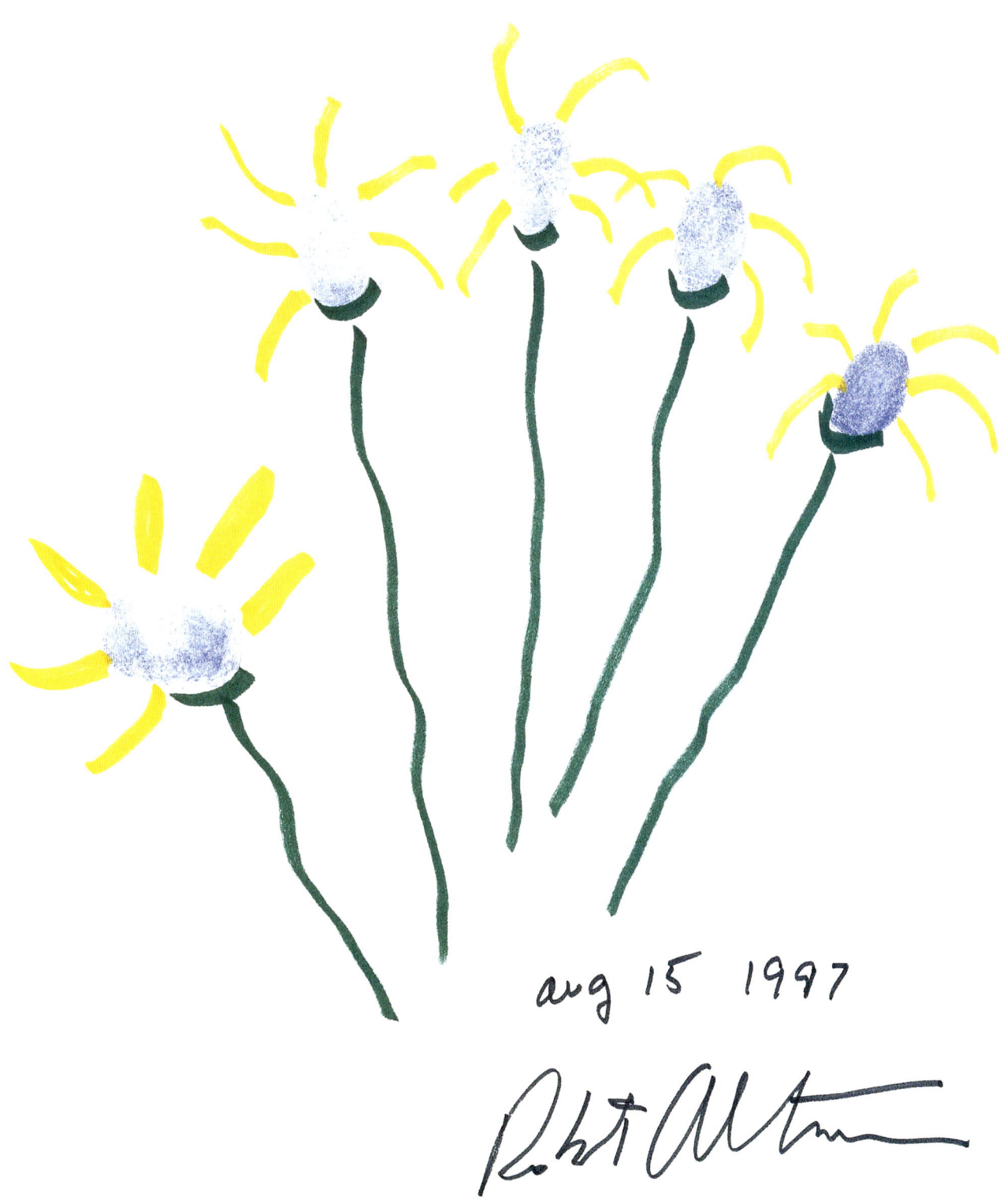

ROBERT ALTMAN | 1997

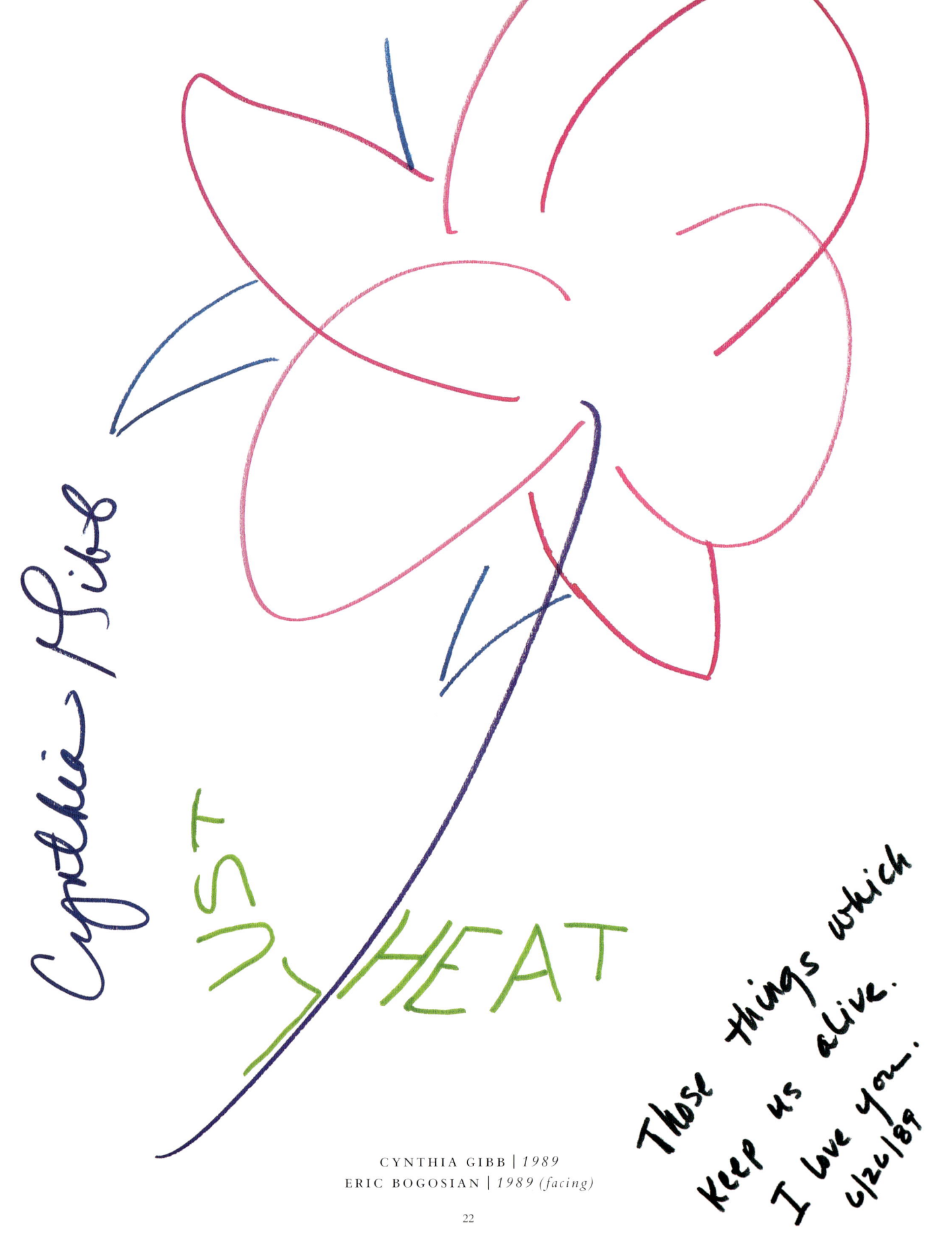

CYNTHIA GIBB | 1989
ERIC BOGOSIAN | 1989 (facing)

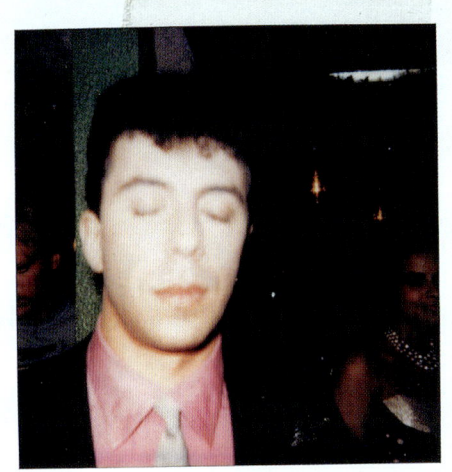

"Crime Story" haircut

Drinking in America run at Americin Place

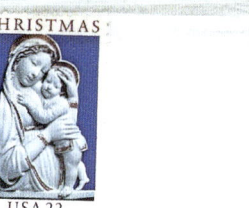
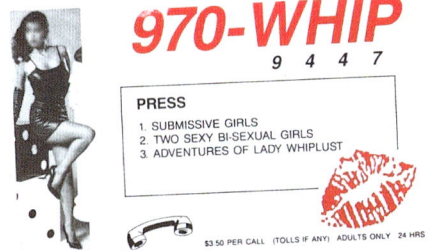

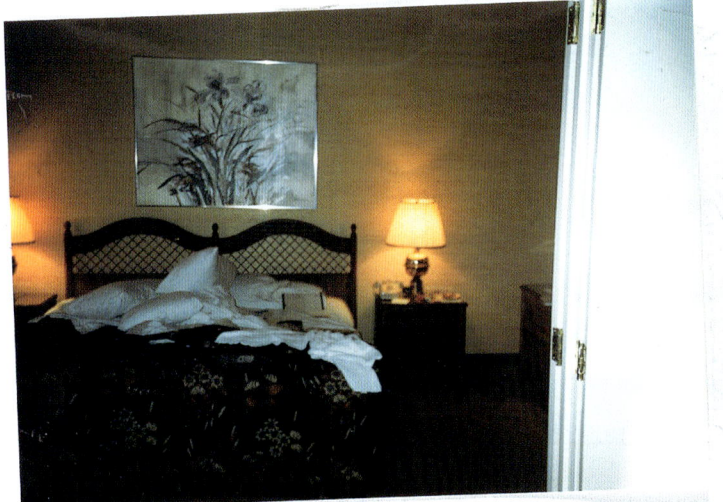

Hotel Room - Promotional Tour - Talk Radio

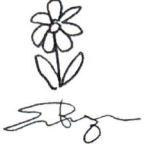

First time I saw Metallica

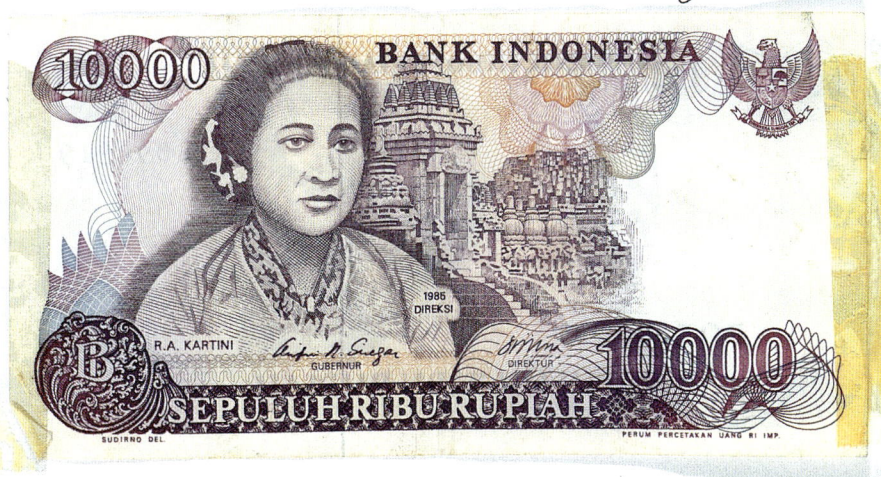

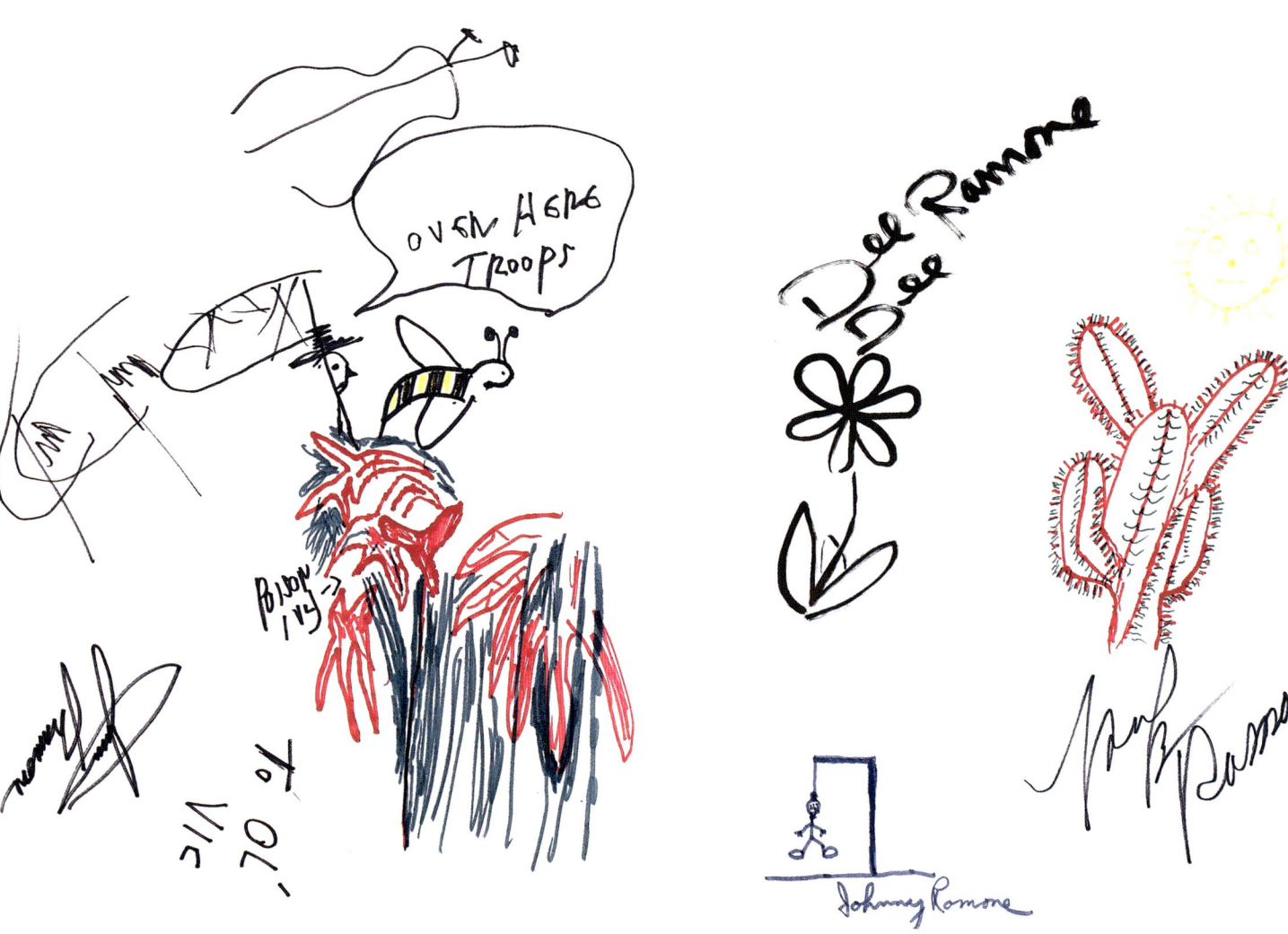

RAMONES | *1982*

I began dating when I was seventeen. My first real date was with artist Arturo Vega, at that time lighting designer for the Ramones. I started going around to various clubs and parties with Arturo, hoping this would become a passion-filled romance. But after a year of an alarmingly platonic relationship, I discovered that he was gay. Having decided up to that point that I must be the most unappealing person in the world, I cried with happiness.

THIS WAS IN the early 1980s. My girlfriends and I were going through our New Wave period, so we basically looked like teased and sprayed transvestite pirates. On any given night we would pile into the back of the band van and go to whatever part of Long Island or Queens the Ramones happened to be playing in. One night before the show started, I was sitting in the green room (which in this case was yellow), my flower book in hand. One of the band members was picking through the bowl of M&M's trying to remember which color he was supposed to remove (brown ones were disliked by Van Halen, I think). He didn't know which band had started the superstition about M&M's, but he was determined the Ramones wouldn't be brought down because of it. I thought a diversion might be in order so I brought out my book and asked them to draw. I didn't know how the leather-clad gurus of punk would react. With the crack of a smile and an "Uh okay," Dee Dee drew a flower, Johnny a hangman, Marky a cactus, and Joey some poison ivy. With a satisfied expression, Joey handed the book back to me saying, "Here ya go, Vic." Clutching the book to my chest, I returned to the thousands of fans out front and slam danced to "I Want to Be Sedated."

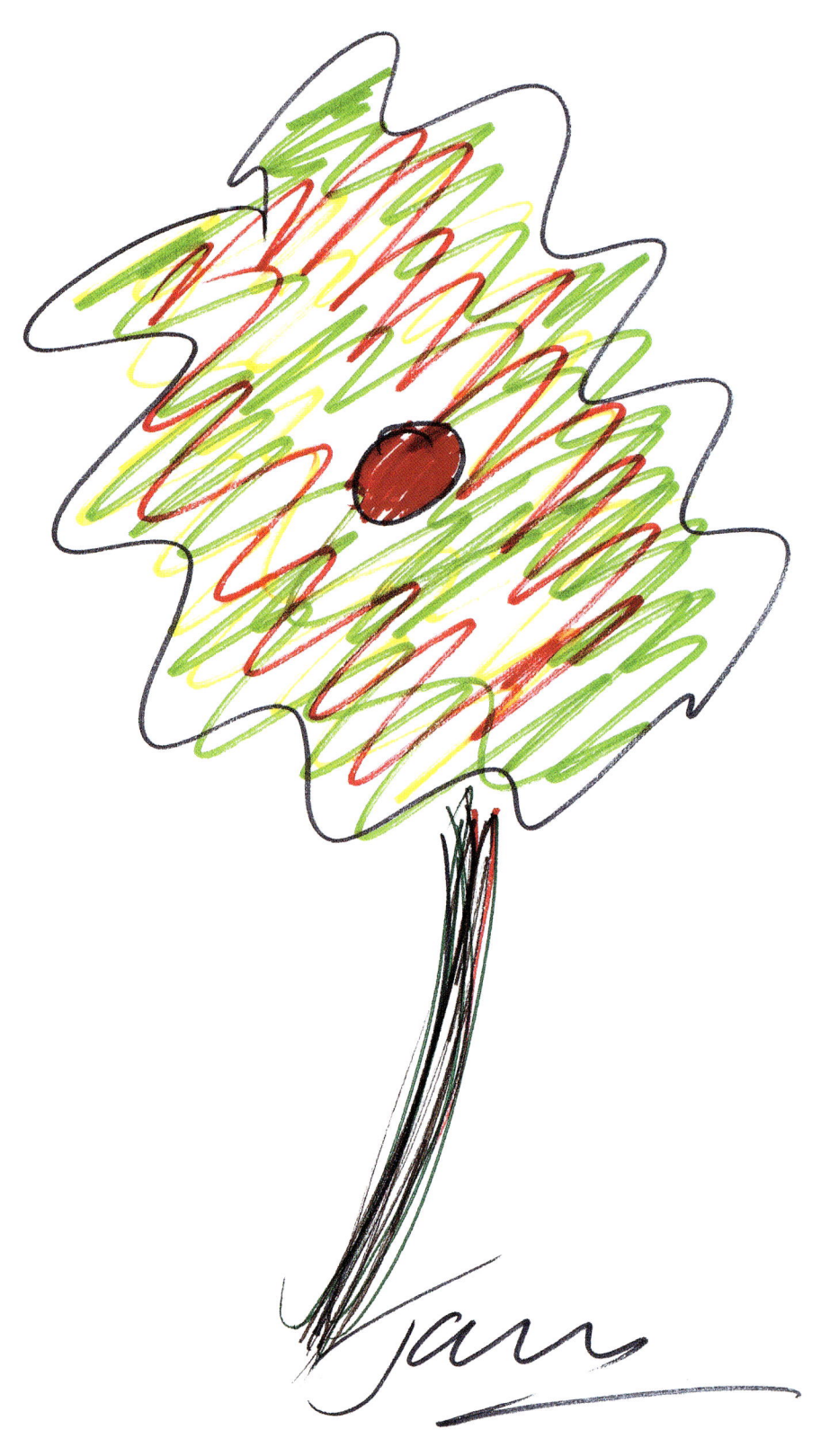

JANN WENNER | *1997*
RICHARD GERE | *1987 (facing)*

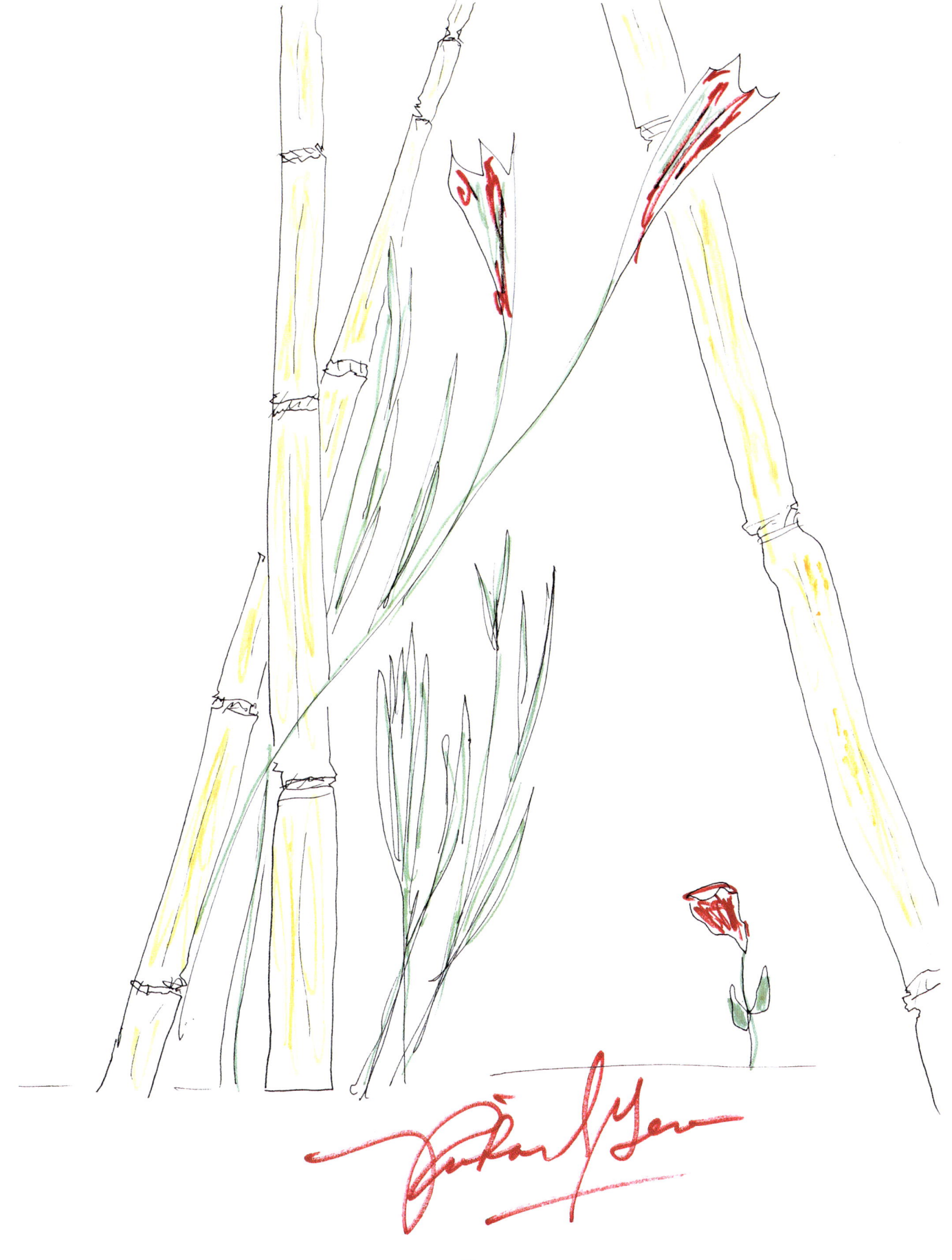

PETER RIEGERT | *1998*
MARY MCCORMACK | *1997 (facing)*

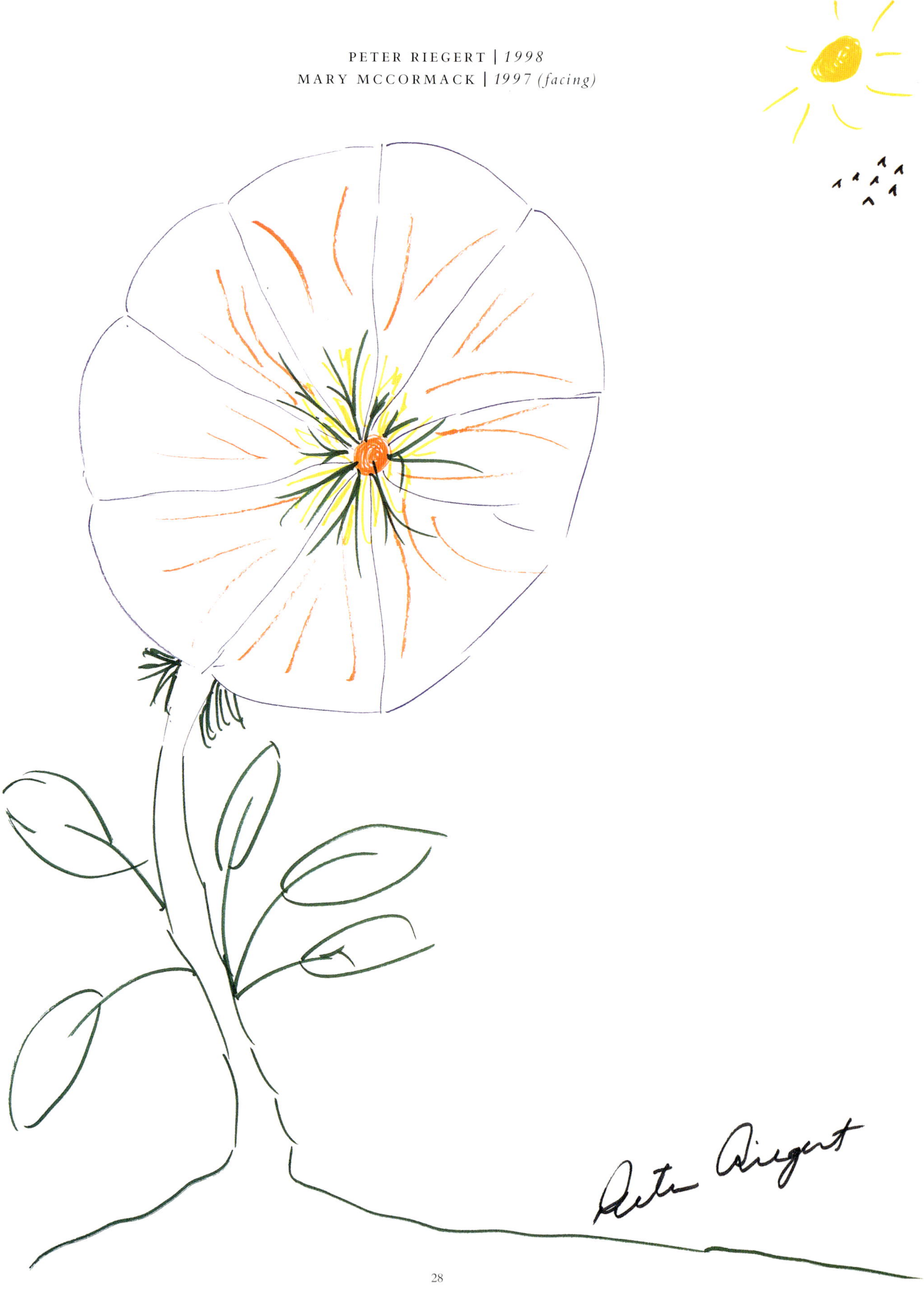

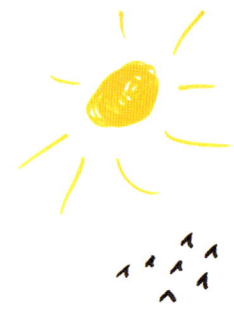

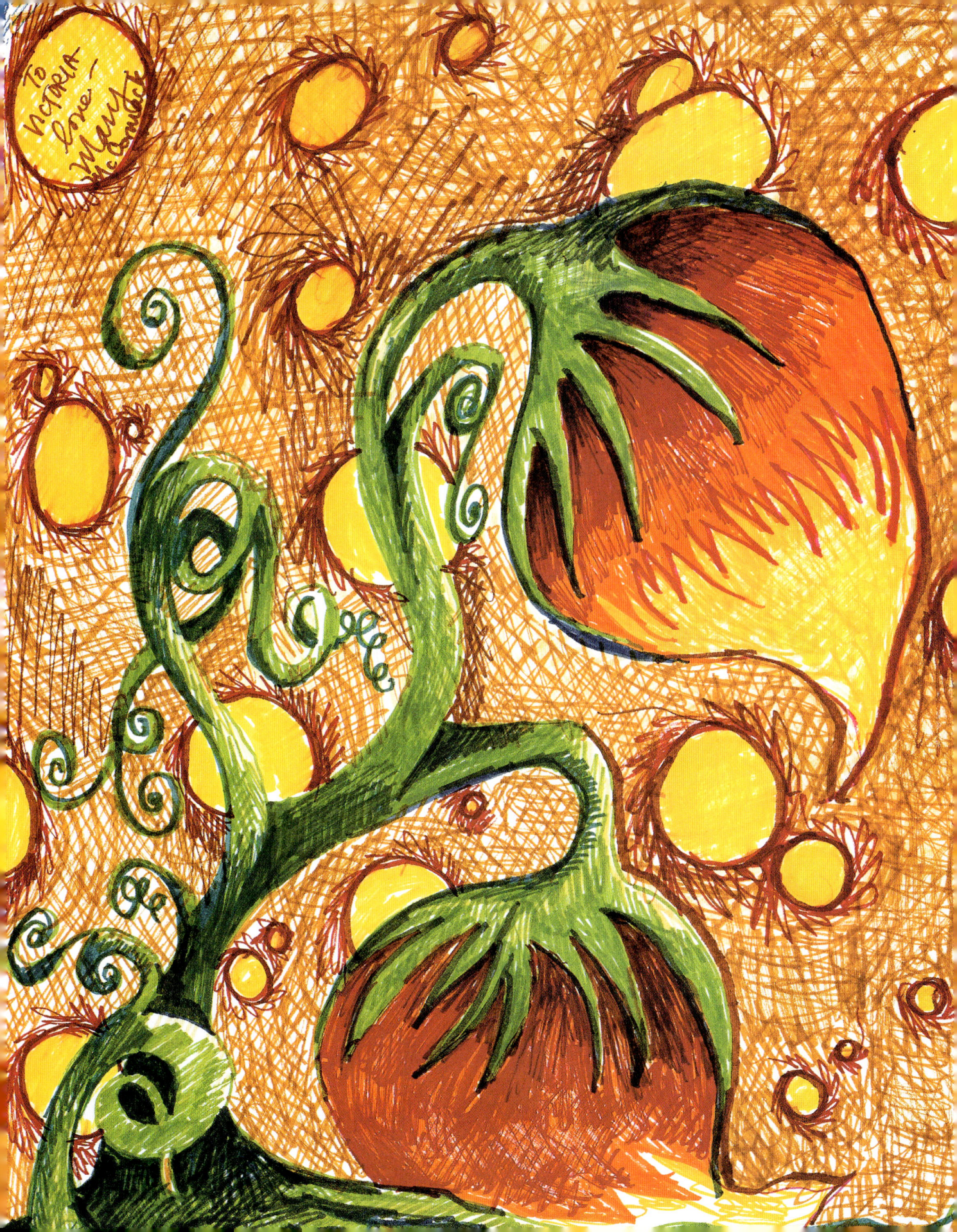

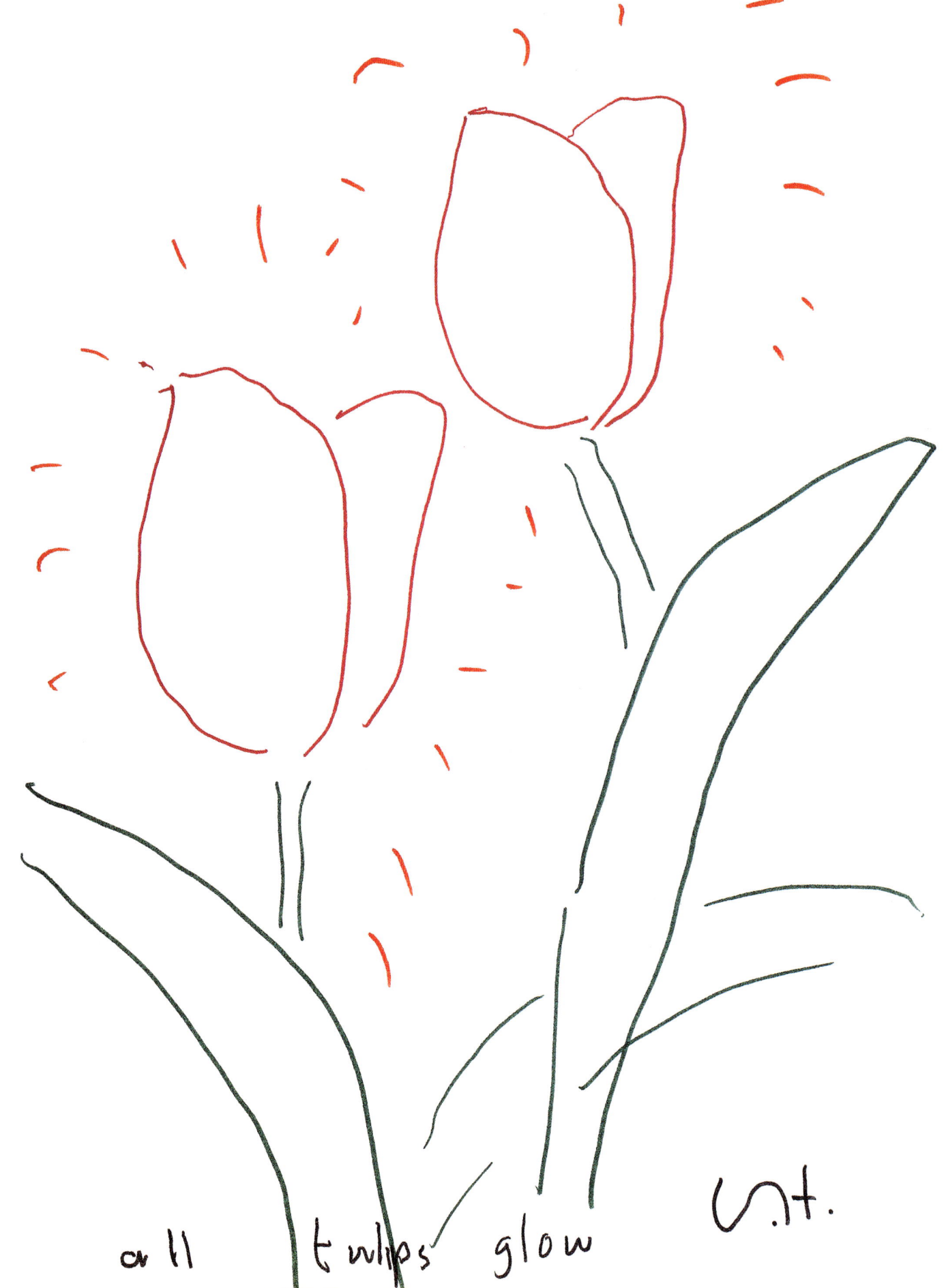

all tulips glow

RICHARD LINKLATER | *1998*
DAVID HOCKNEY | *1982 (facing)*

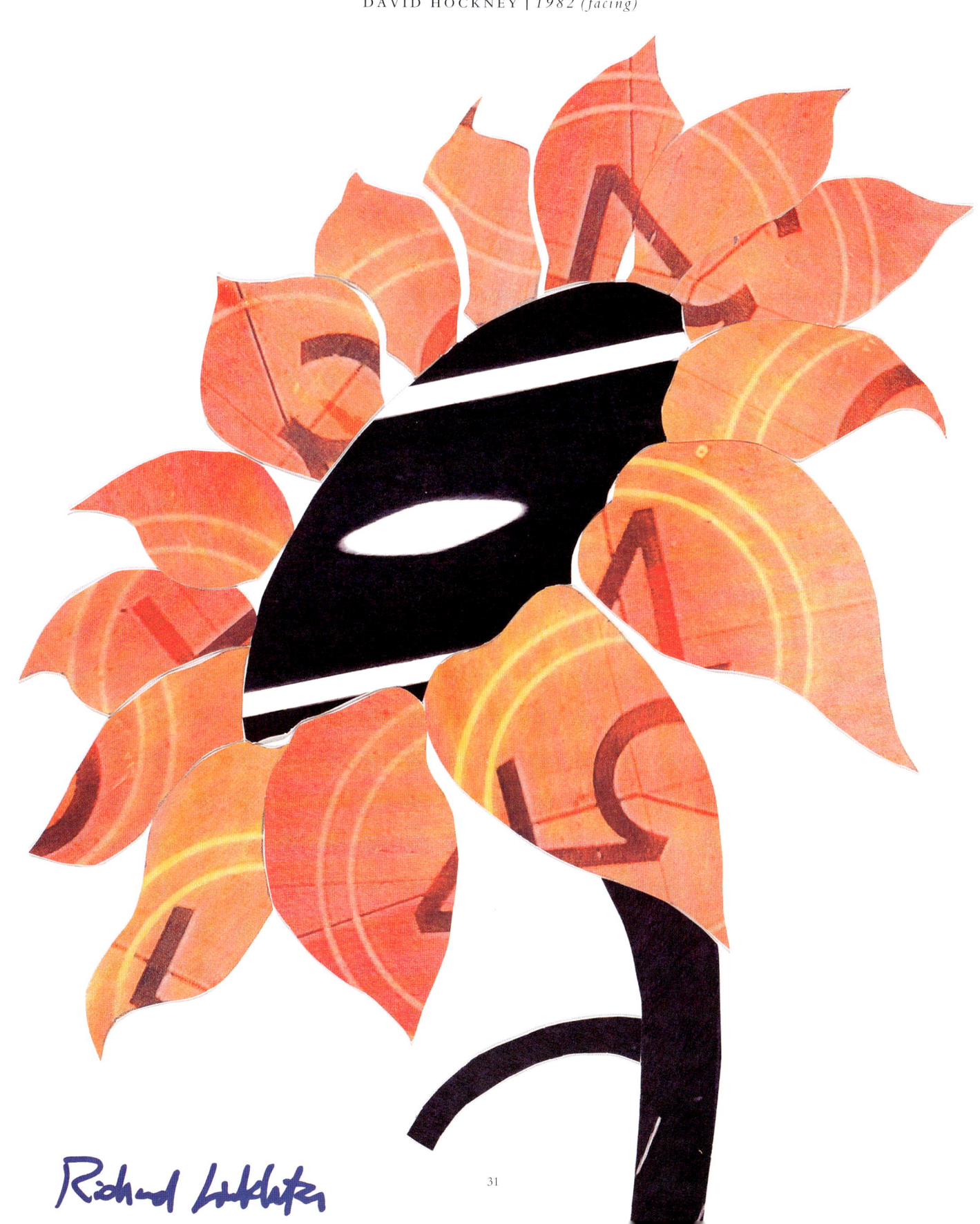

BARBARA WALTERS | *1979*

WALTER CRONKITE | *1982*

DICK CLARK | *1981*

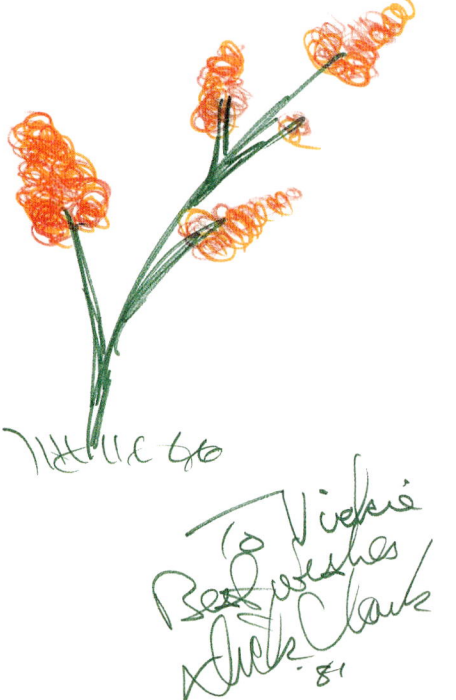

REX REED | *1982*

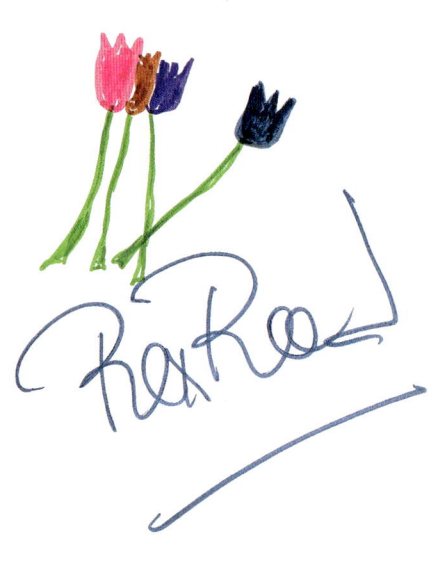

GUS VAN SANT | *1991*

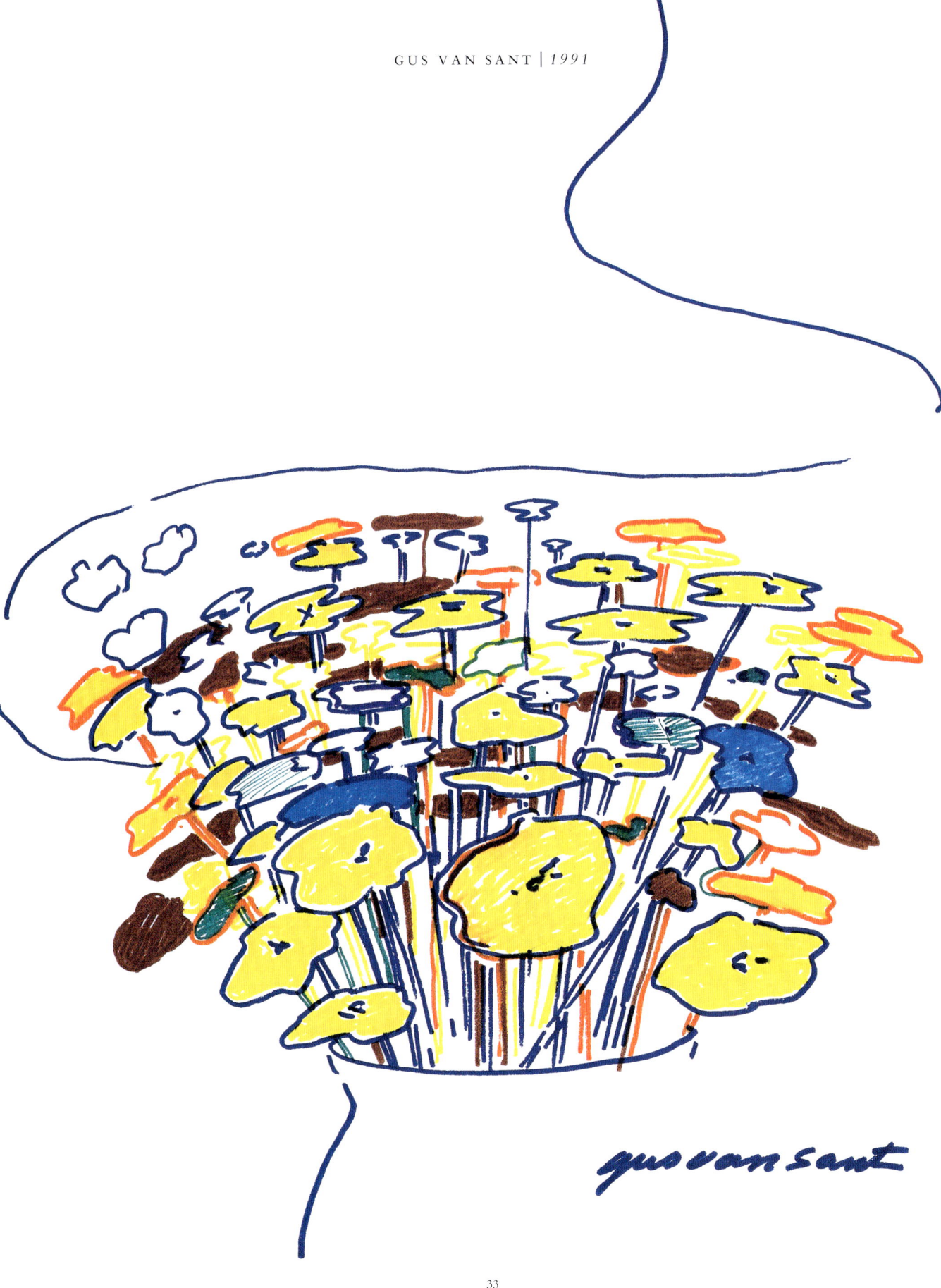

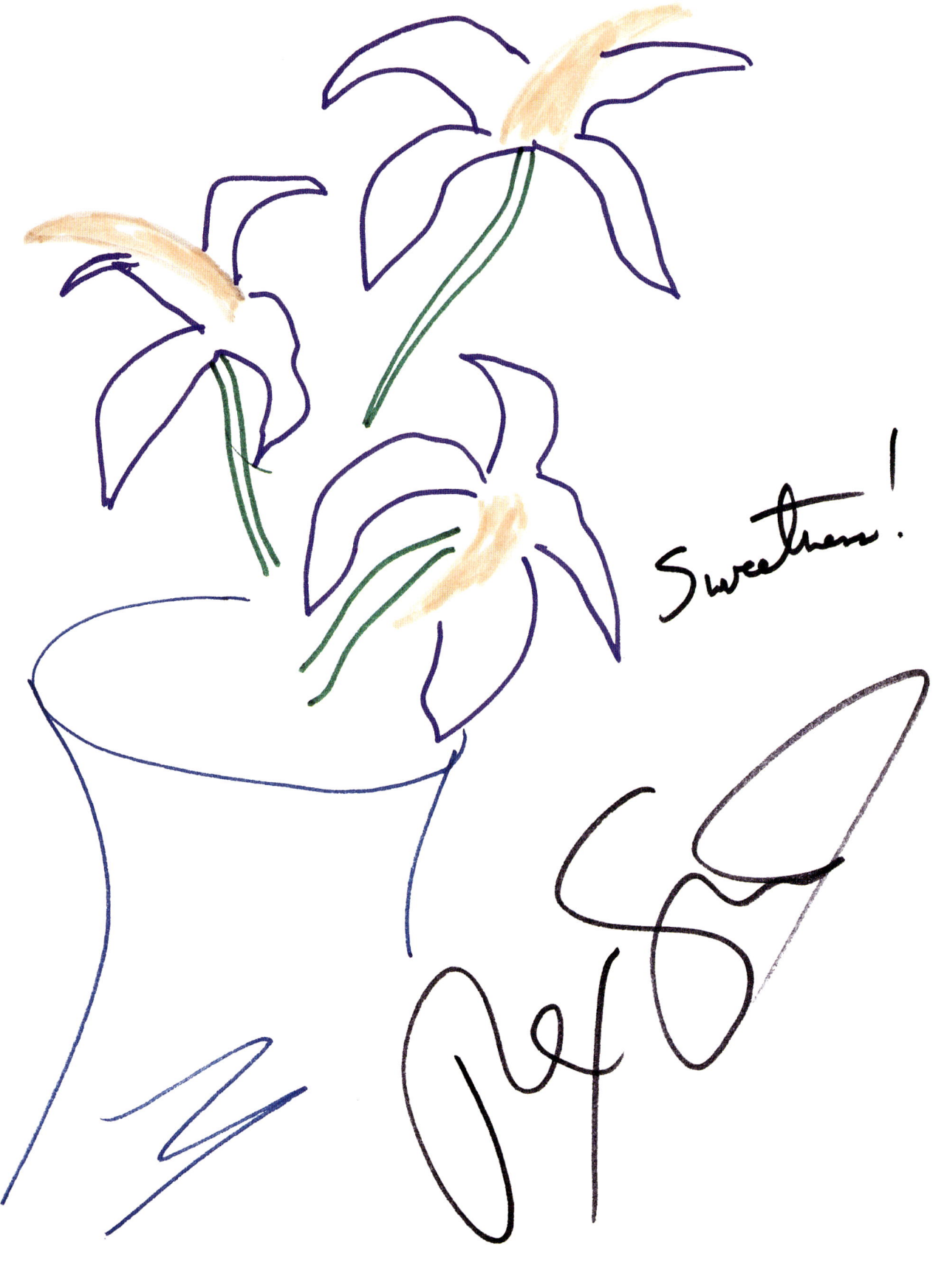

REX SMITH | 1982

The Tony Awards were a big event at our house every year. My mother would be in bed, and I would get dressed up in a party dress, pull out a director's chair, and drink 7UP from a champagne glass.

WHEN I WAS eighteen, I decided I wanted to see the Tonys live. I sent a letter to Alex Cohen, the producer that year, asking if there was any way I could attend. A few days later I received a note saying that he couldn't get me into the show, but that I was welcome at the dress rehearsal.

ALTHOUGH THIS WASN'T the real thing, I was thrilled. While there, I picked up a program, which gave me an idea.

THAT NIGHT, AS the awards were being presented on television, I made myself up, styled my hair, and put on a vintage lavender-and-gold-striped ball gown I'd bought with the money I'd earned as an Avon lady. When the award ceremony was over, I headed for the party at the Waldorf-Astoria. At the moment when everyone was arriving from the theater I tossed my mother's black velvet coat with mink trim over my arm, clutched my program, threw myself into the rush, and walked right into the party.

SO FAR SO good. As everyone else kissed and greeted one another and sat down at their tables, I realized I hadn't considered something. Where was I to sit? I had to think fast. I asked to speak to the headwaiter.

"Is there a problem, Madame?"

I HAD BROUGHT myself to the verge of tears. "Yes! I've had a terrible row with my boyfriend, and I just can't sit at the same table with him. He refuses to leave, and I don't think I should have to leave just because he is being unreasonable. Could you possibly find me another place to sit?"

"Of course, Madame, right this way."

THE NEXT THING I knew, I was seated at a table with teen heartthrob Rex Smith (who at that time was appearing on Broadway in *The Pirates of Penzance*), Pam Dawber of the television show *Mork and Mindy*, Kevin Kline, and the senior staff of *Playbill* magazine. They were all eyeing me, wondering, Who is this girl? I was getting nervous. All of a sudden, a waiter approached very excitedly and asked for my autograph.

"Oh! Of course!"

I SIGNED IT, "Thank you more than you know! Victoria Leacock."

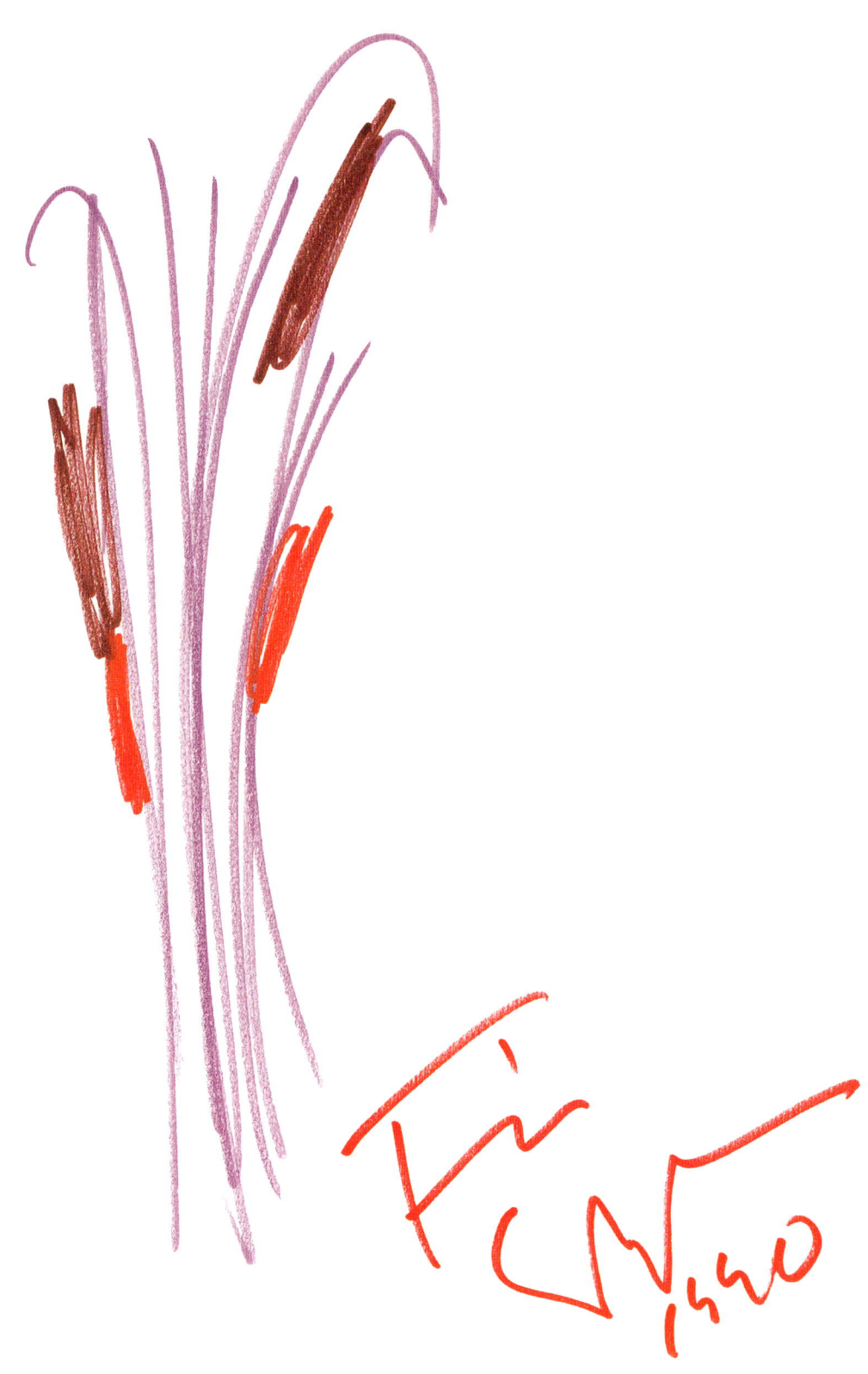

FRANCIS FORD COPPOLA | *1990*

STEPHEN SPROUSE | *1991*

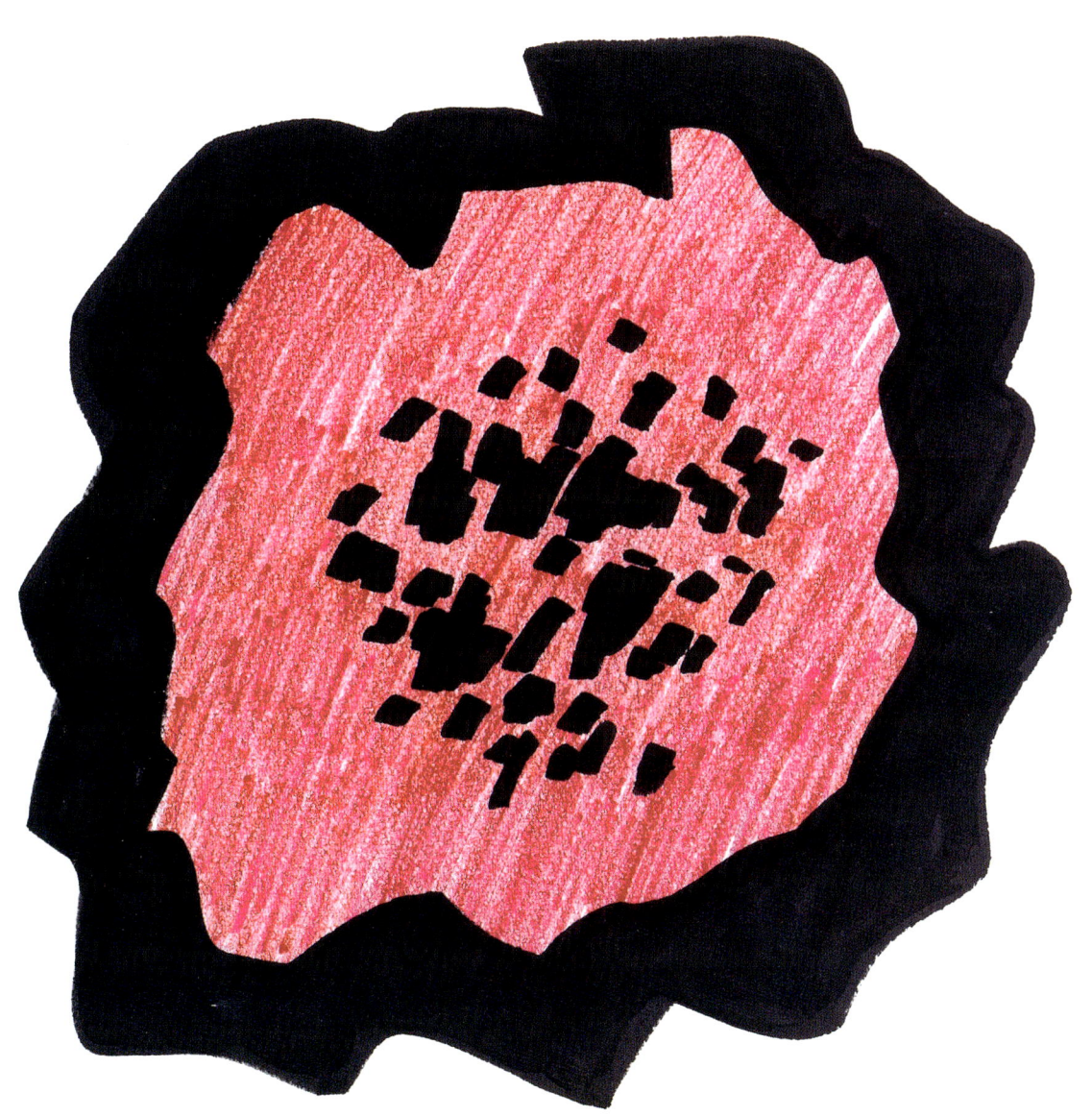

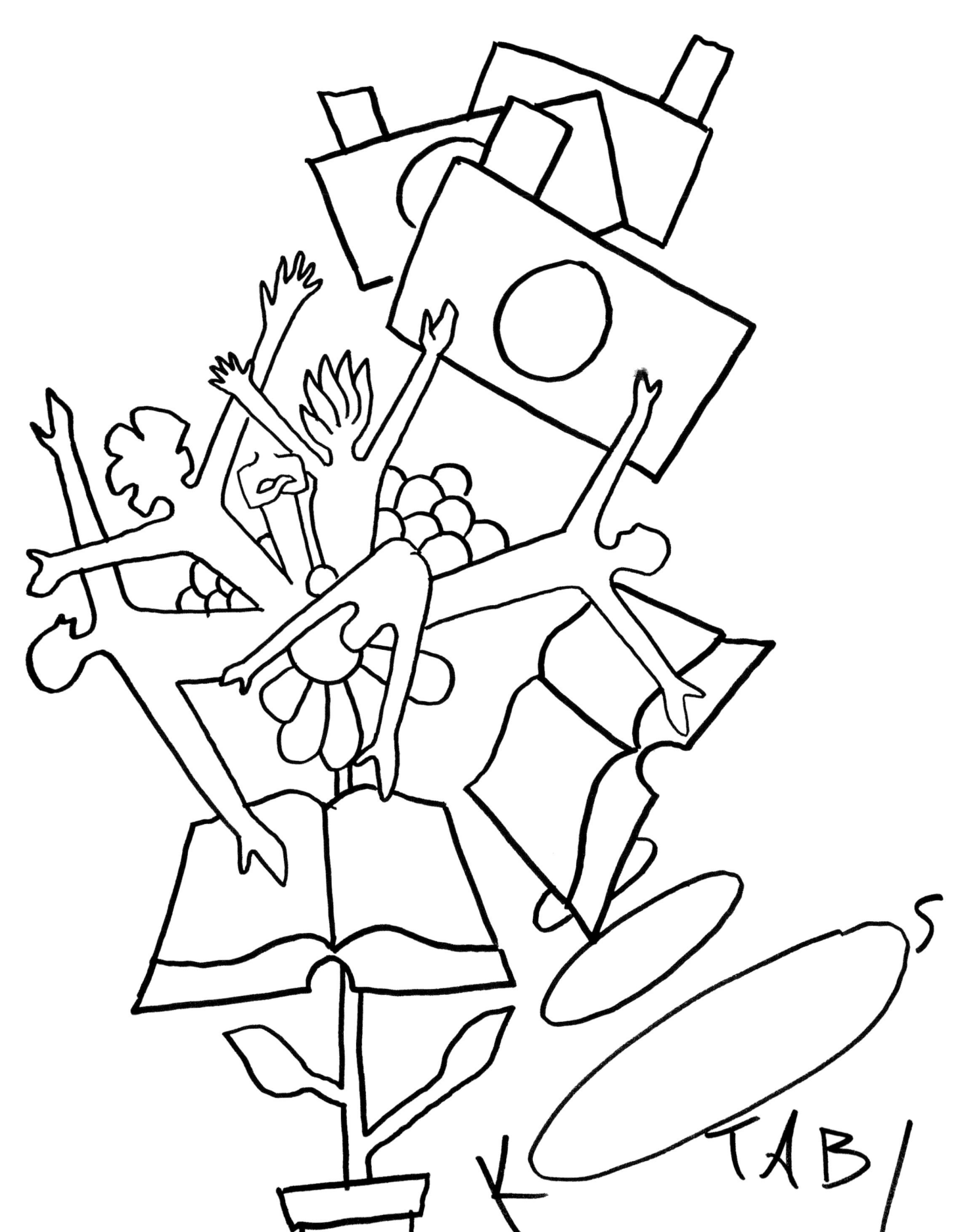

ELIZABETH TAYLOR | *1981*
MARK KOSTABI | *1988 (facing)*

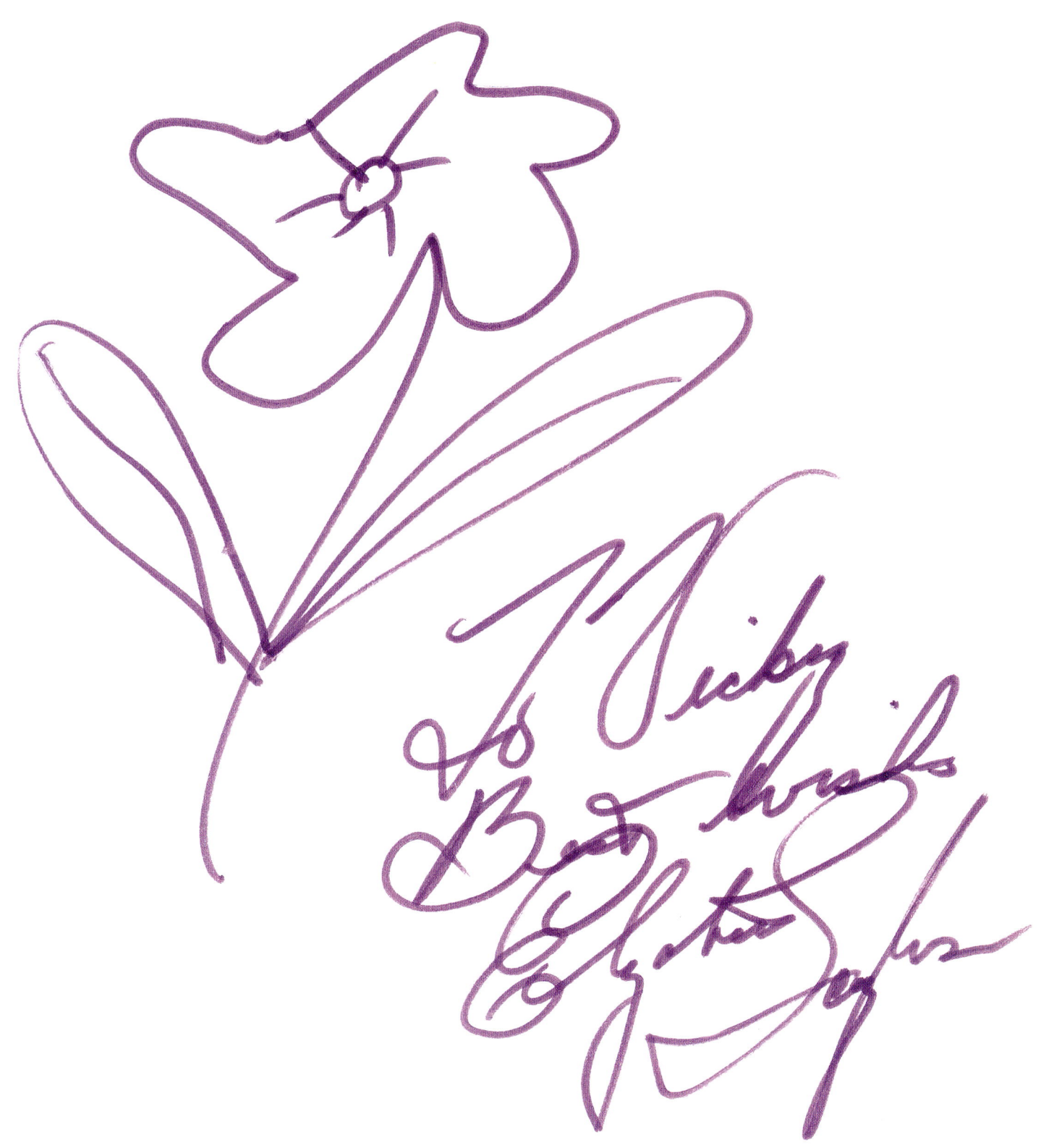

SARAH MCLACHLAN | *1998*
MOLLY RINGWALD | *1997 (facing)*

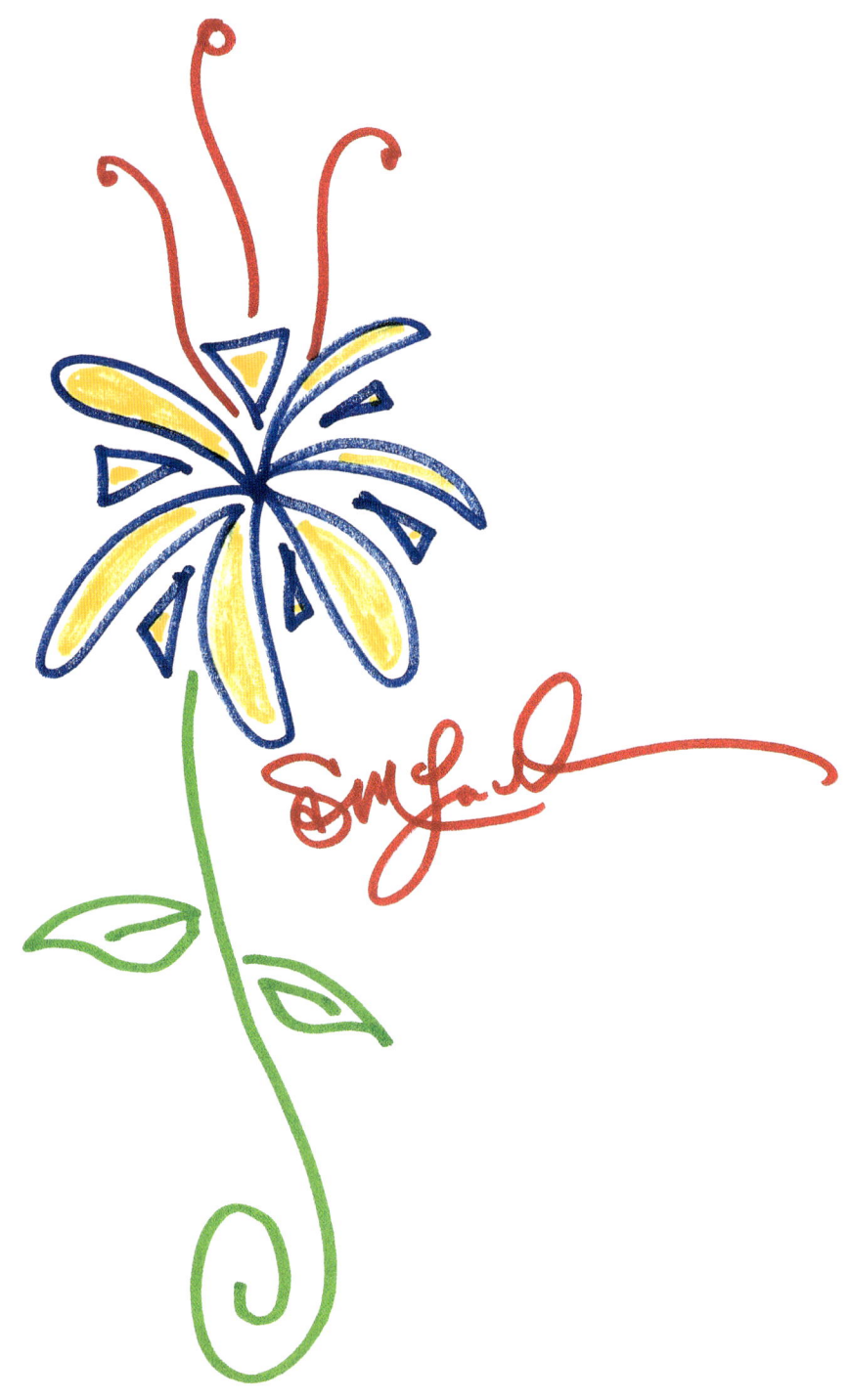

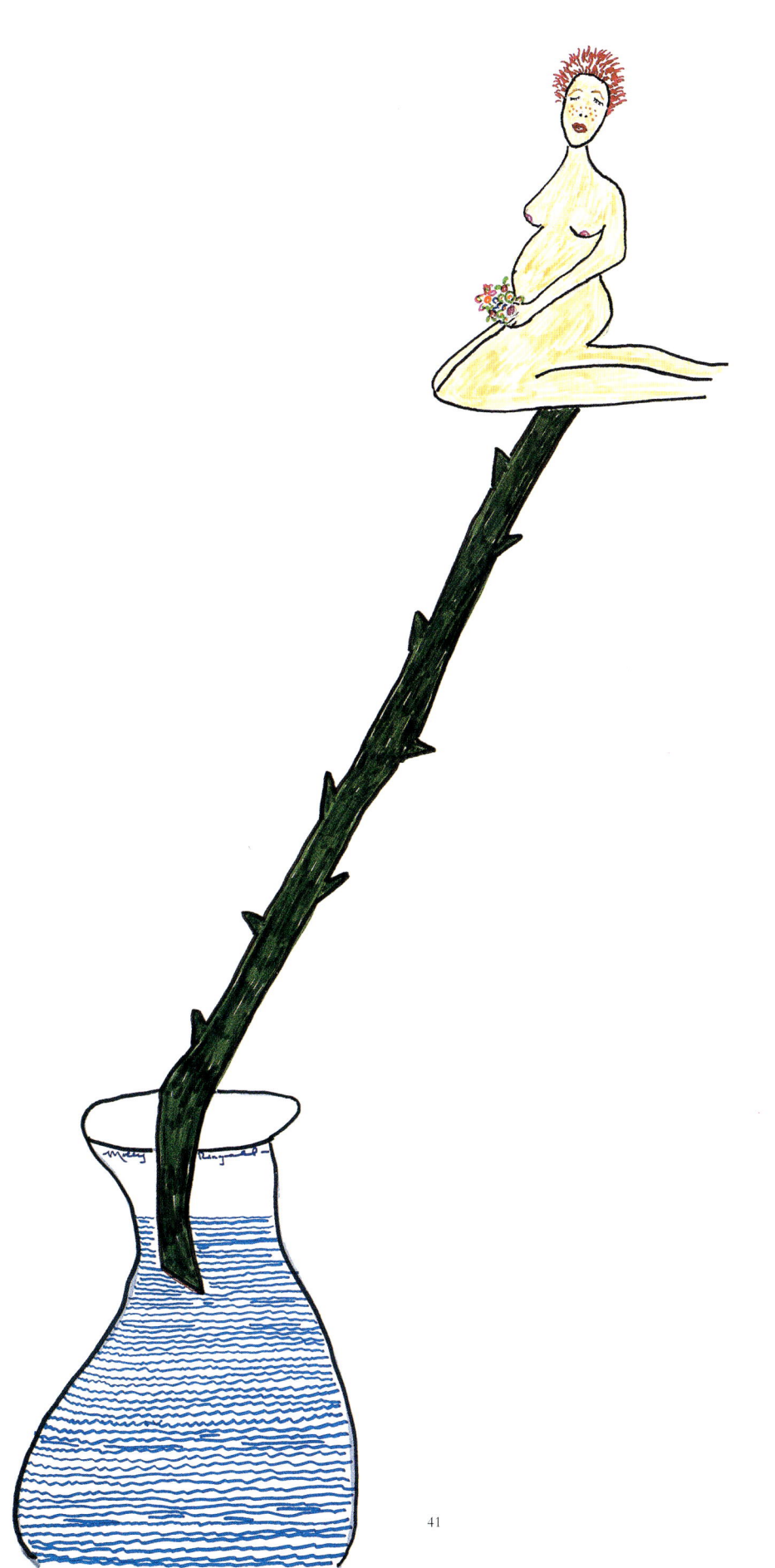

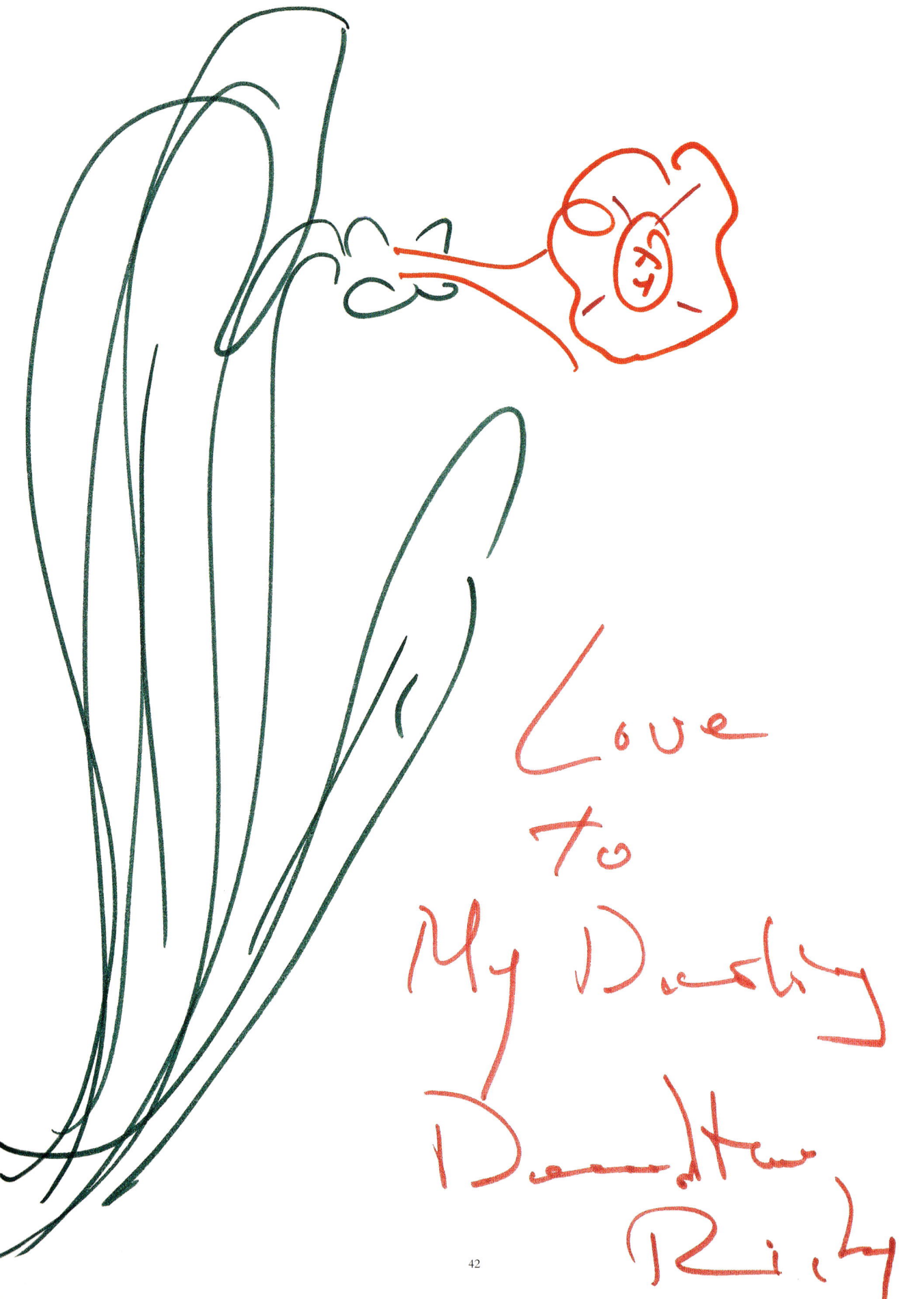

RICHARD LEACOCK | *1982*

I think my father is the best filmmaker in the world. And perhaps that is as it should be.

BORN IN LONDON to English parents, he was raised in the Canary Islands on his father's banana plantation. But paradise doesn't last forever, and at the age of six he was shipped off to boarding school. Since his classmates never quite understood the island life he spoke of, he bought a small 16-mm camera when he was fourteen and set out to share the experience with them. What resulted was his first film, *Canary Bananas,* a vivid 16-minute documentary that evoked the feeling of being there.

ROBERT FLAHERTY, THE father of one of his classmates, saw the film and said, "Young man, if you are still interested in film when you grow up, come and work with me." Flaherty was one of the great documentary pioneers of the century. Dad did continue filming. He filmed the unusual sight of a bird using a "tool" while on David Lack's 1938–39 expedition to the Galapagos Islands when he was seventeen, and during World War II he spent four years walking across Burma, documenting the war. When he returned, Flaherty hired him to film *Louisiana Story* without seeing any of his work since their first meeting. He filmed the media frenzy around such key moments of the 1960s as the Wisconsin primary race between Hubert Humphrey and John F. Kennedy, the birth of the Fischer quintuplets, and the Monterey Jazz Festival. He spent three months living with the Ku Klux Klan making *The Hidden Empire* and examined the nature of faith in Muncie, Indiana, in *Community of Praise*. He works in digital video now, trying to capture life as it is, in its simplest and most complex form.

I USED TO have him on a pedestal. Everyone said that this was bad, take him down. So finally I did. What I found was a great father.

JUSTIN BOND | *1998*
MIKE NEWELL | *1996 (facing)*

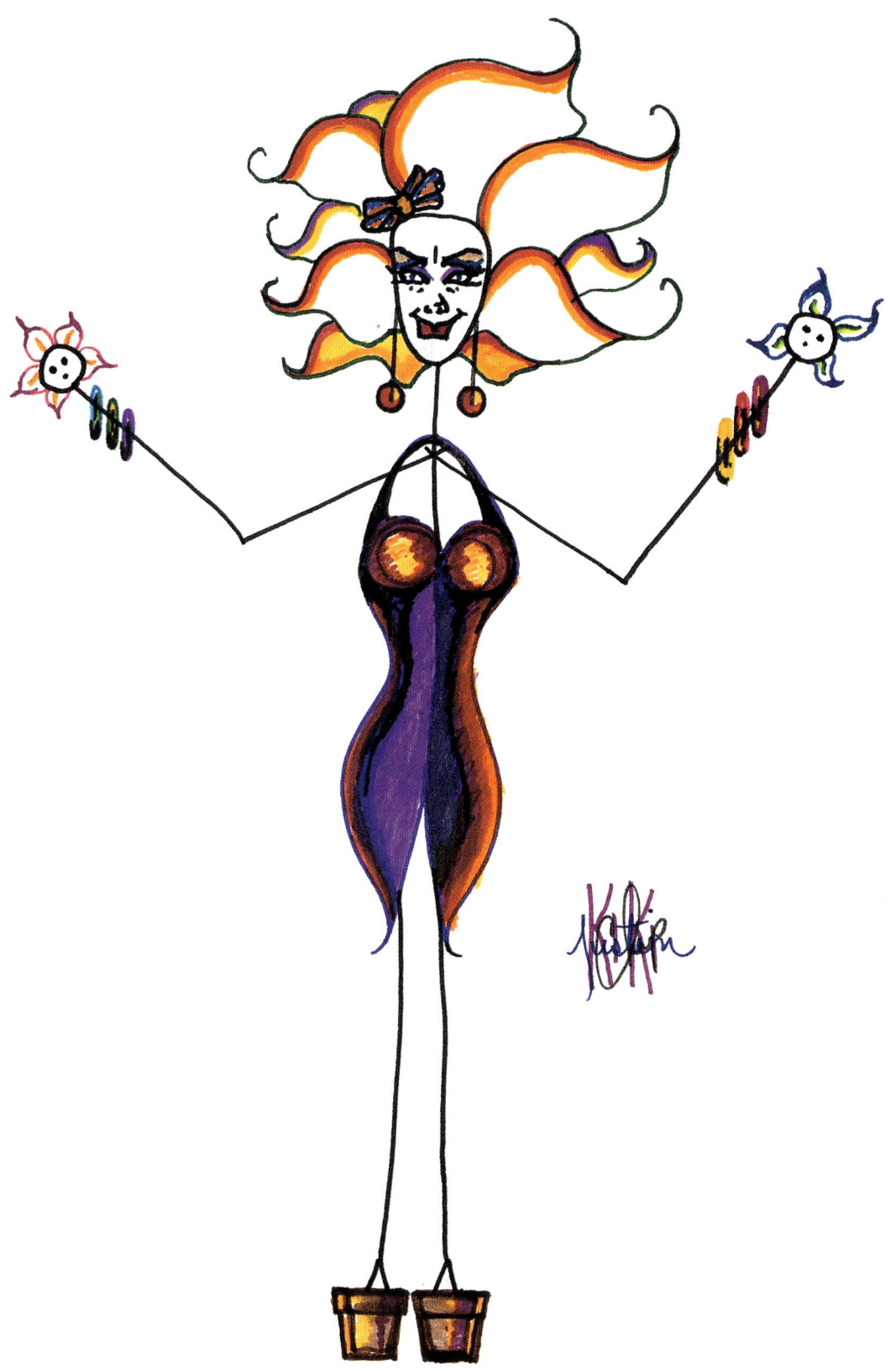

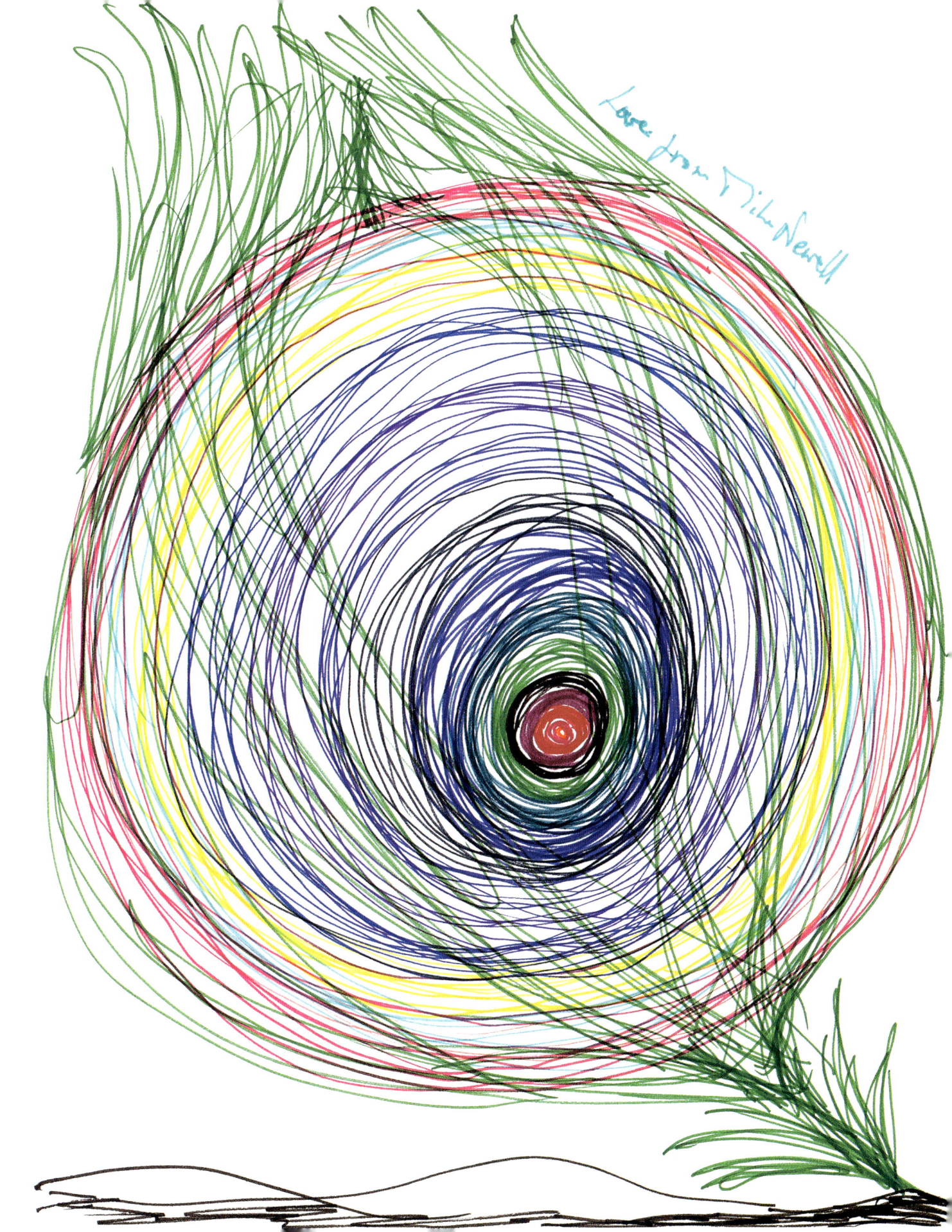

DANNY DEVITO | *1982*

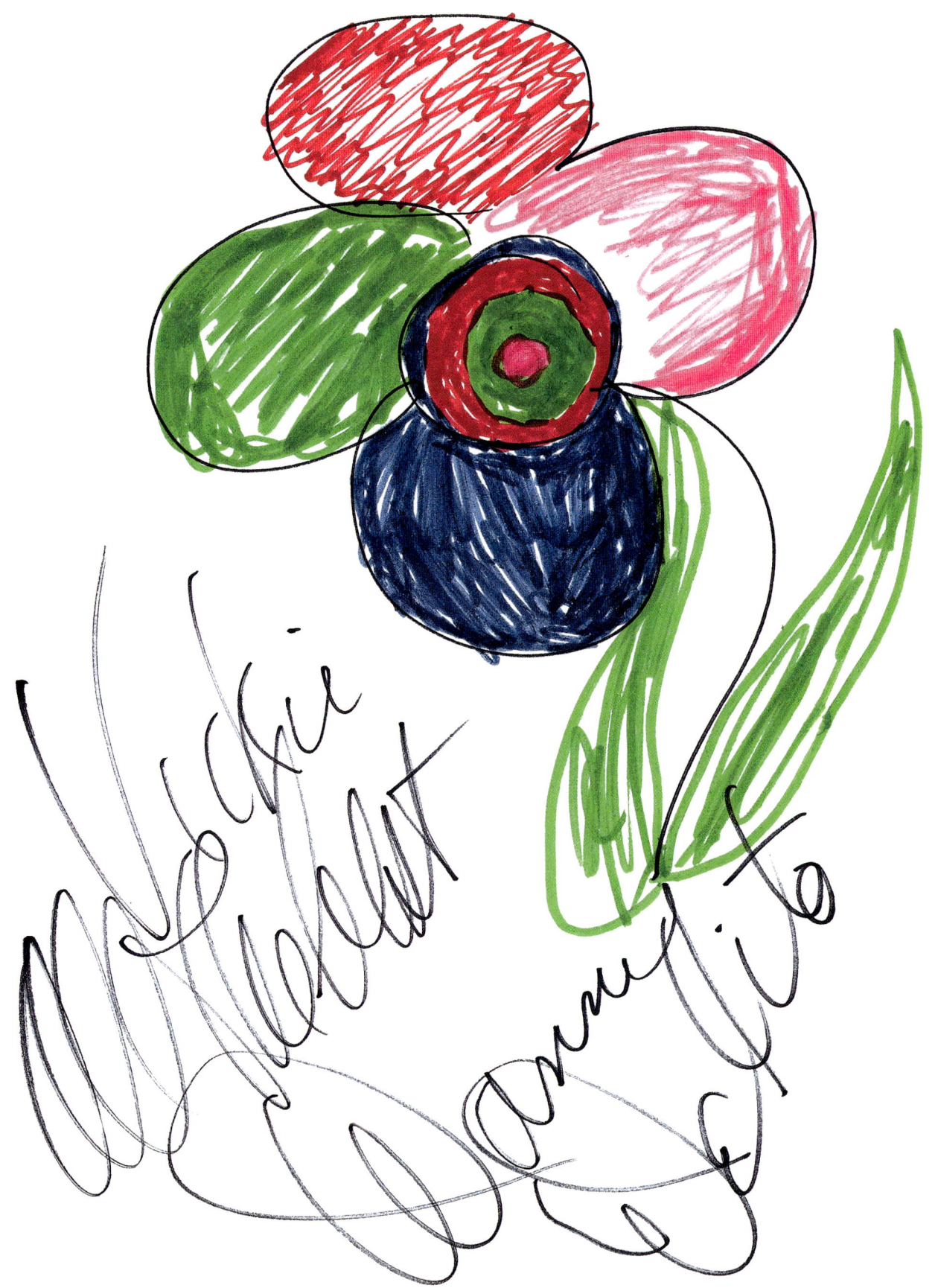

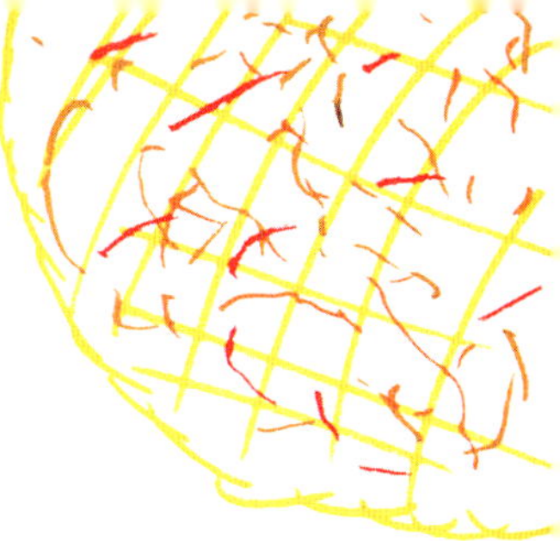

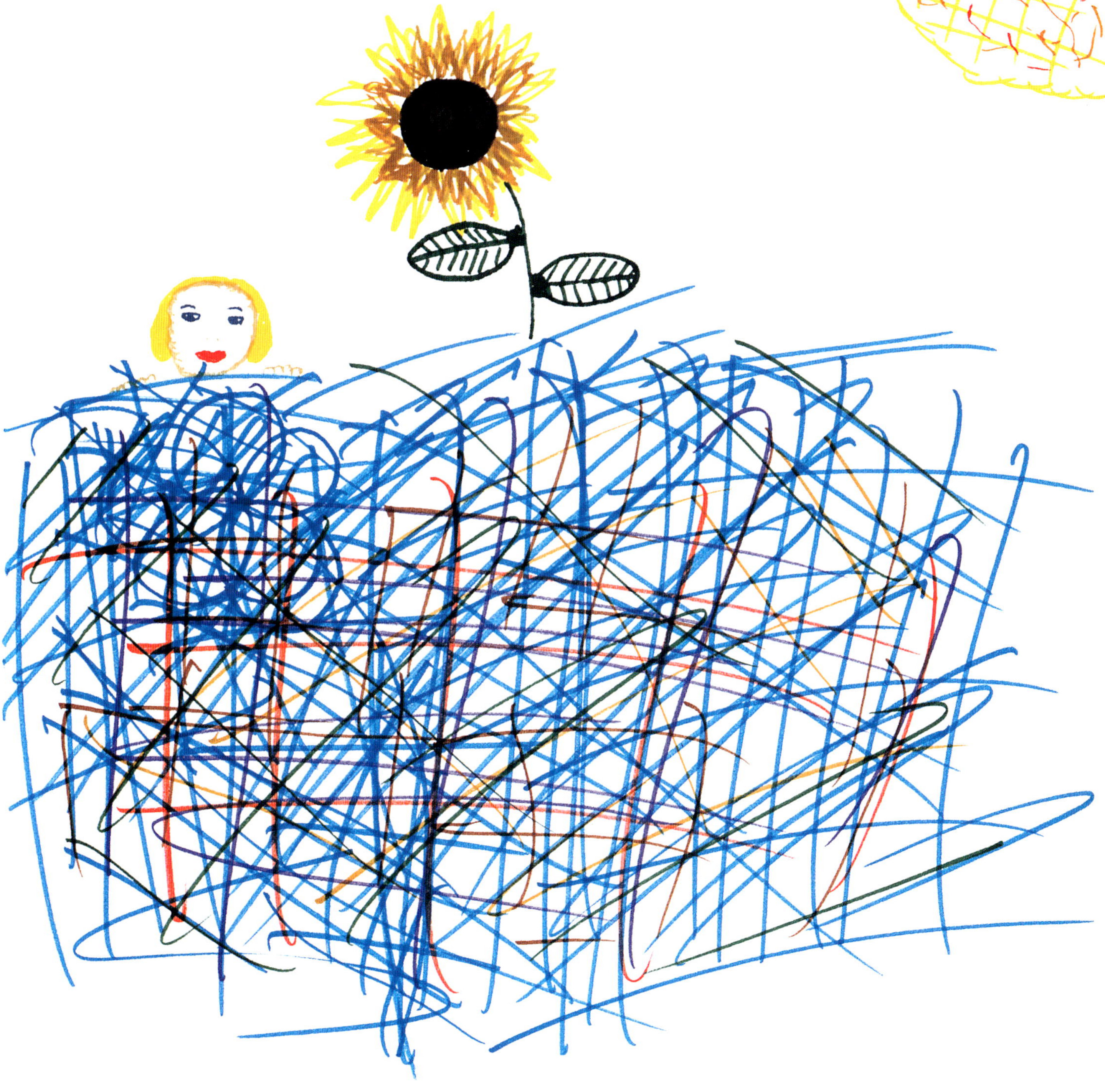

BETTE MIDLER | *1998*

Aloha & All good things to those who love the natural world

Bette Midler

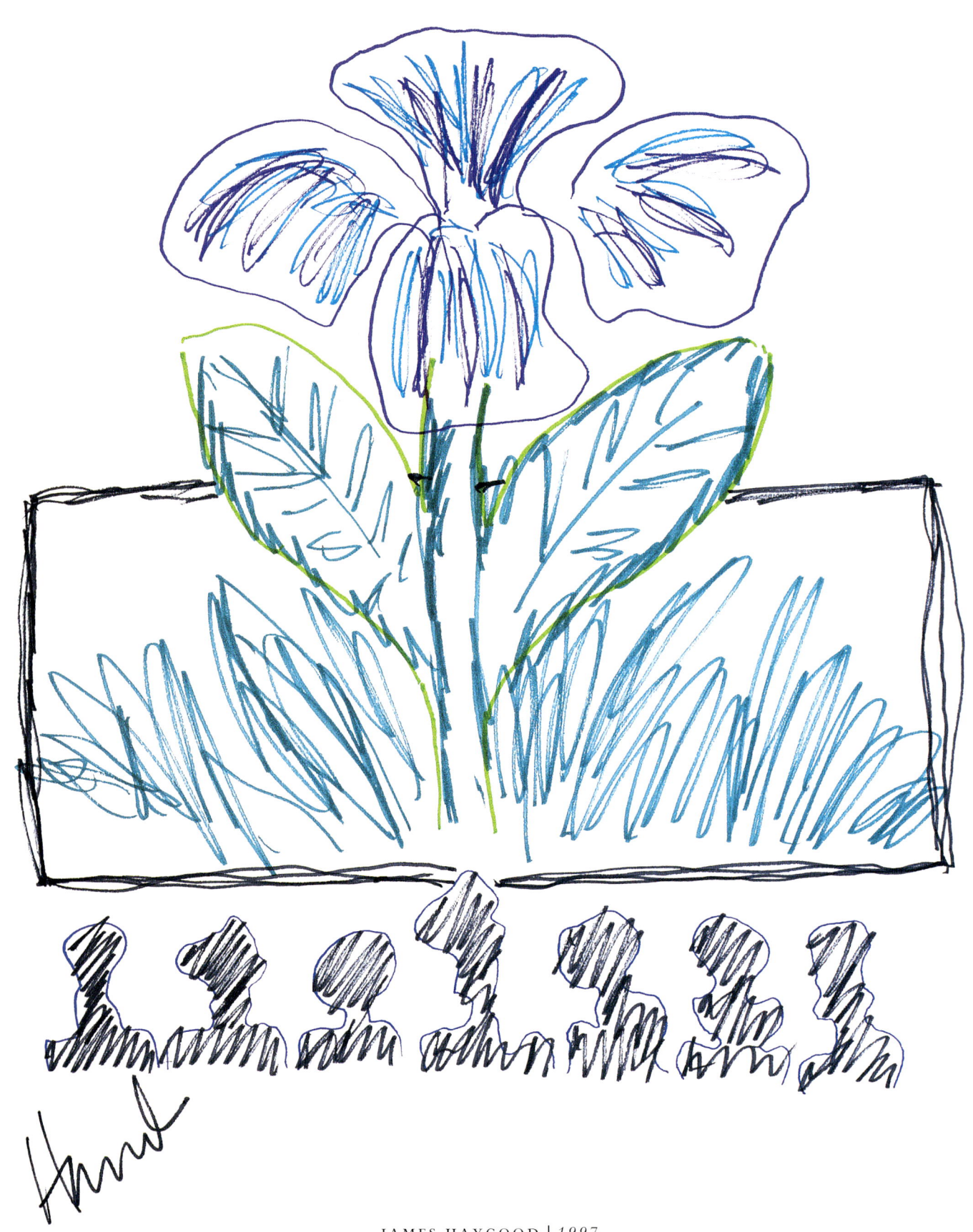

JAMES HAYGOOD | *1997*

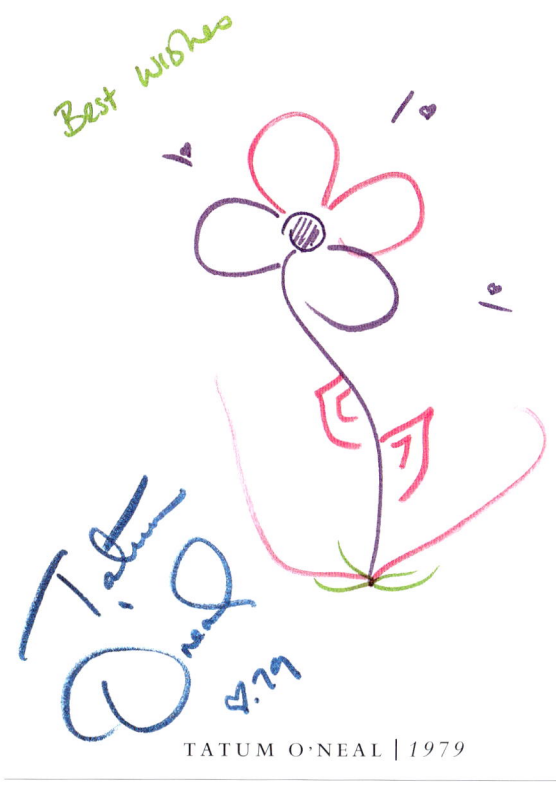

TATUM O'NEAL | *1979*

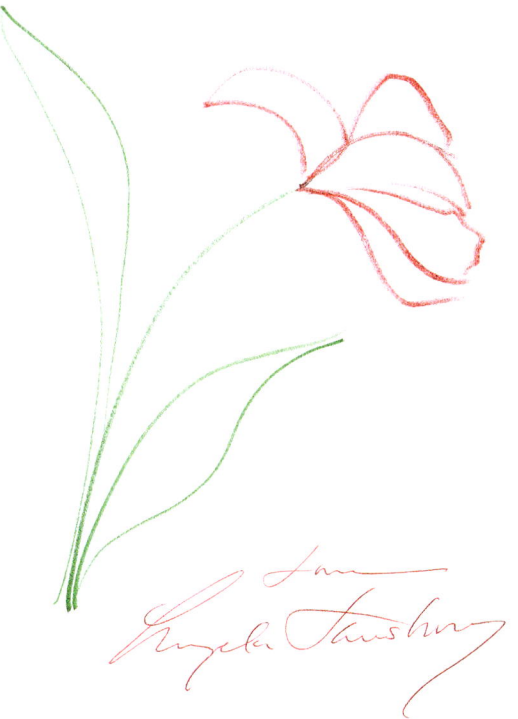

LAUREN BACALL | *1980*

DEBORAH HARRY | *1980*

ANGELA LANSBURY | *1980*

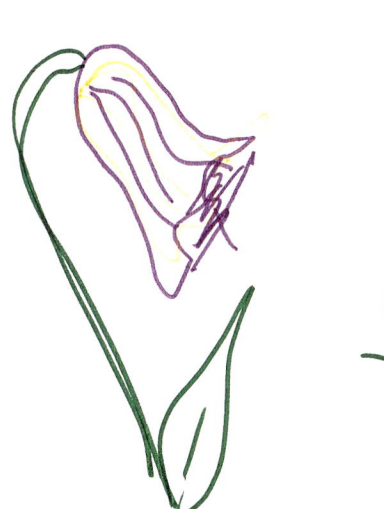
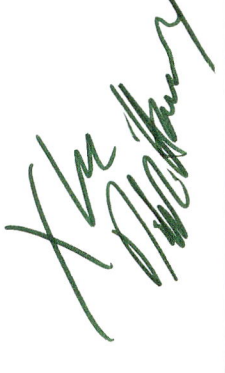

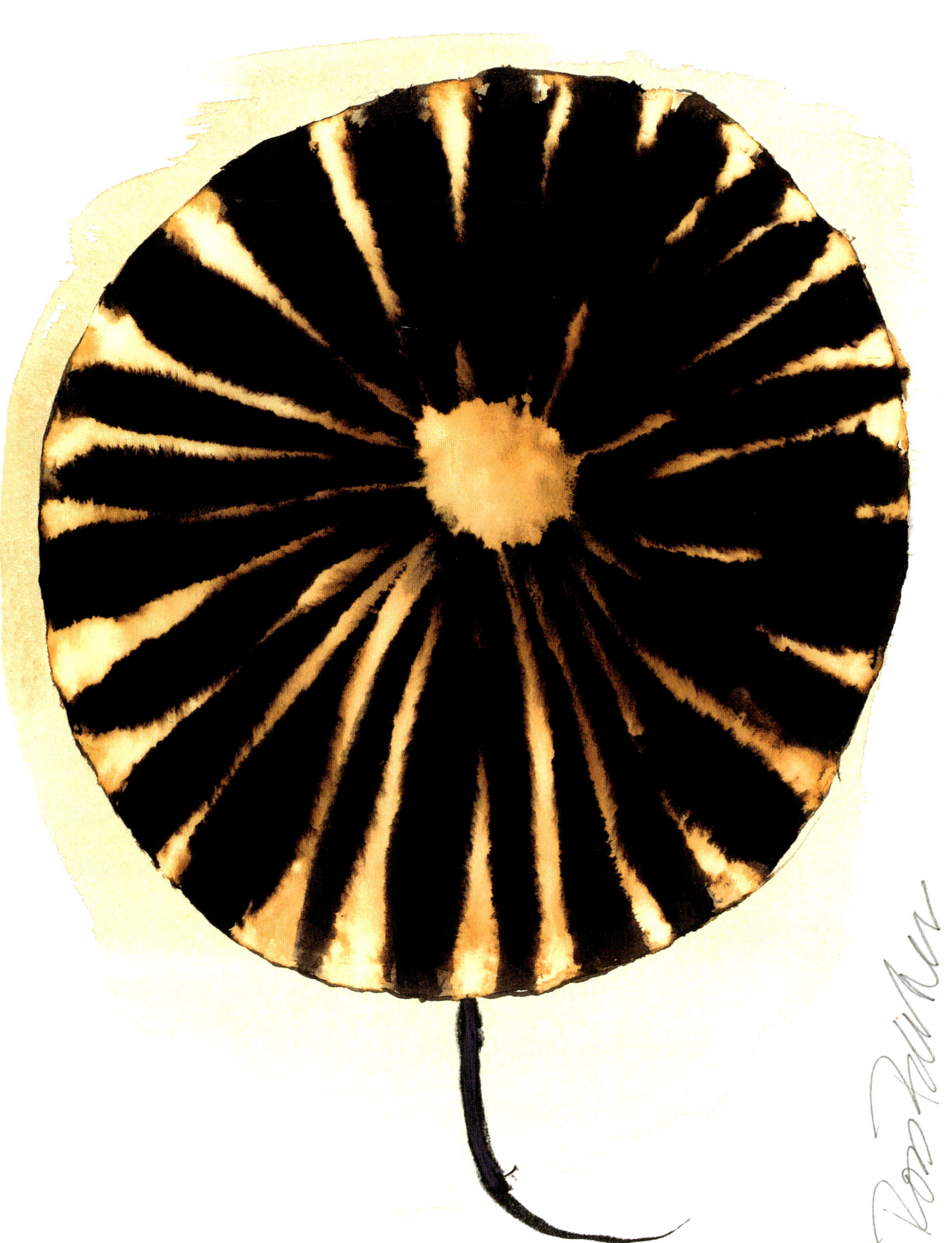

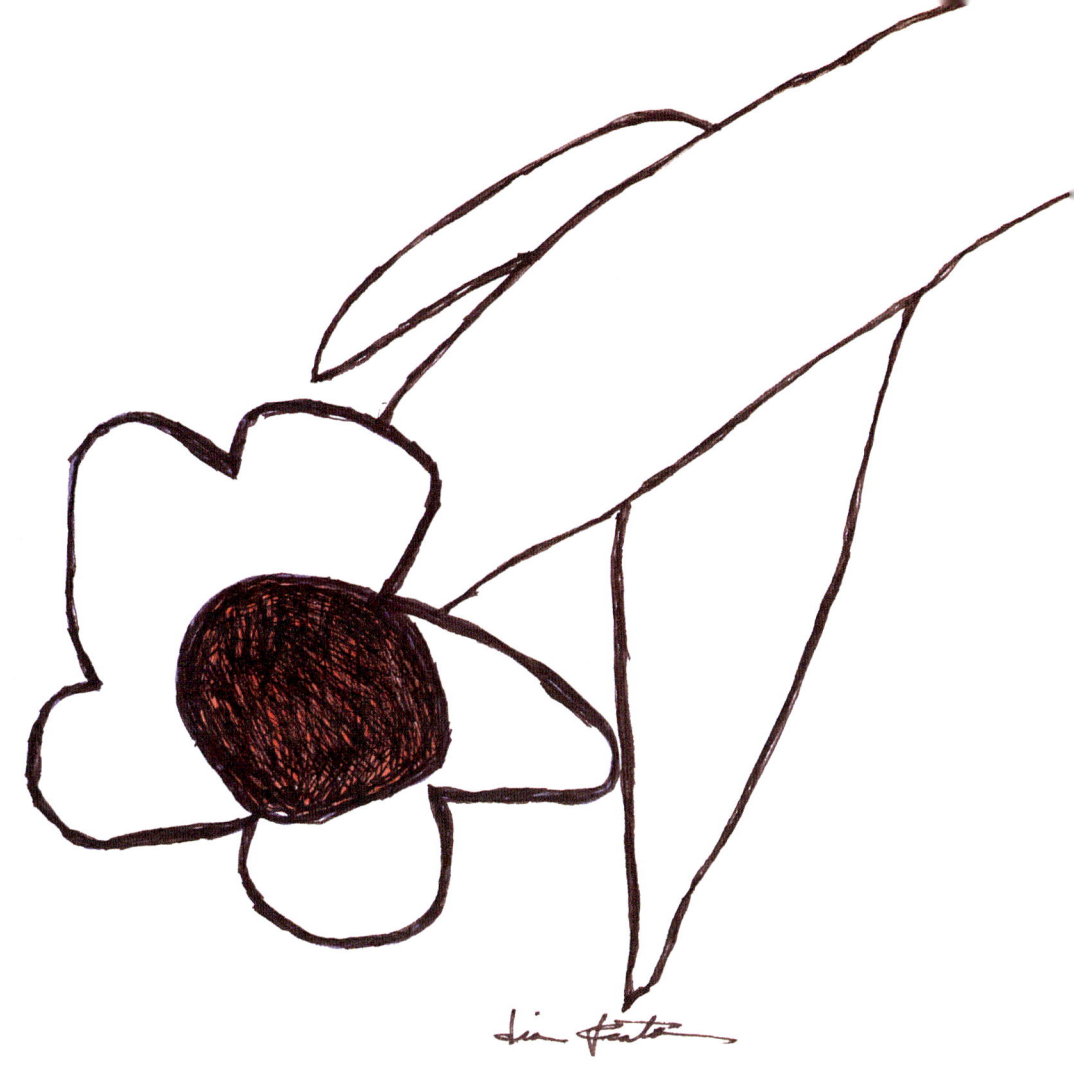

DIANE KEATON | *1983*
ROSS BLECKNER | *1996 (facing)*

FLORA

FLORA

To satisfy Prospero's imagination, the chaste spirits that walked about the glades in the forest behind the library walls were never seen to eat, to spit, to urinate, to defecate, to curse. Perhaps they never did these things. Prospero caught one with a butterfly clenched between her lips and teeth. Its wings were beating frantically on her cheek. He prised open her mouth with his finger and found a mouth full of moths, butterflies and gaudy beetles, all broken backed and half-drowned in spittle, beyond repair. She lived on insects. She was insectivorous. Did her gut collect the chitinous fragments, the beetle legs, the crumpled antennae, the brittle wings, and throw them out, like an owl throws out what it cannot digest, in pellets, smoothed and shaped like small, rough-formed eggs, blunt at one end, tapered at the other? She was not going to throw up a parcel of insect remains for Prospero. Prospero smacked her bottom, leaving a pink handprint, and she ran off weeping into the forest. Or was it laughing?

One creature that lived in the shadow between two library buttresses, had a heavy mane of dark hair. In the twilight the hair was violet and at dusk when the sun went down, it was purple. At night, it was heavier still and purple almost to black. Maybe it was not her own hair, but leased from Night, kept hung by day on a wooden stand in a hollow tree. Her skin was pale yellow and her figure was slim with small breasts whose pink nipples never knew how to harden. Of this child, Prospero fashioned an idea of Flora, personification of Spring. He gave her a small bunch of bright flowers to carry in procession. Lilies and lilac, both strongly and antagonistically scented. This creature, like Spring, was a little mad. Prospero waited for Spring every year as though Spring was a simple moment and when it came he wanted it to stay, Freshness, Spontaneity, Newness, Vitality, Hope. All allegorical possibilities. Spring always passed into summer before Prospero could welcome it - maybe the transience was the quality to be cherished. He thought of tieing Flora down and watching she did not run away to summer. He did not. She would

PETER GREENAWAY | *1991*

One creature that lived in the shadow between u[...]
a heavy mane of dark hair. In the twilight the hair [...]
dusk when the sun went down, it was purple. At night, [...]
still and purple almost to black. Maybe it was not her own hair,
leased from Night, kept hung by day on a wooden stand in a hollow tree.
Her skin was pale yellow and her figure was slim with small breasts whose
pink nipples never knew how to harden. Of this child, Prospero fashioned
an idea of Flora, personification of Spring. He gave her a small bunch of
bright flowers to carry in procession. Lilies and lilac, both strongly
and antagonistically scented. This creature, like Spring, was a little
mad. Prospero waited for Spring every year as though Spring was a simple
moment and when it came he wanted it to stay, Freshness, Spontaneity,
Newness, Vitality, Hope. All allegorical possibilities. Spring always
passed into summer before Prospero could welcome it - maybe the
transience was the quality to be cherished. He thought of tieing Flora
down and watching she did not run away to summer. He did not. She would

Peter Greenaway
Sept. '91.

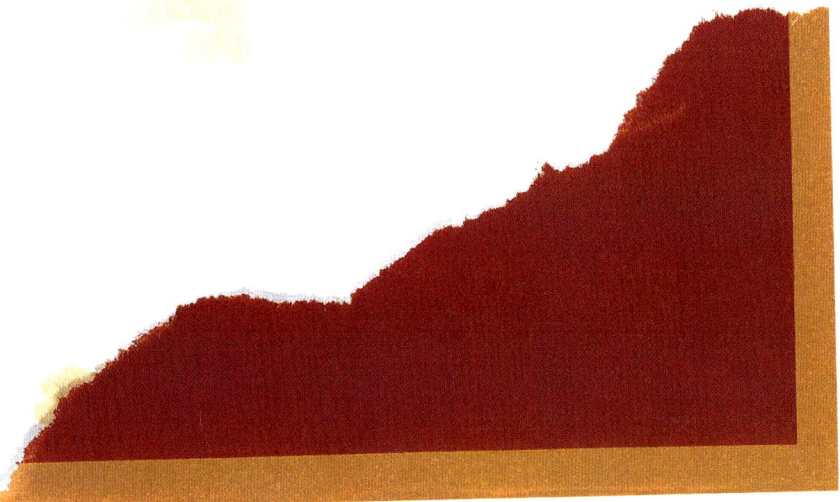

For Victoria: appropriate draft pages for a floral in memoriam?
... and the pages are stuck down with Rosey - Australian Wild Honey!

PAUL SHAFFER | *1988*
SHAWN COLVIN | *1998 (facing)*

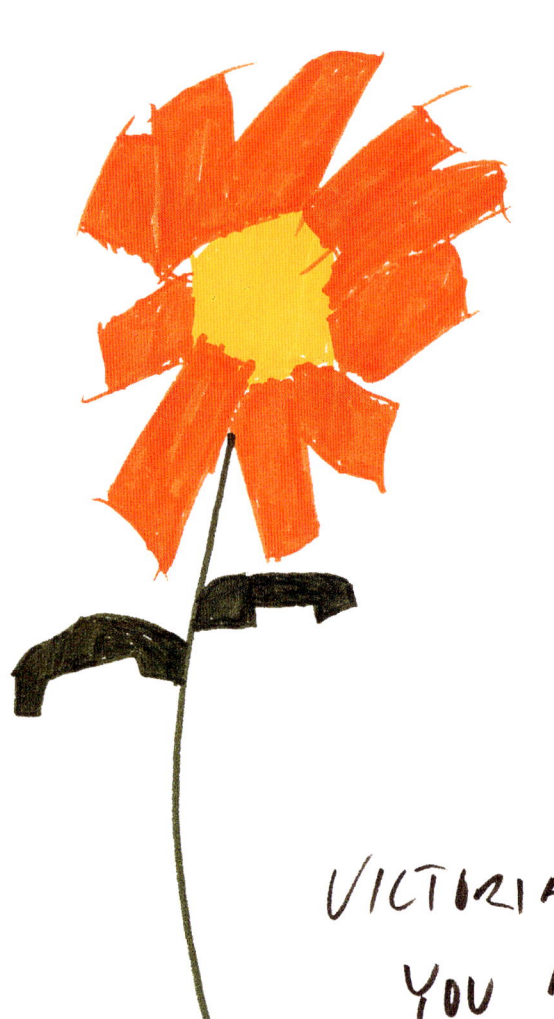

VICTORIA —
YOU ARE THE
FLOWER, BABE.
LOVE,
Paul Shaffer

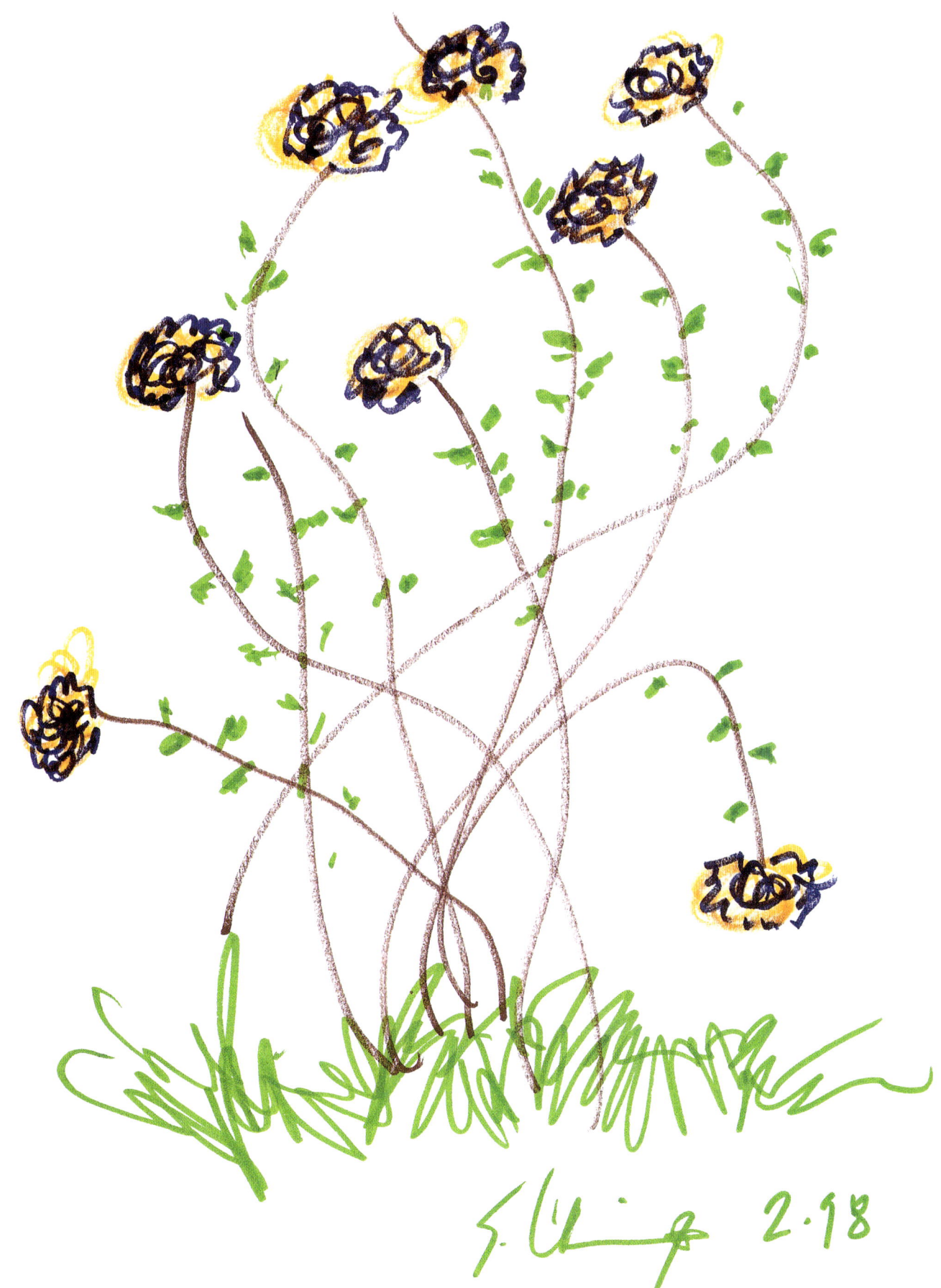

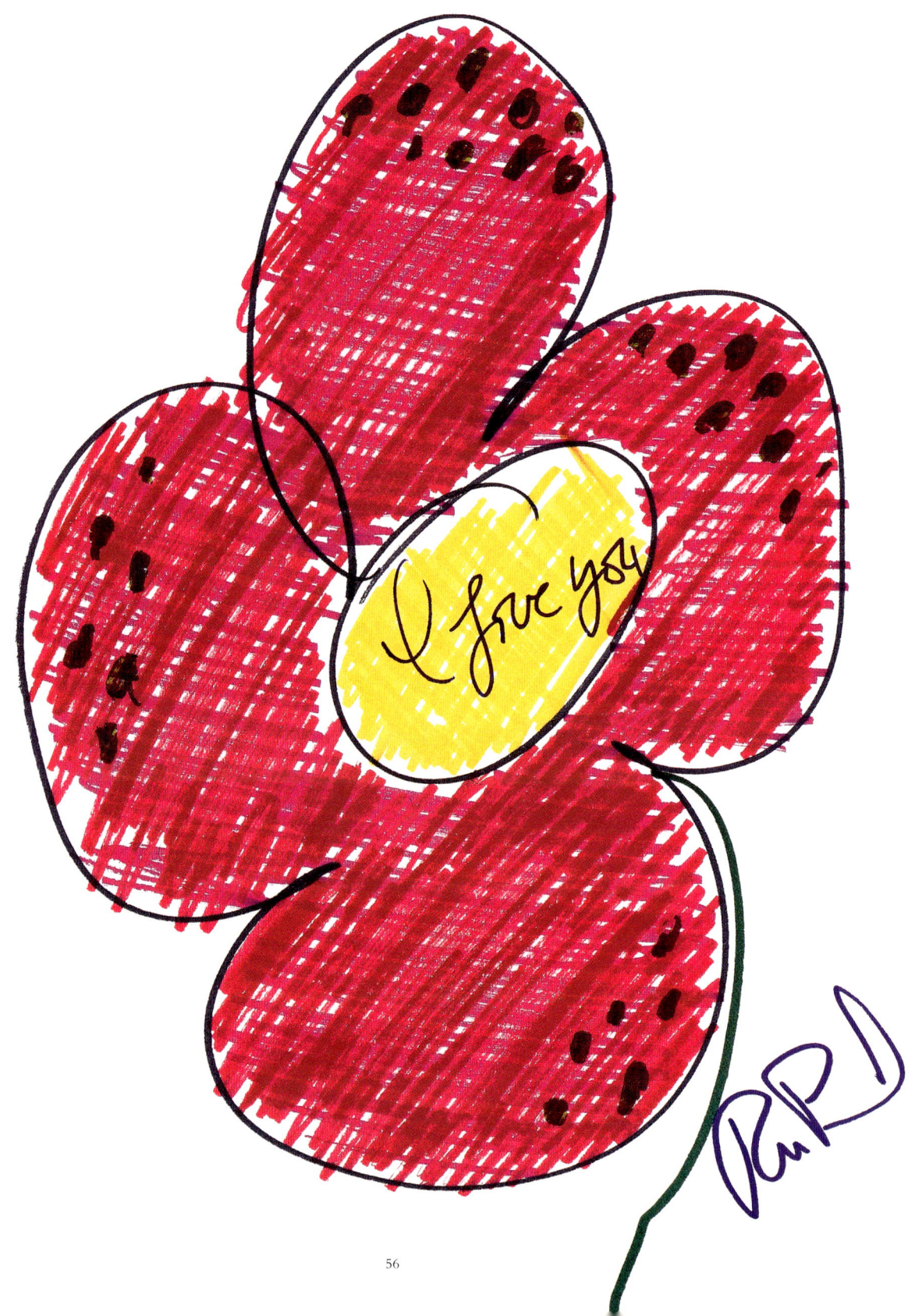

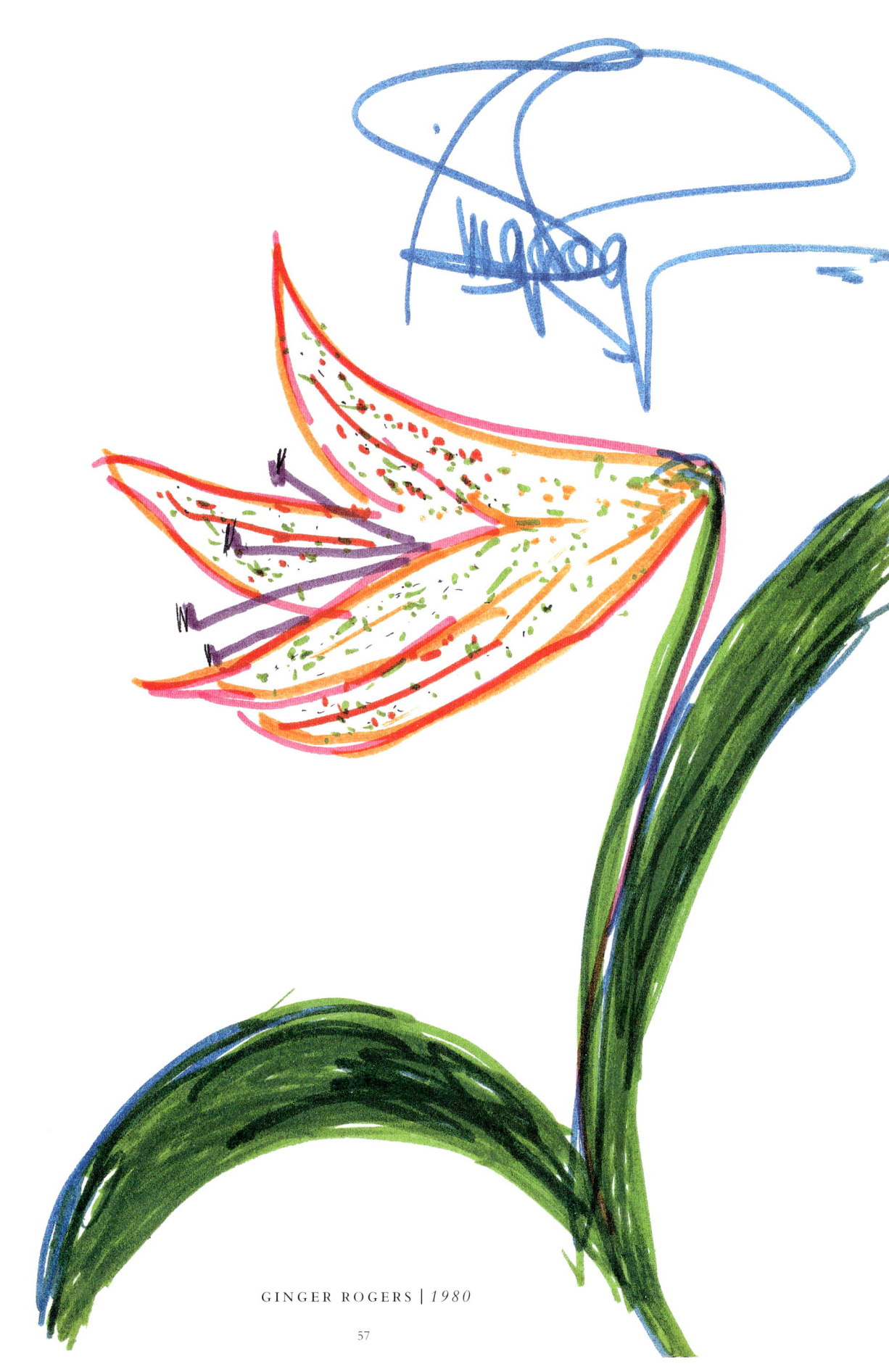

GINGER ROGERS | *1980*

KEITH HARING | *1984*

In April 1984 while I was a theater student in London, I flew back to New York for a brief visit. I dropped by Andy Warhol's studio to show him how my latest flower book was coming along and to ask him to start a fourth one for me. He invited me to stay for lunch and introduced me to his other guest, a talented young artist named Keith Haring. I was a fan of Haring's work, having seen it on the subways and in the streets for some time, so I was very excited to meet him.

DURING LUNCH ANDY suggested that Keith draw a flower. When Keith handed me his drawing I was overwhelmed. It was a beautiful, dancing flower, brimming with life and energy. It was the kind of flower I wished everyone could create—happy and vital.

AFTER THAT INITIAL meeting I ran into Keith quite a lot, sometimes at parties, but more often on the street. Keith was a very warm person who was always friendly and generous with his time.

A FEW YEARS later Andy was dead. My fourth flower book was full, and I was having a hard time starting another one without him. He had been such an important figure in my life, and one of my great joys was sharing these books with him. I didn't know what to do. Then I thought of Keith.

IT WAS DECEMBER 1988 when I went to his studio on Broadway. By this time he was truly famous, but as always he was very genuine and down-to-earth. He asked me to leave the book for a few hours. I went back later that night to find him surrounded by friends, casually working on another project and listening to music. He presented me with a second flower (see the front endpaper), and I was stunned. It wasn't what I had expected at all, nothing like his first drawing, which was so energetic and full of life. This picture was just as moving, but it was sad, almost vicious. The flowers had been deliberately cut down in full bloom.

I DIDN'T UNDERSTAND until later when Keith announced that he had AIDS. When I saw him that December night he seemed fine, he looked great. But I guess it's true—art never lies. The flowers said it all.

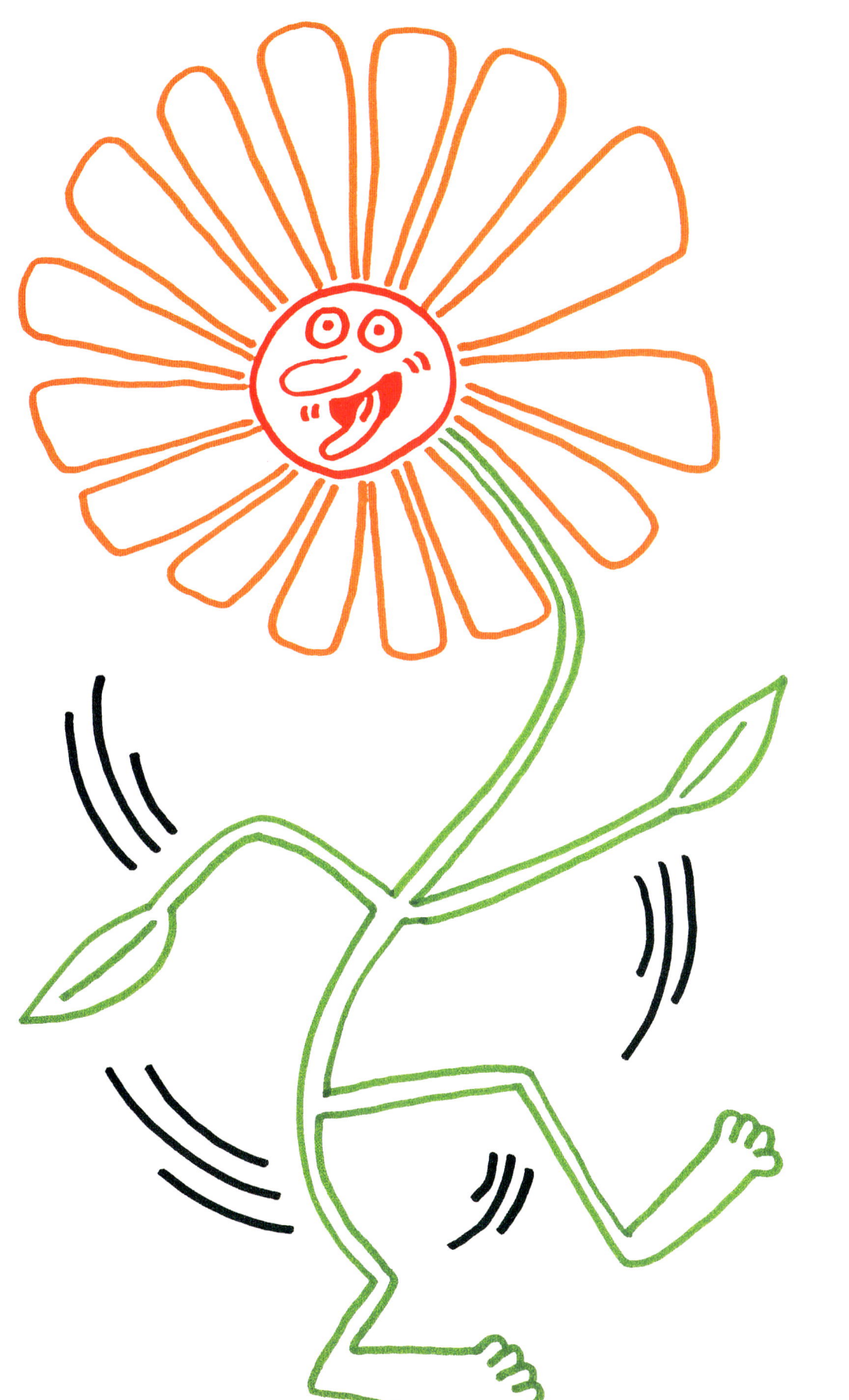

JOHN HUSTON | *1980*

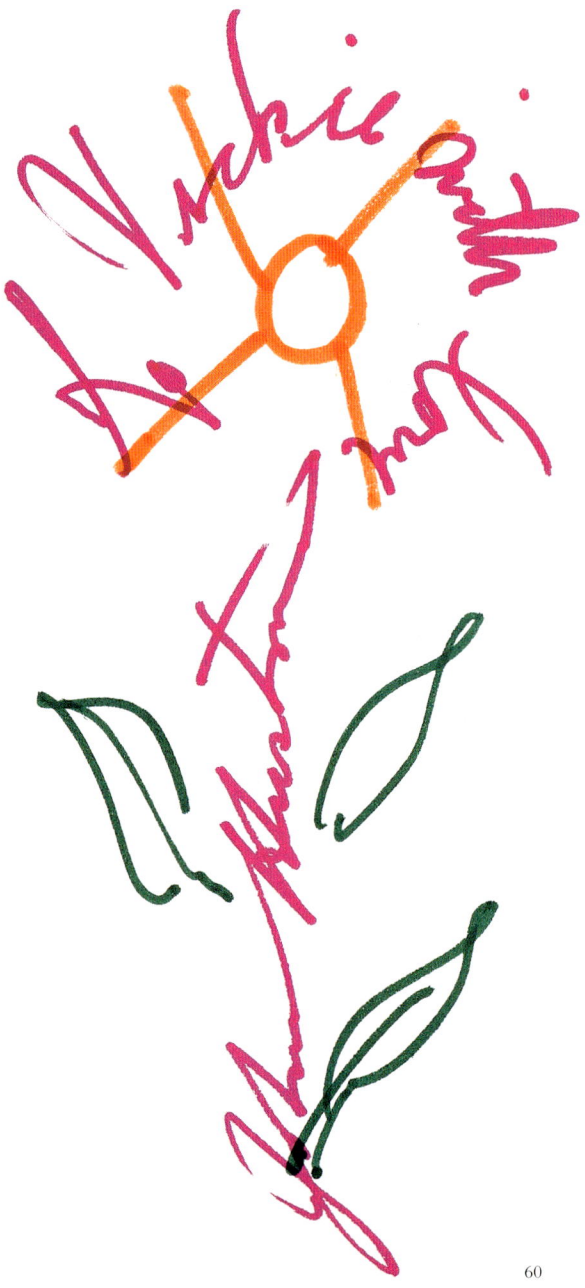

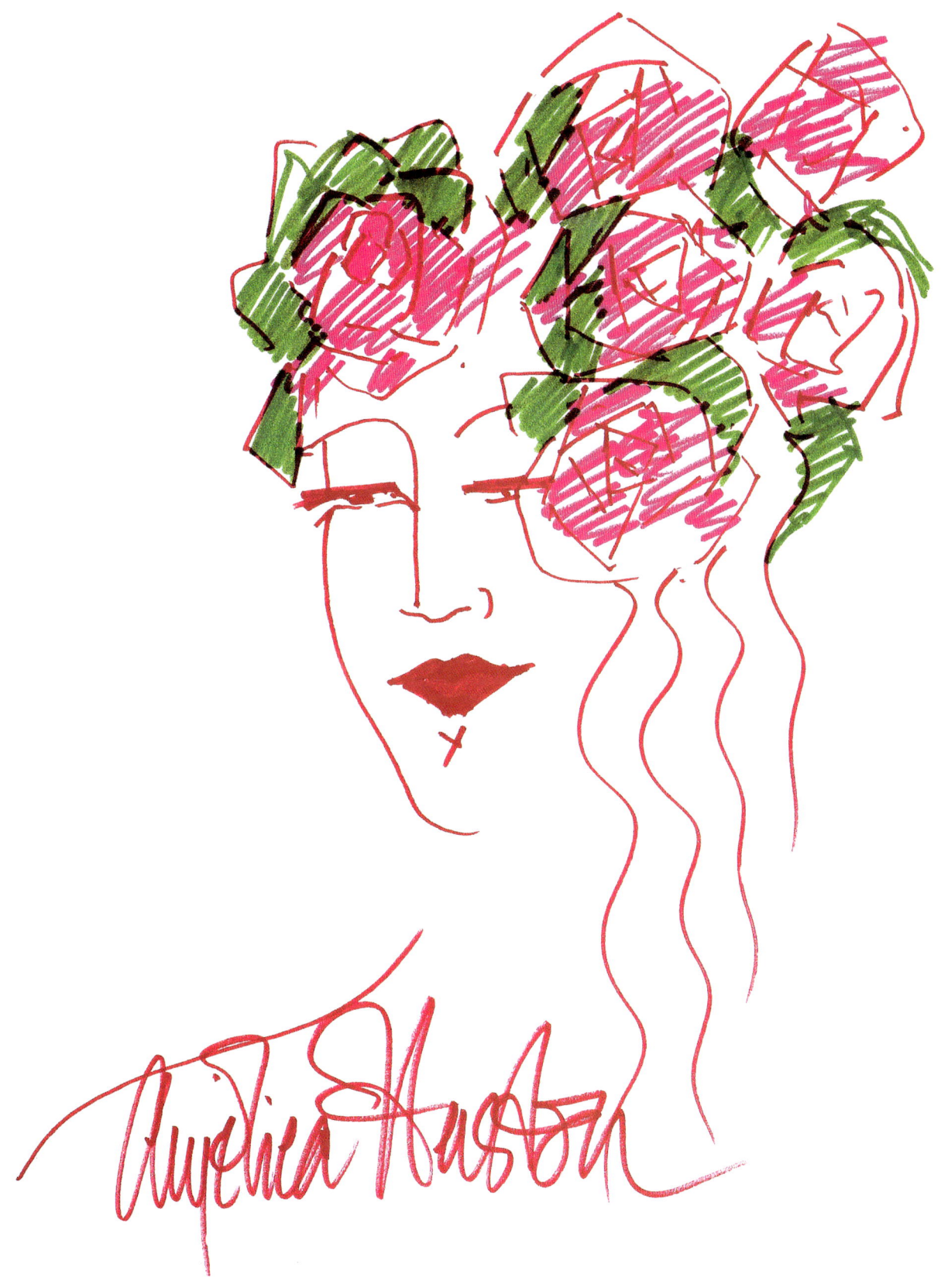

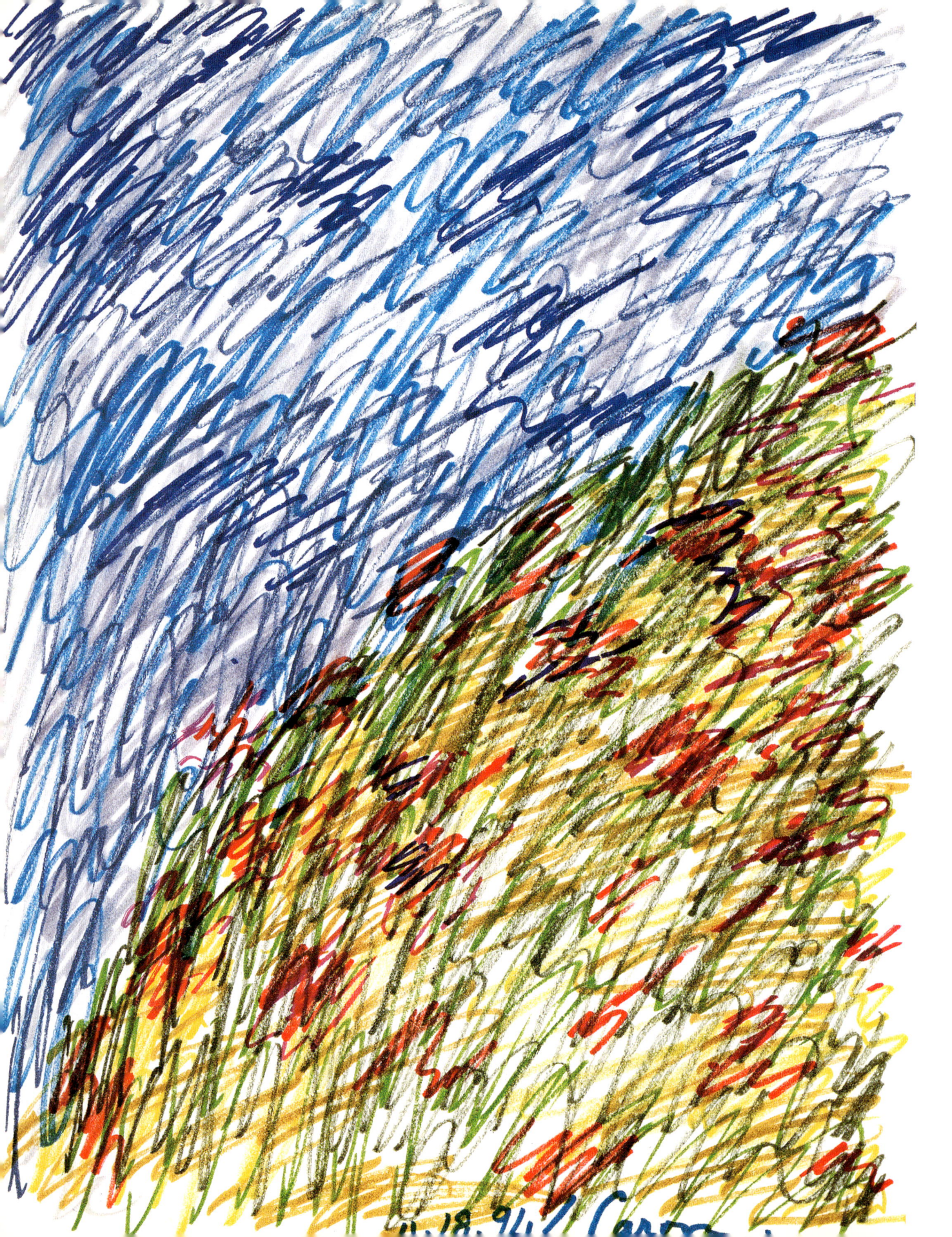

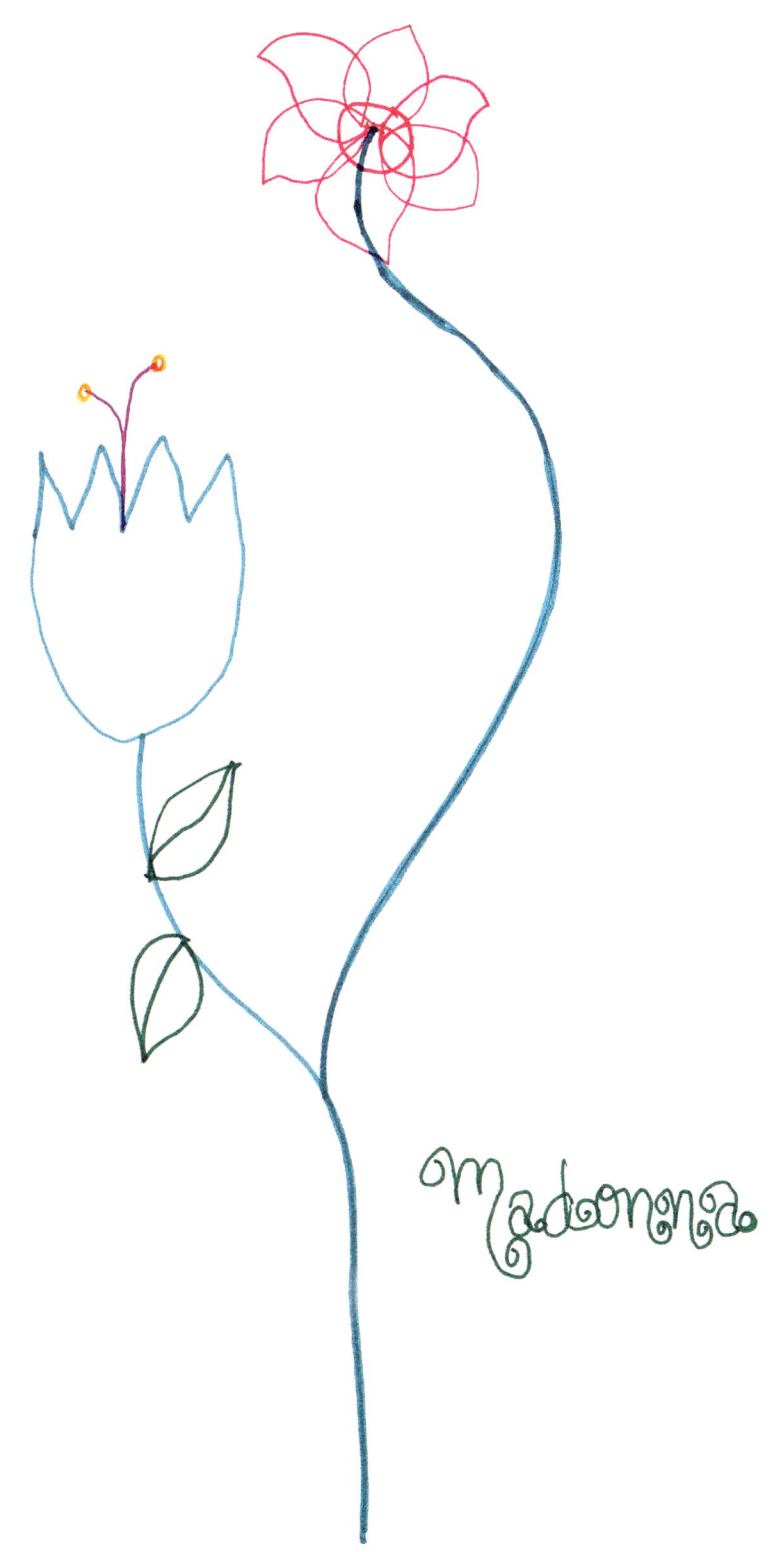

MADONNA | 1997
LESLIE CARON | 1994 (facing)

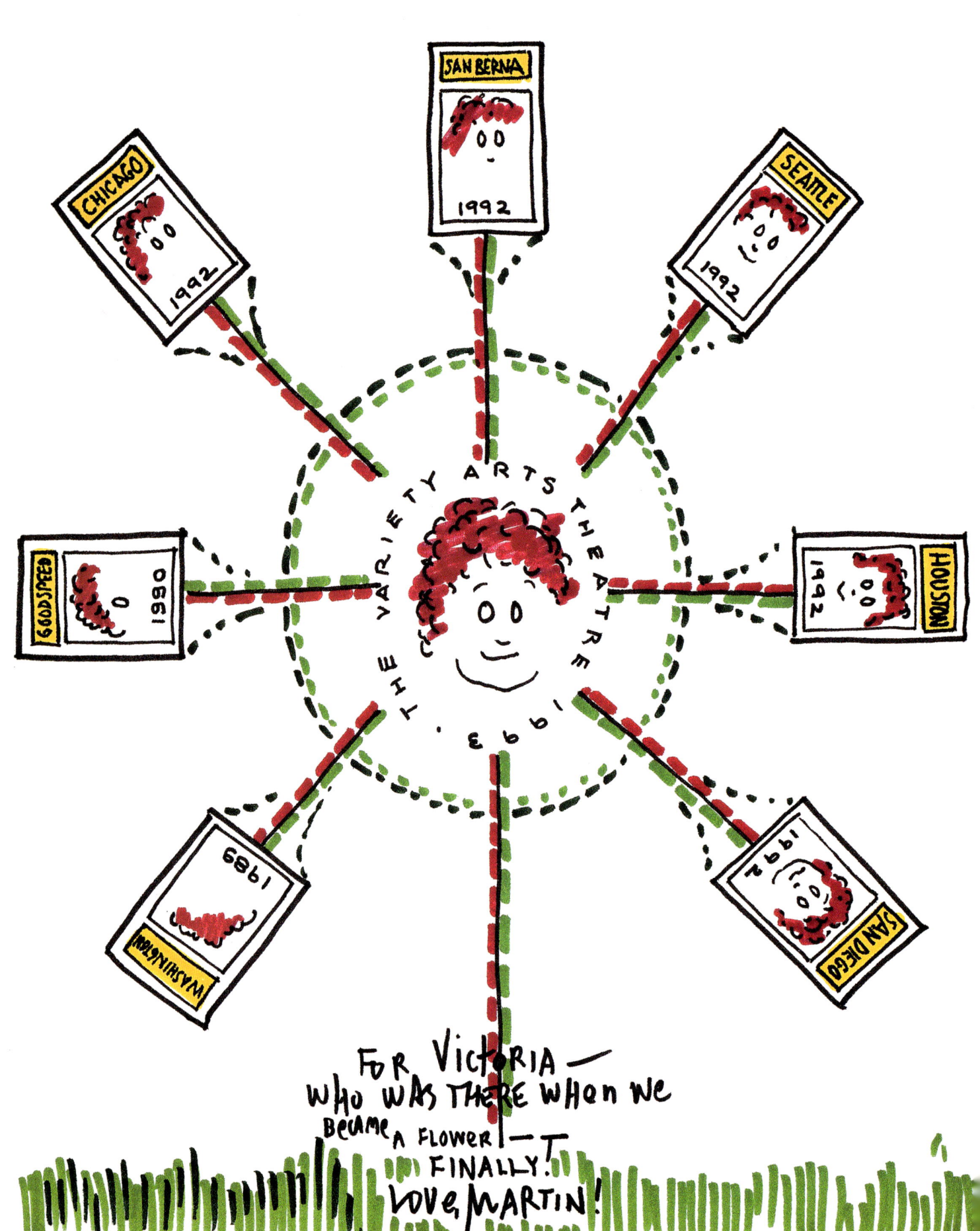

CELINE DION | *1998*
MARTIN CHARNIN | *1993 (facing)*

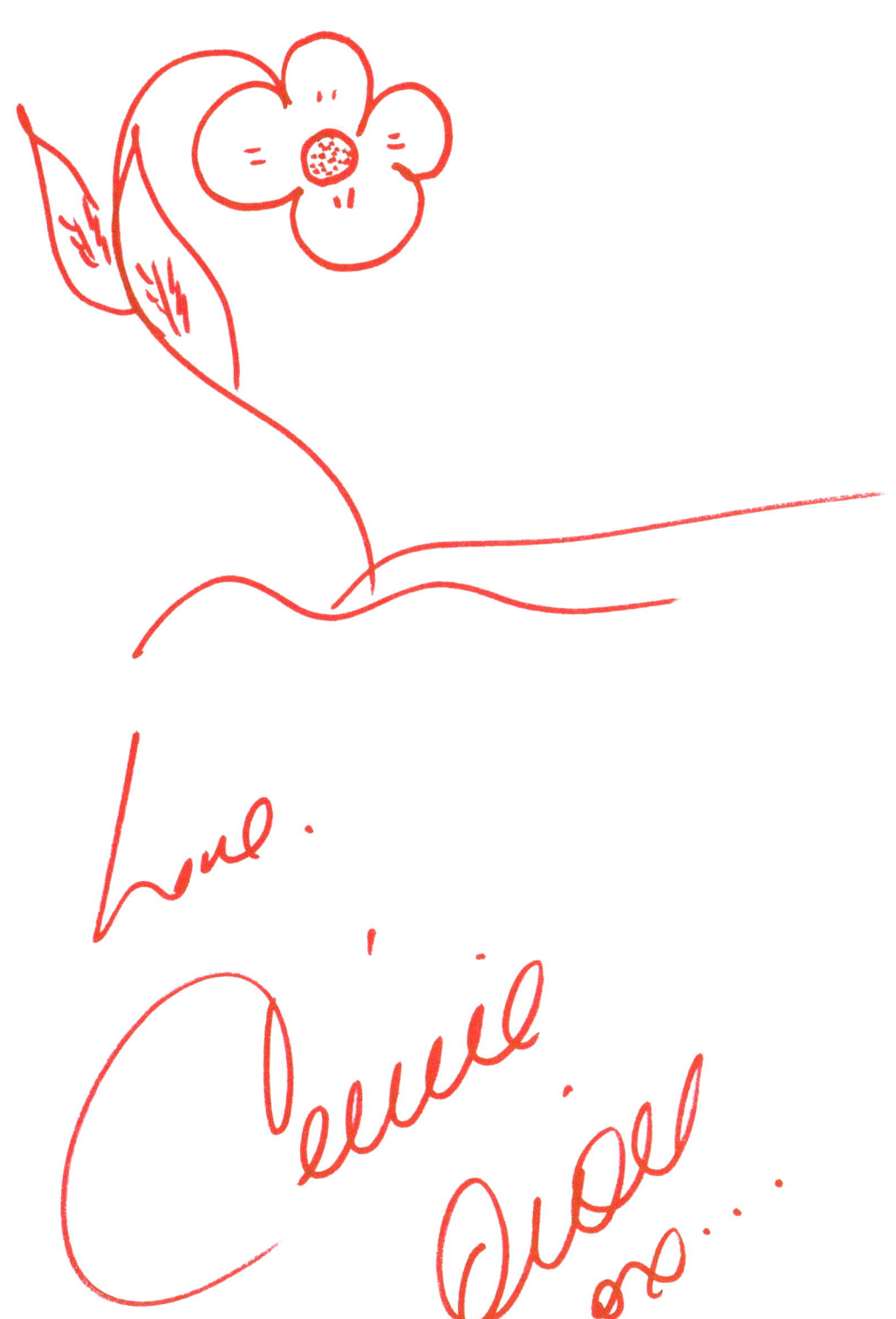

MAY 15 1989

THIS IS ONLY A RECORD OF A REQUEST OF A FLOWER. RENEE IS SITTING AND RENEE IS HERE IN "ODEON" THE DAY AFTER MOTHERS DAY AND VICTORIA IS SAYING "BUT, PLEASE, DRAW A FLOWER...", AND RENEE IS SAYING "PLEASE, WHATEVER YOU DO IT QUICKLY BECAUSE SHE HAS A REAL BAD SORE THROAT AFTER HER BEST FRIENDS WEDDING

OVER

AND I KEEP THINKING THE HEADLINES I SHOULD / WILL READ AFTER "GAL" HOSPITALIZED — OR "GIRL" BEST FRIENDS WEDDING "HOSPITALIZED" NOT YET MARRIED... DAMN BUT VICKY SAYS "AND I KNOW A FLOWER TAKES TIME A FLOWER... FLOWER TO GROW TO..... FLOWER. I'M STILL HAPPY - STUCK IN "WORDS"

Spud Gray

SPALDING GRAY | 1989

LILI TAYLOR | *1997*
PATRICK STEWART | *1994 (facing)*

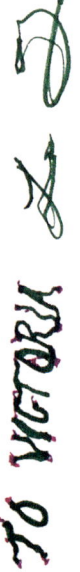
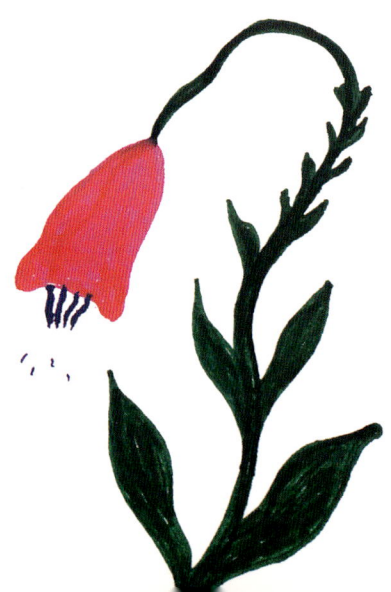

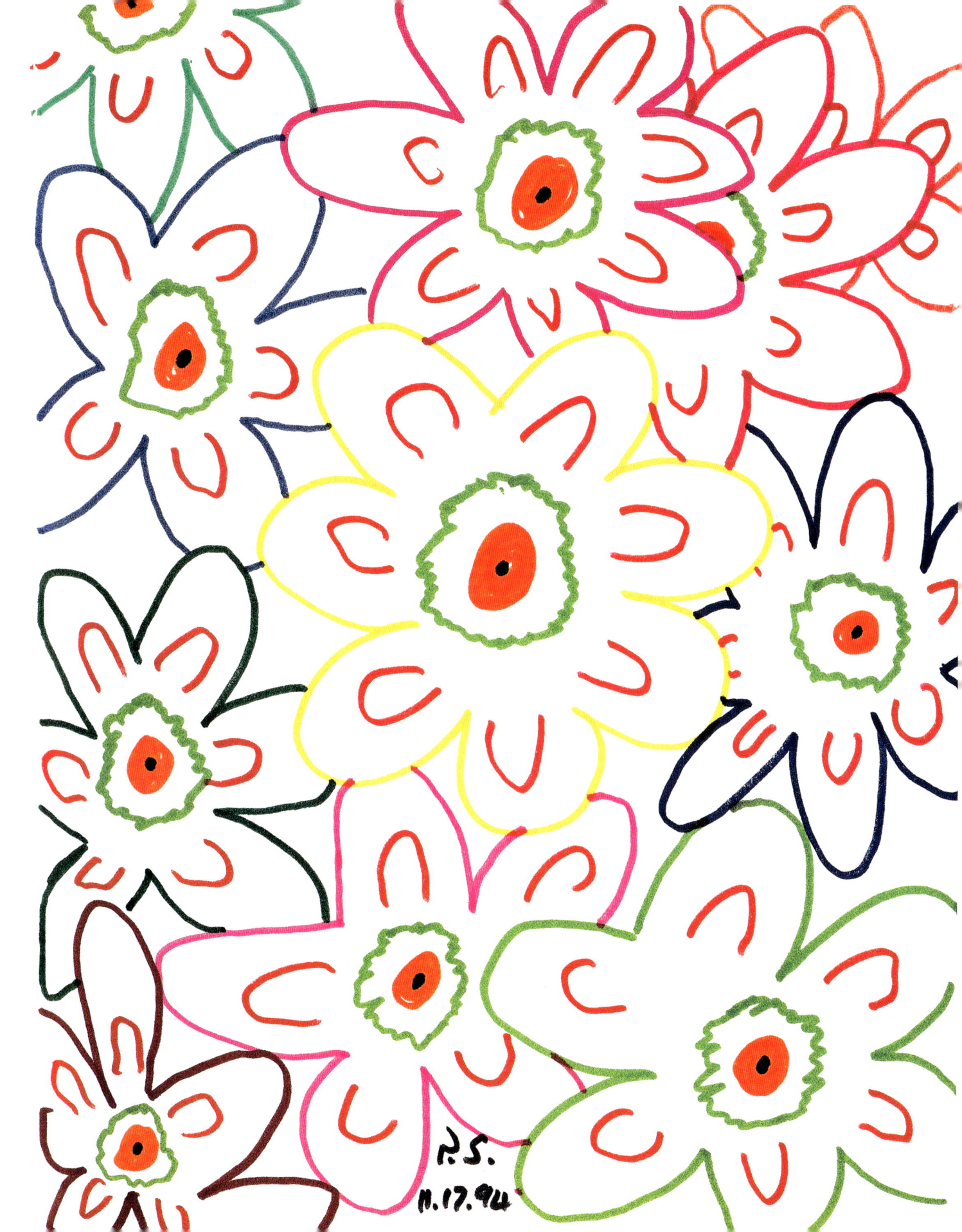

SUSAN SAINT JAMES | *1982*

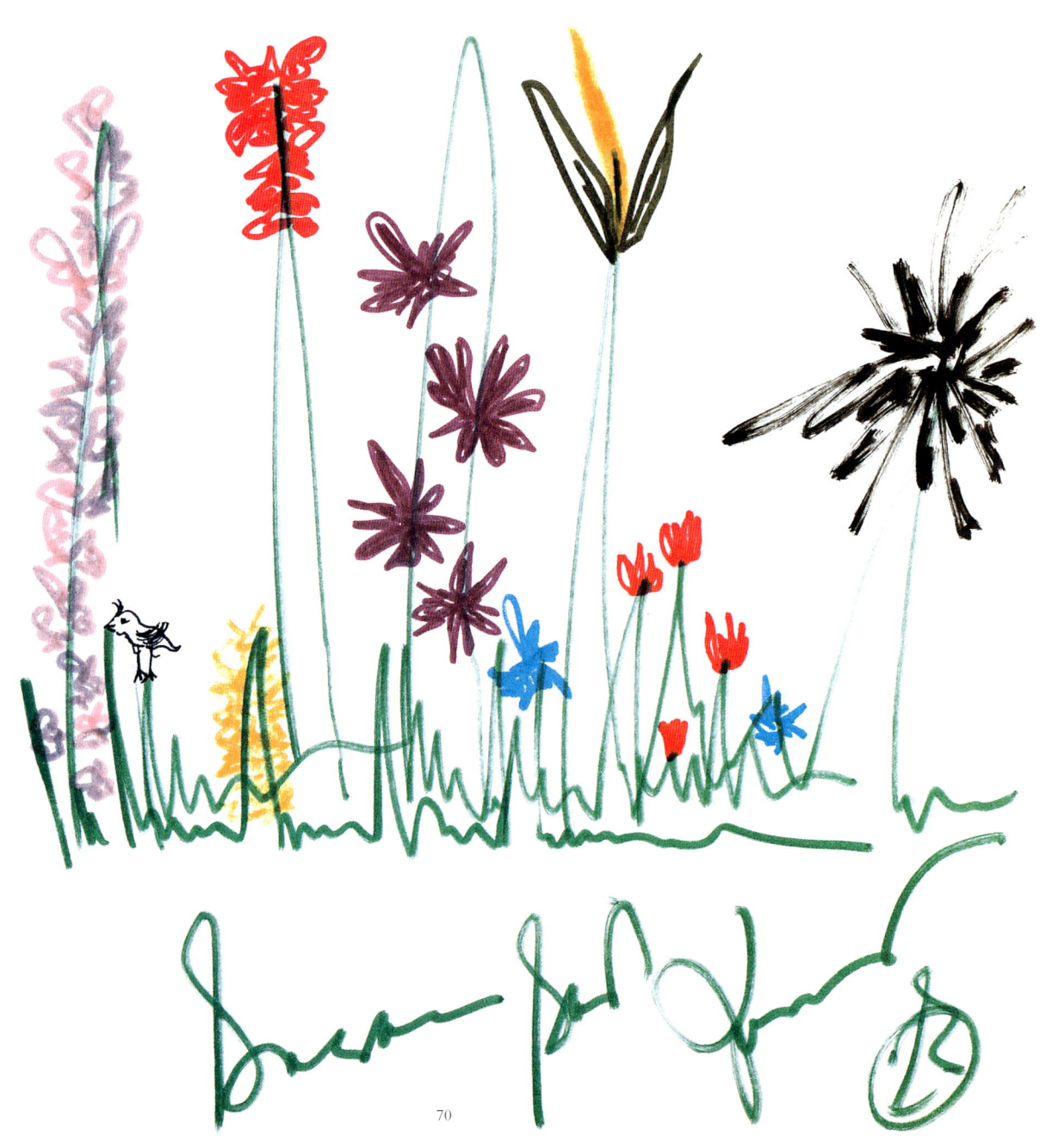

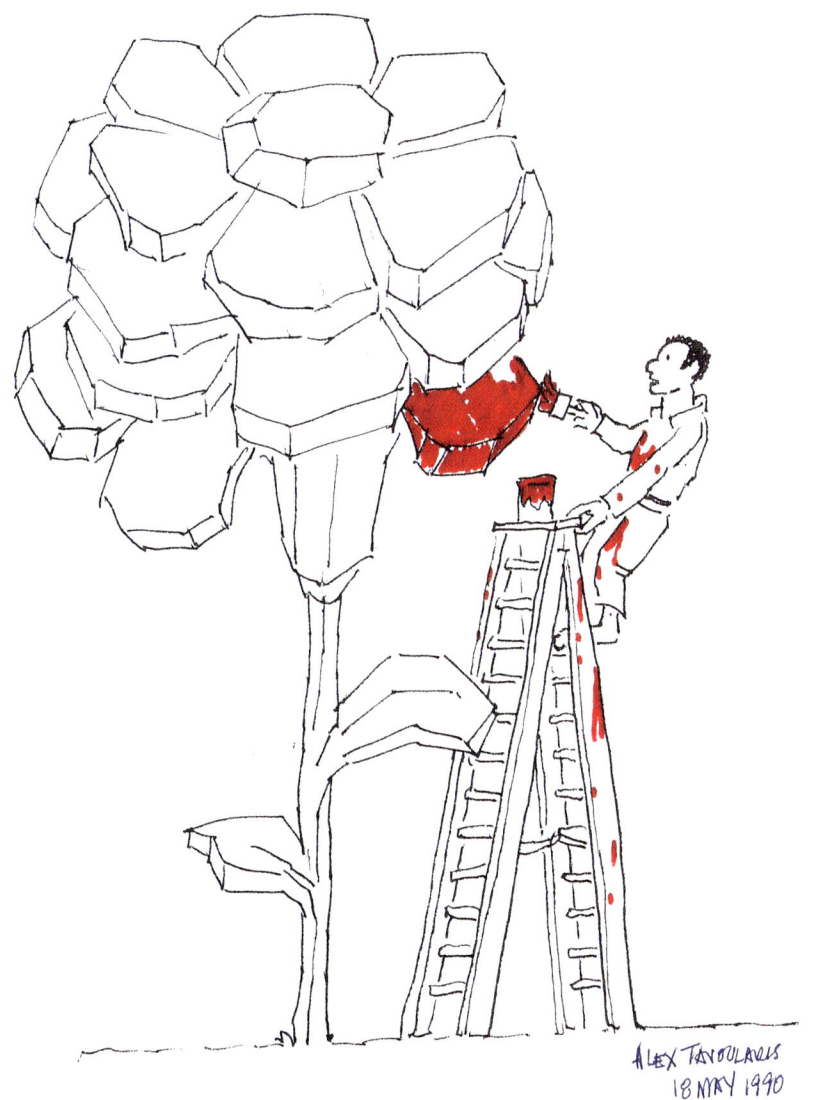

ALEX TAVOULARIS | *1990*

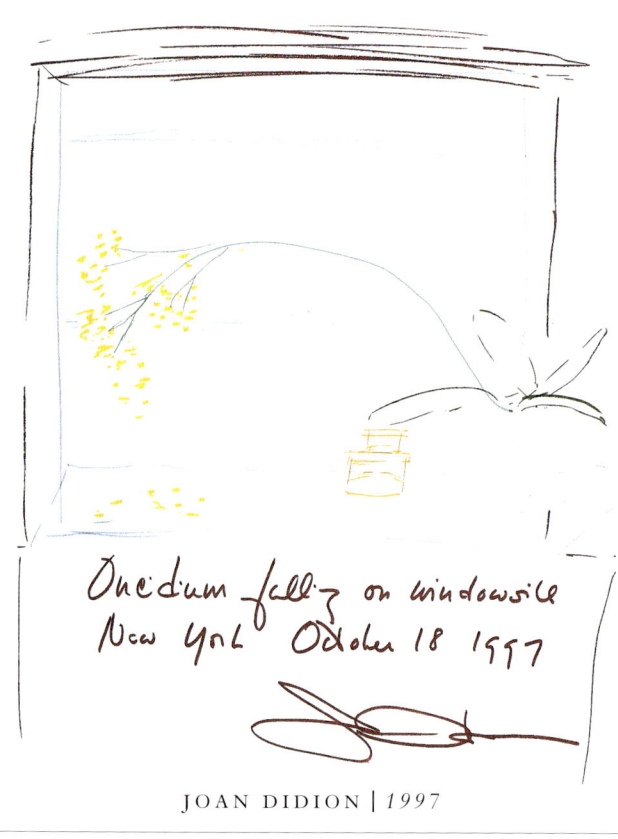

JOAN DIDION | *1997*

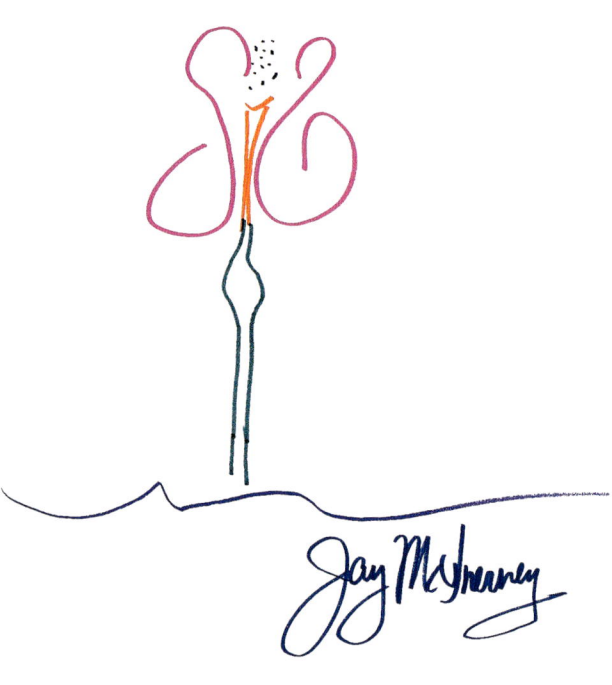

JAY MCINERNEY | *1988*

BRET EASTON ELLIS | *1988*

JON ROBIN BAITZ | *1990*

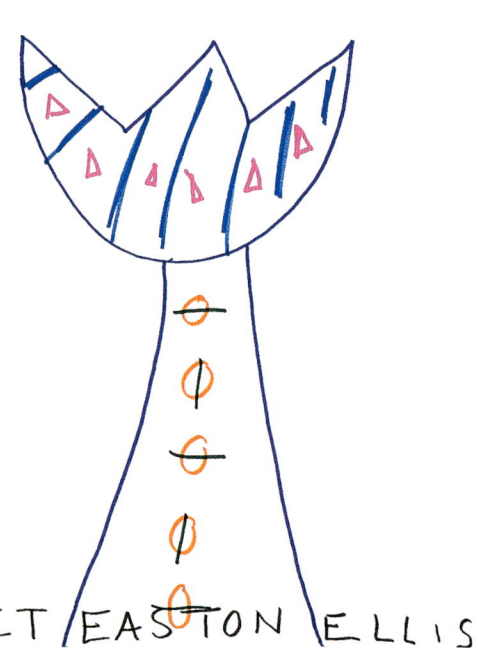

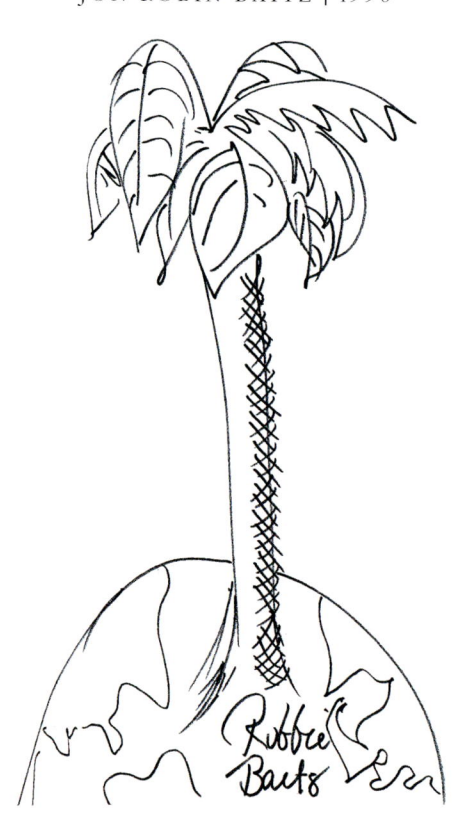

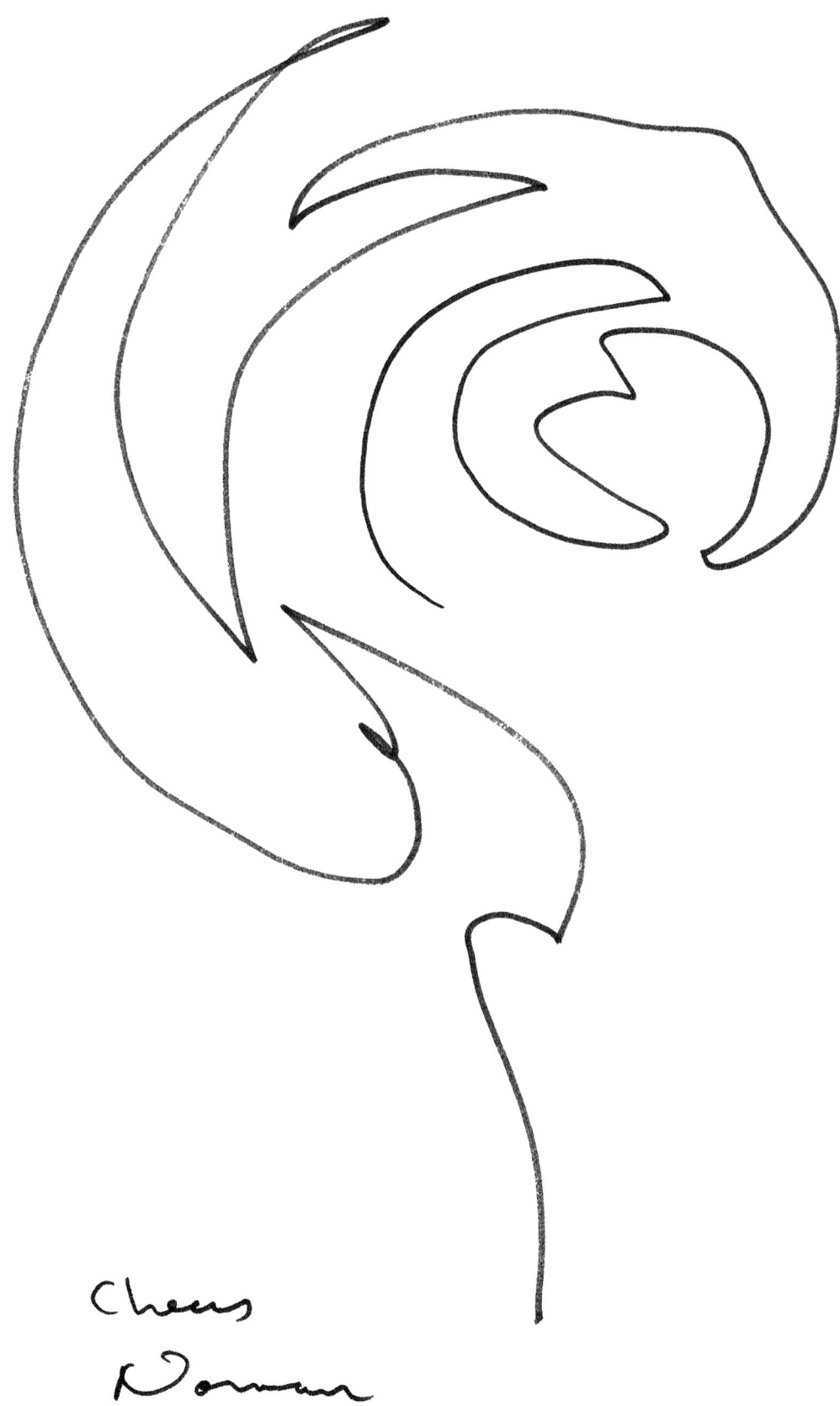

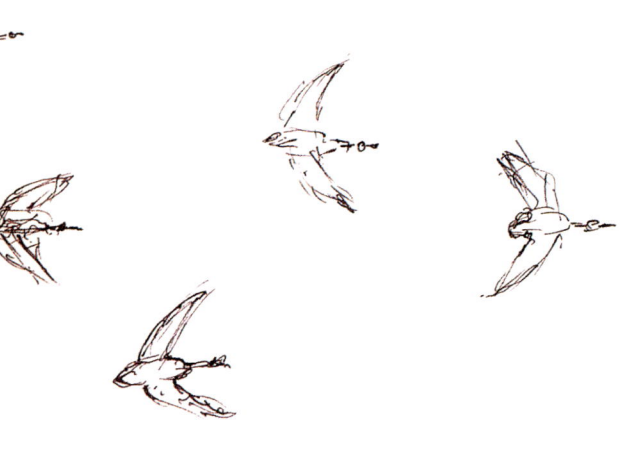

GEORGE PLIMPTON | *1988*

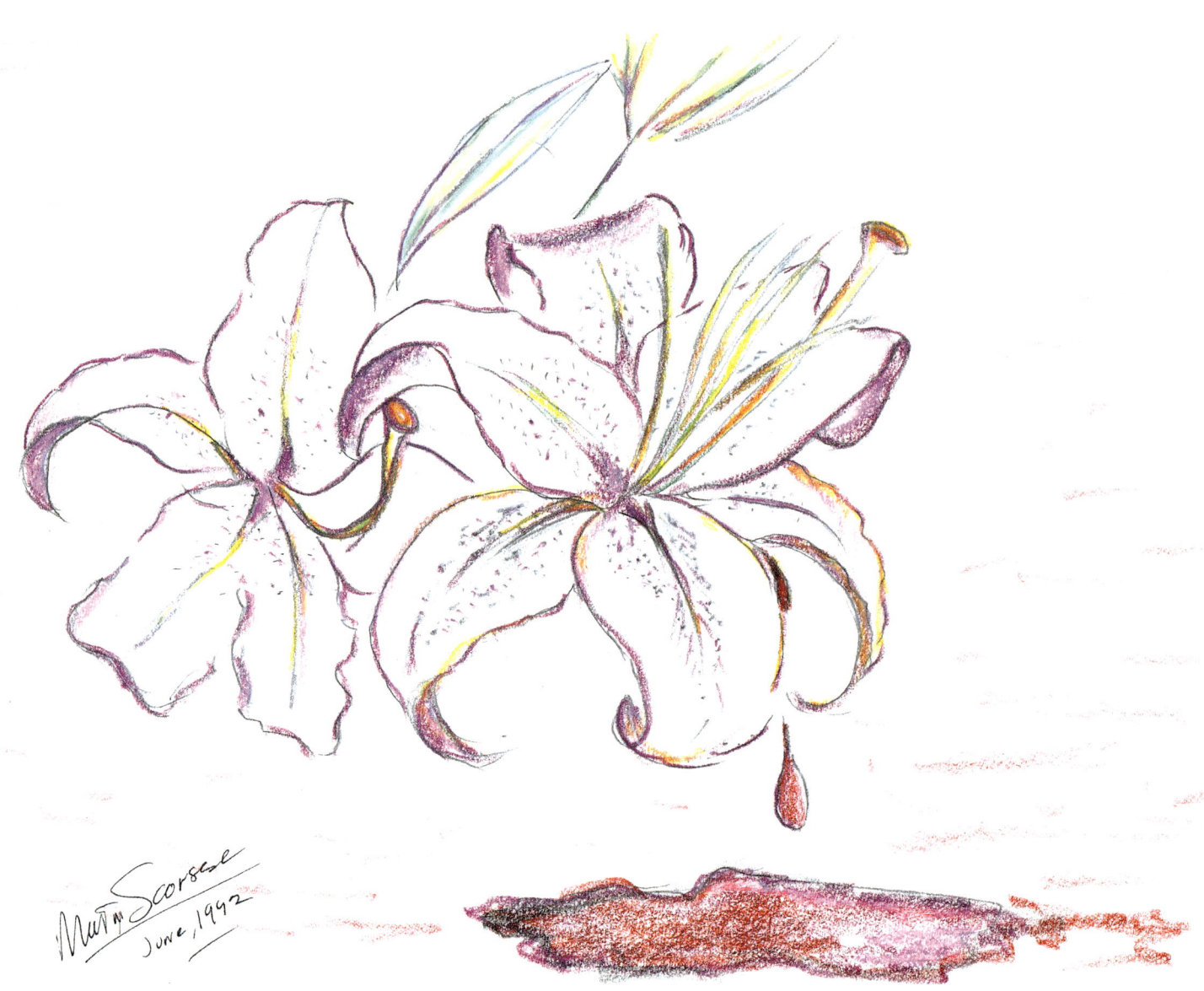

MARTIN SCORSESE | *1992*

Aside from my father, Martin Scorsese has always been my favorite director. My experience as a thirteen-year-old at the premiere of *New York, New York* opened a world of possibilities to me, including inspiring me to pursue filmmaking as a career.

IN 1991, ANTHOLOGY Film Archives, an organization in New York dedicated to preserving and exhibiting avant-garde and experimental film, was honoring Scorsese for his heroic work in film preservation at their annual awards dinner. As festival director, it was up to me to organize the event.

ON THE BIG night I arrived at Tavern on the Green with my hair piled into a huge beehive and wearing false eyelashes you could hang a hat on. I sat down at the head table, introduced myself to the guest of honor, and we began a conversation in which Scorsese talked about how much he admired my father's work. He was very charming, but I was becoming increasingly tense about the fact that as Mistress of Ceremonies I would soon have to get up in front of all these people and coordinate the award presentations for the evening. Sensing my distress he began coaching me, trying to soothe my frazzled nerves. The evening turned out to be a great success, and at the end I asked if he would draw a flower.

SIX MONTHS LATER I was on the set of *The Age of Innocence*, book in hand, watching the filming of a gorgeous nineteenth-century ballroom scene. Scorsese was in a corner watching the action on monitors. He looked up and invited me to join him. It was exciting for me, as a young filmmaker, to be able to watch a great director at work. I gave him the book and he invited me to visit him during the editing of the film.

SIX MORE MONTHS passed and on the appointed day I went uptown to the editing suite. Unfortunately, I got there just as Scorsese was editing the last shot of the film. Concerned about spoiling the whole movie by showing me the end first, he refused to let me into the editing room, but apologized profusely and asked if he could make it up to me with dinner.

NINE MONTHS AND many scheduling conflicts later, we finally sat down to dinner at his incredibly elegant town house. We talked for hours about everything from films to how much we both hate licorice.

HE PRESENTED ME with the flower book, which now contained two beautiful new drawings. One was of a white lily oozing crimson blood, the other was an almost cinematic rendering of the first flowers of the season in his town-house garden.

MARTIN SCORSESE IS every bit as fascinating, layered, and full of surprises as his films. It had taken a year and nine months, but I had gotten two of the most beautiful flowers in my collection. They were definitely worth the wait.

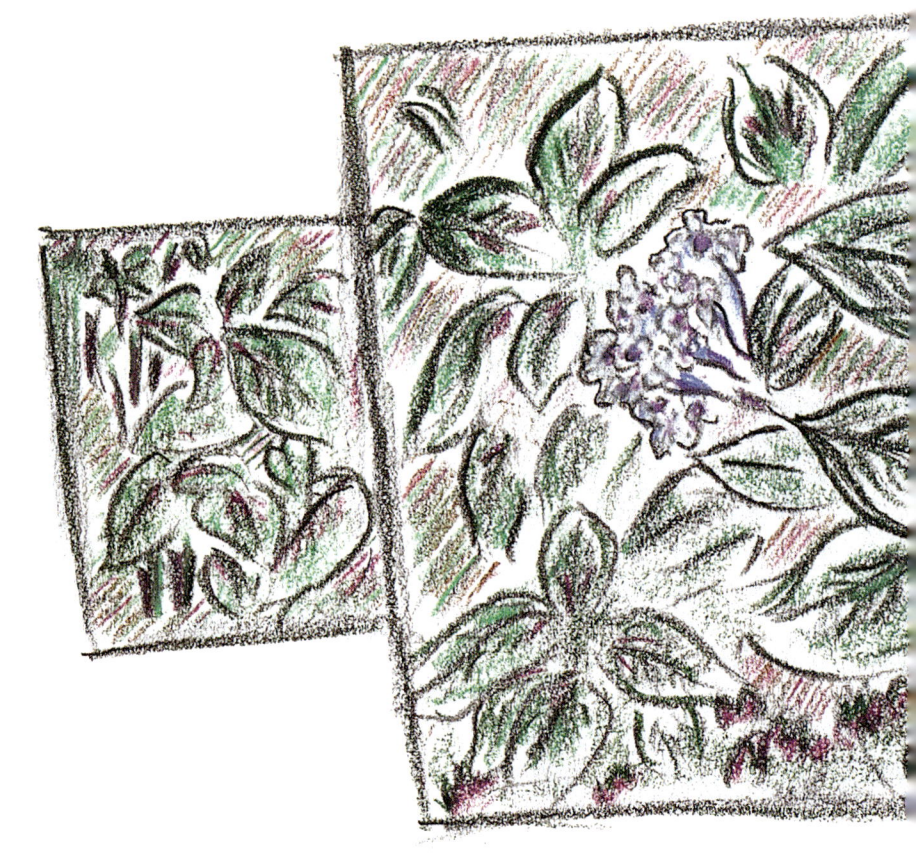

Martin Scorsese
June, 1992
1st Flower in New Garden - N.Y.C.

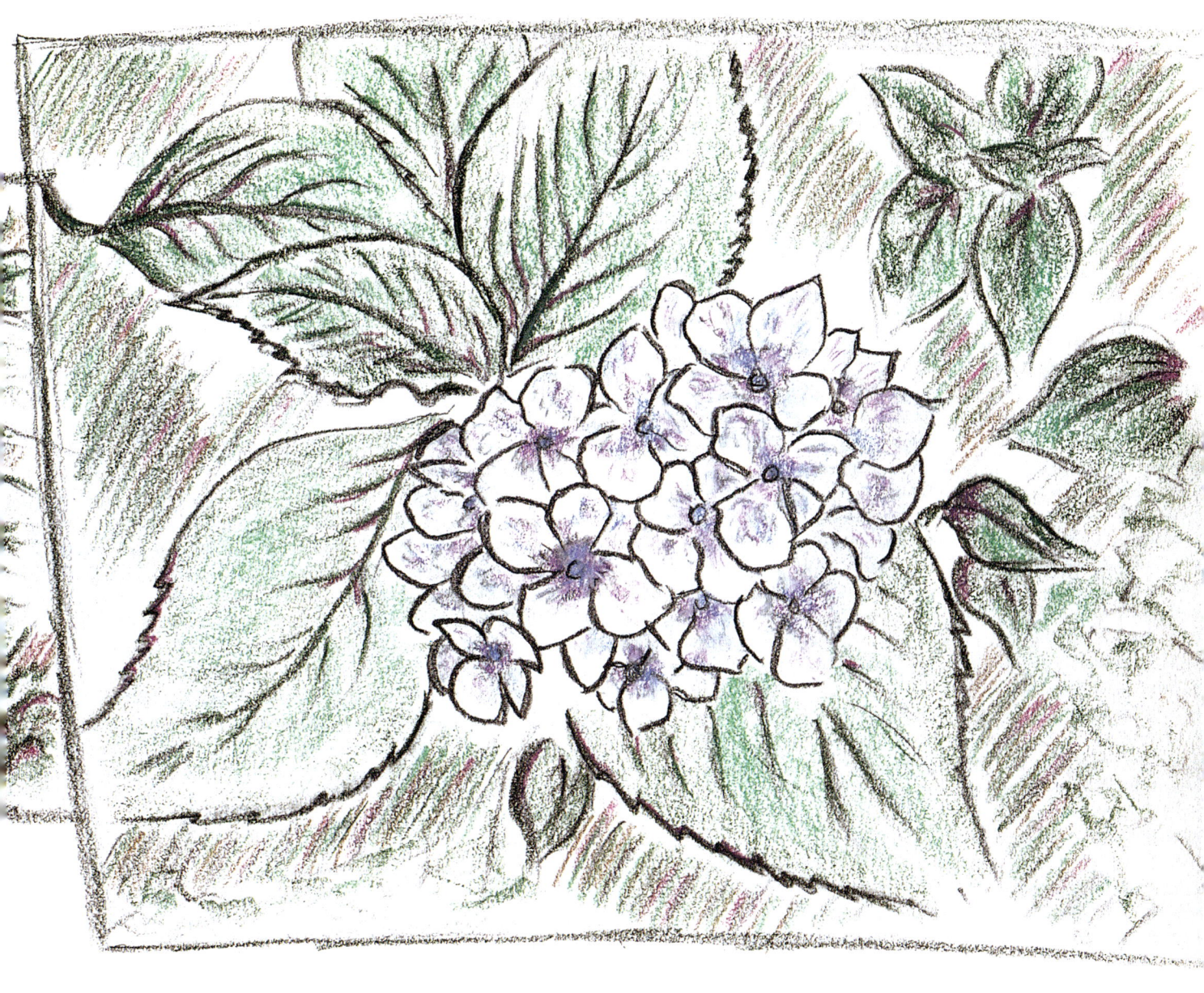

MARTIN SCORSESE | *1992*

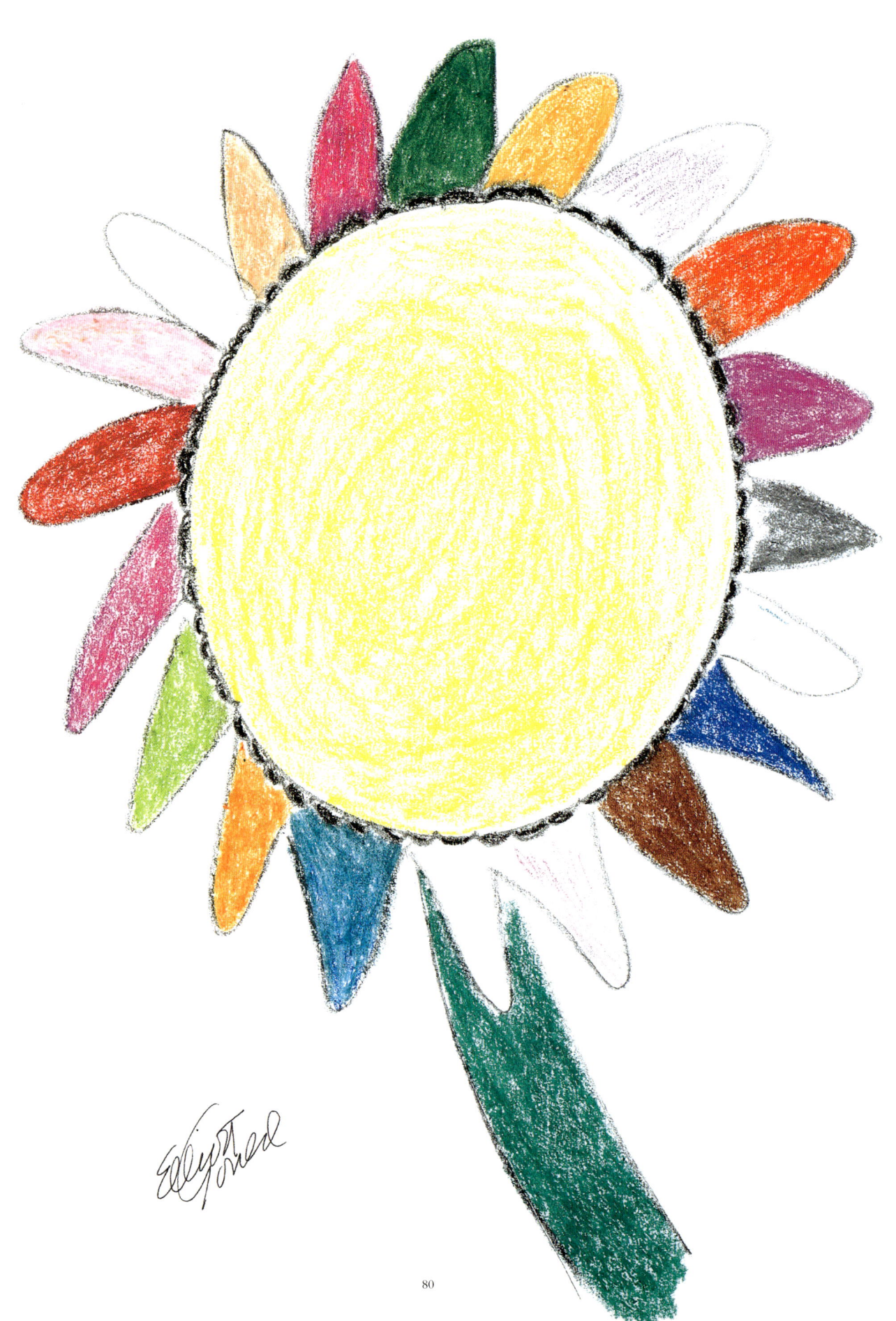

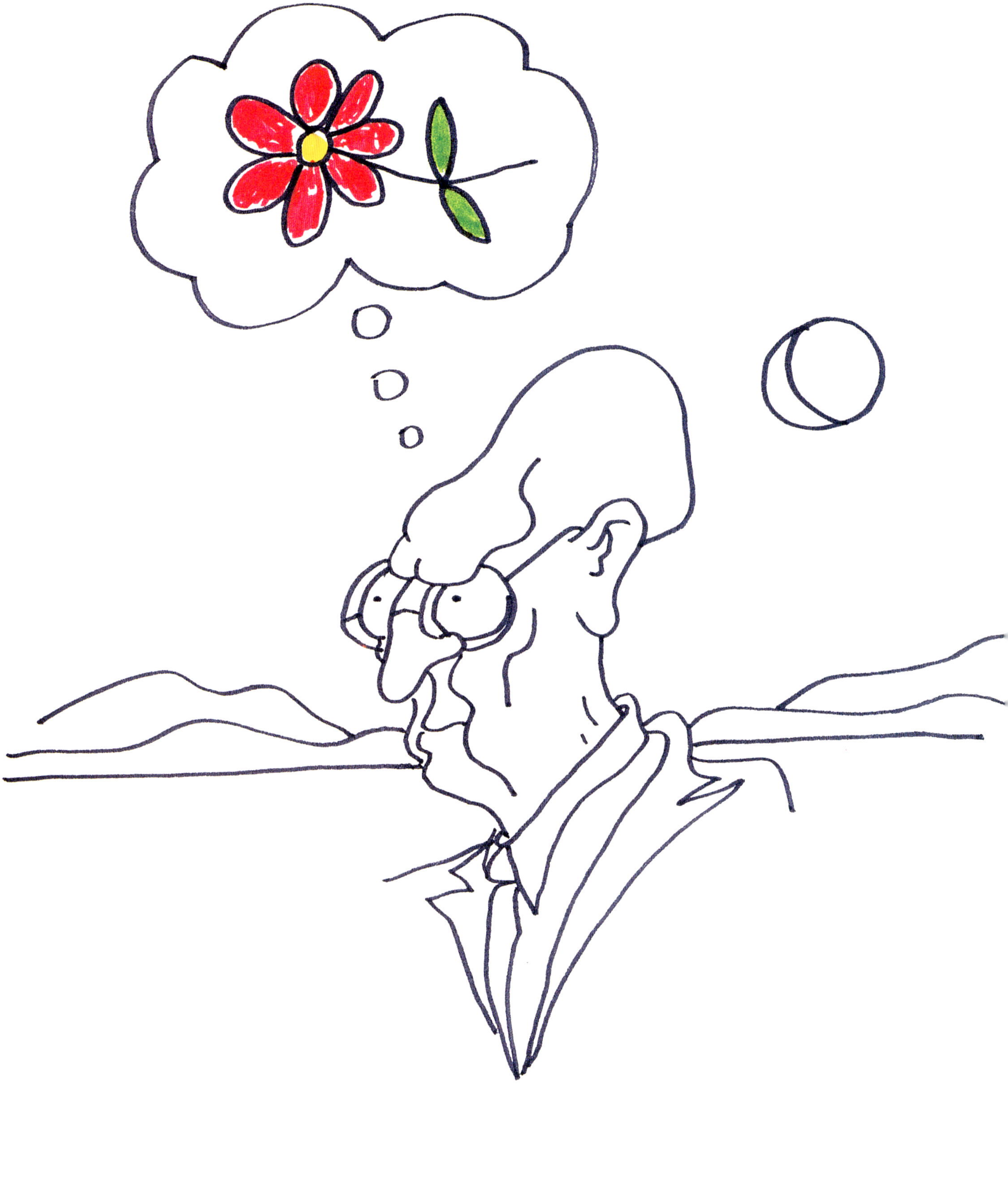

MARK ROMANEK | *1997*
ELLIOTT GOULD | *1995 (facing)*

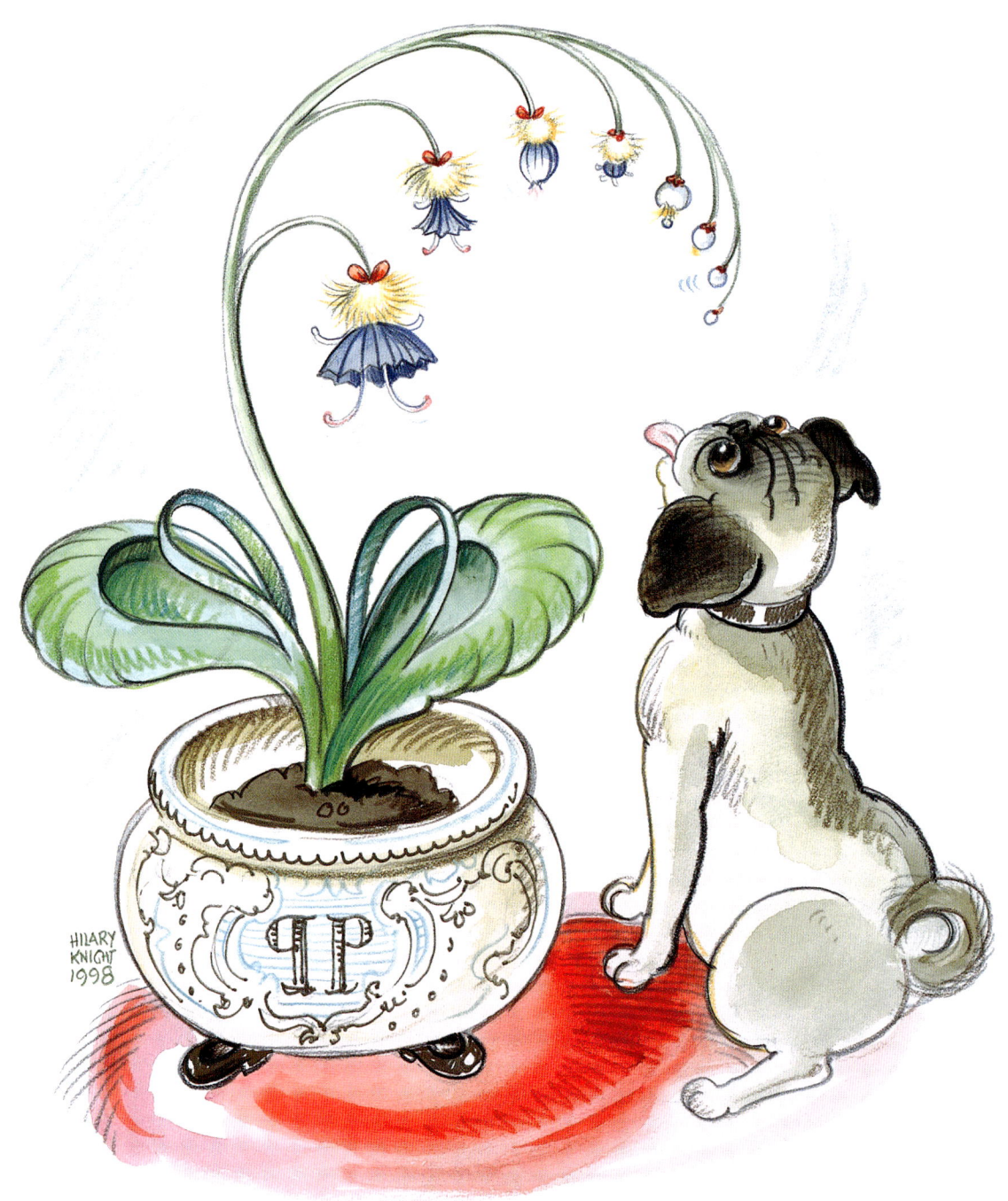

A VERY RARE ORCHID·
The eloisia horriblis

LENA HORNE | *1984*

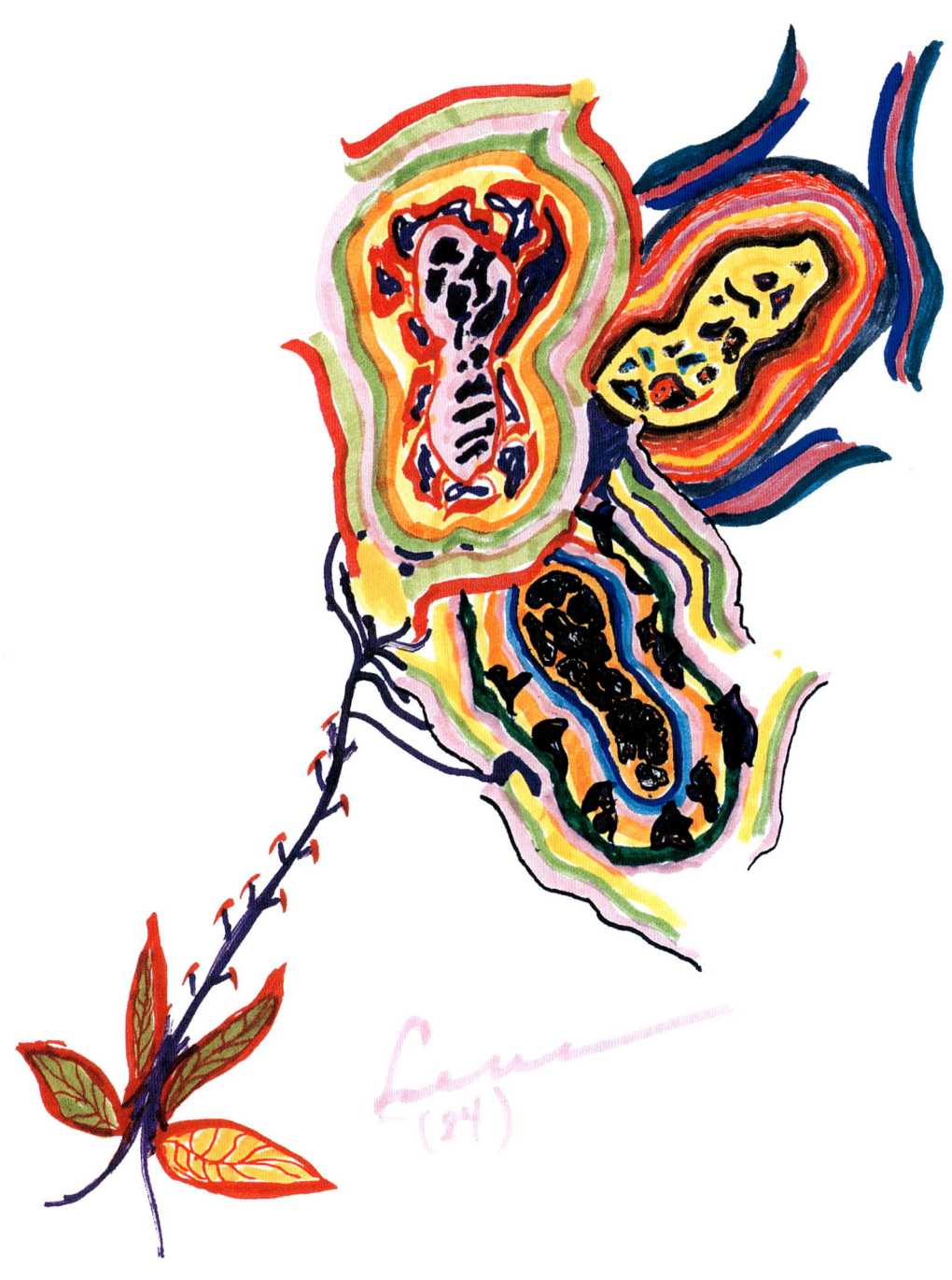

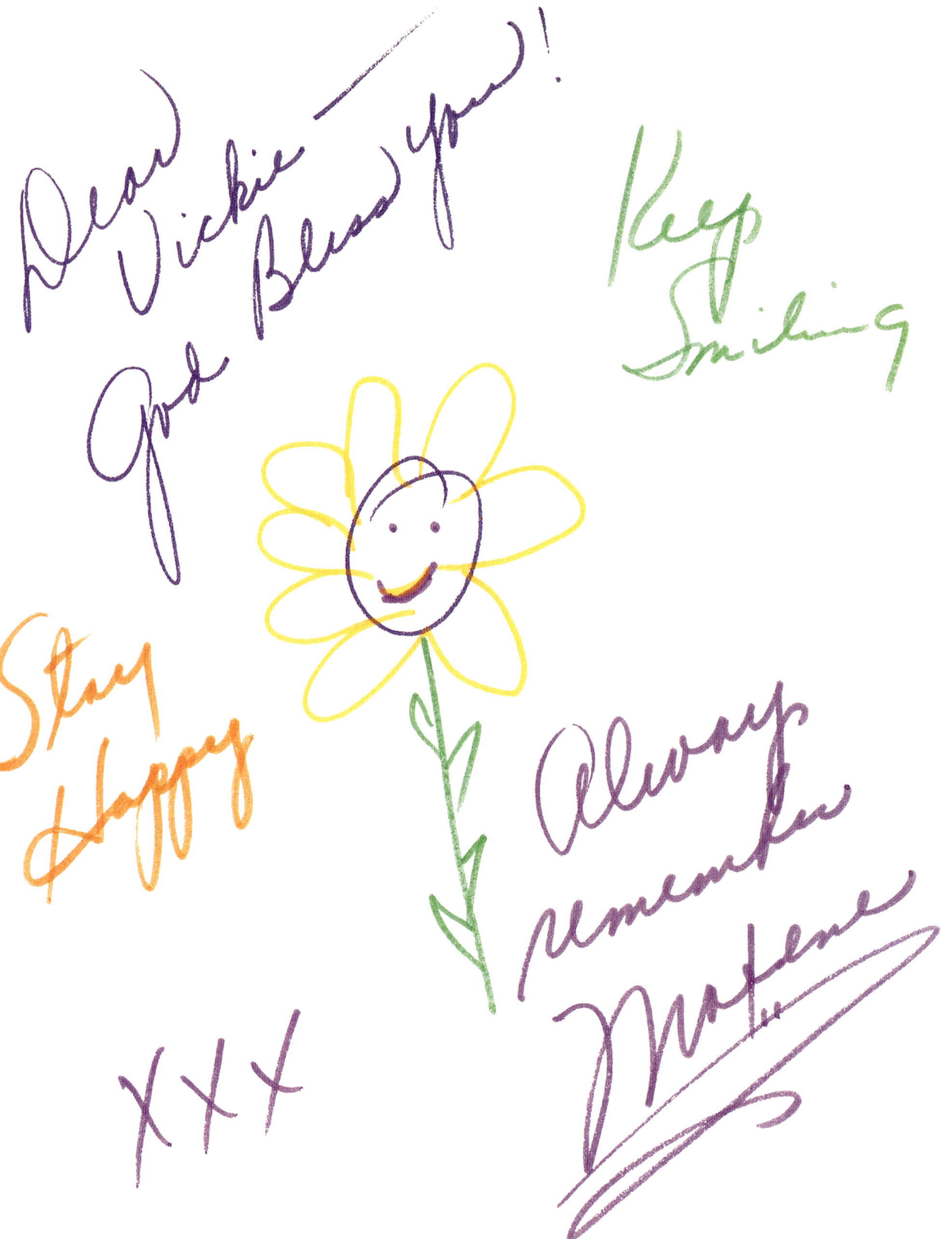

MAXENE ANDREWS | 1980

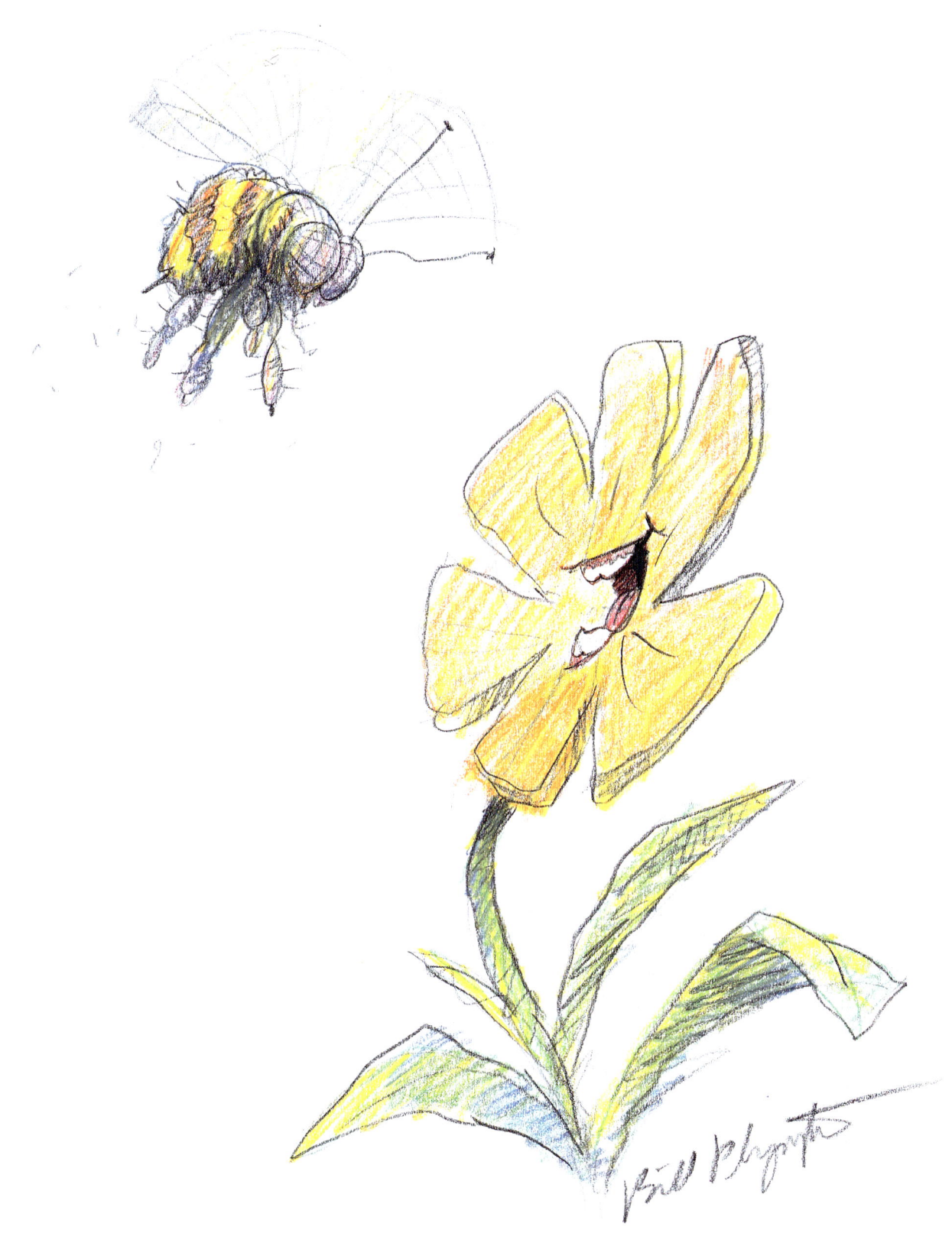

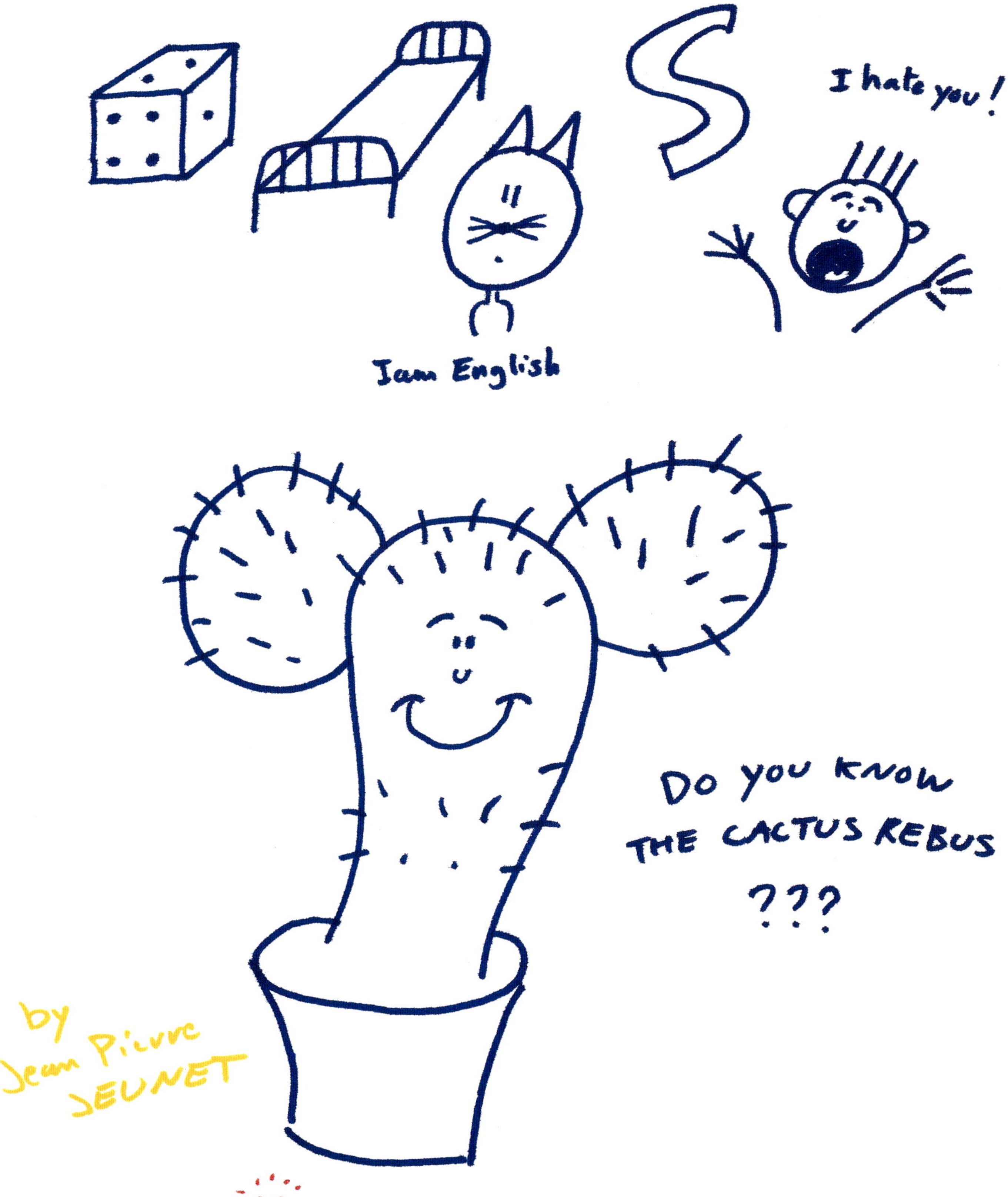

JEAN PIERRE JEUNET | *1991*
BEN STILLER | *1997 (facing)*

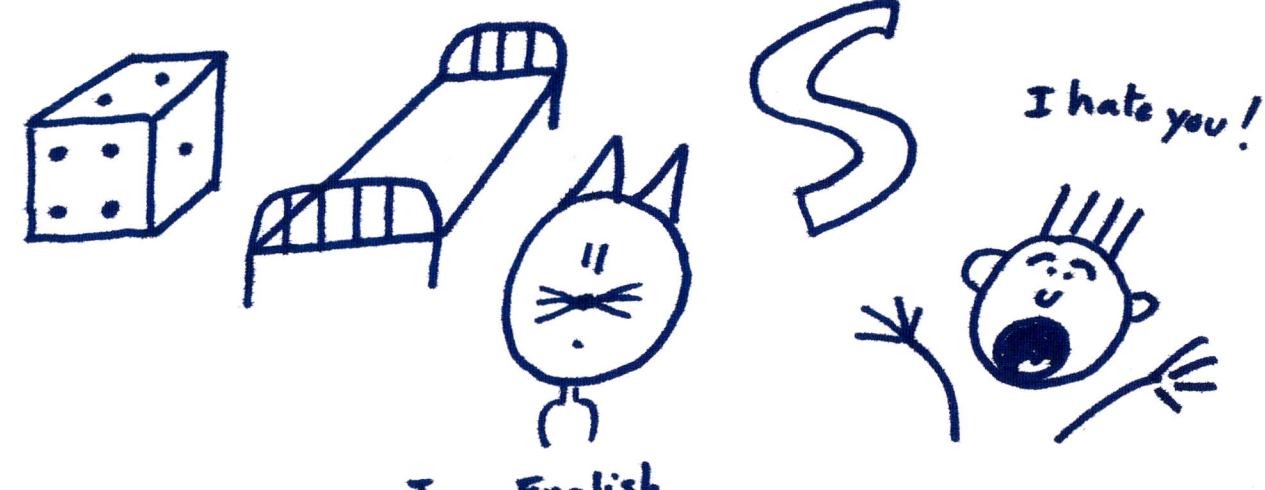

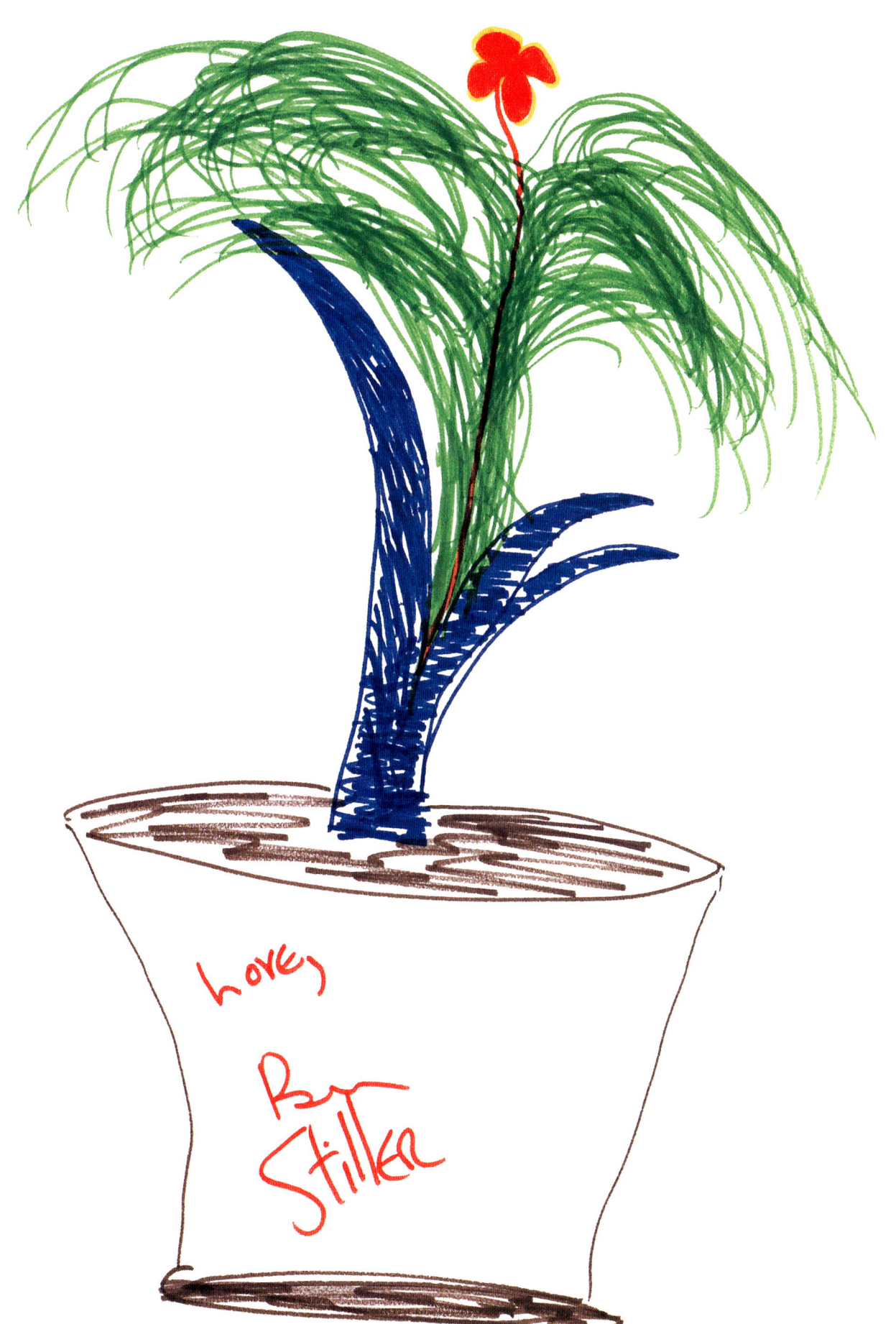

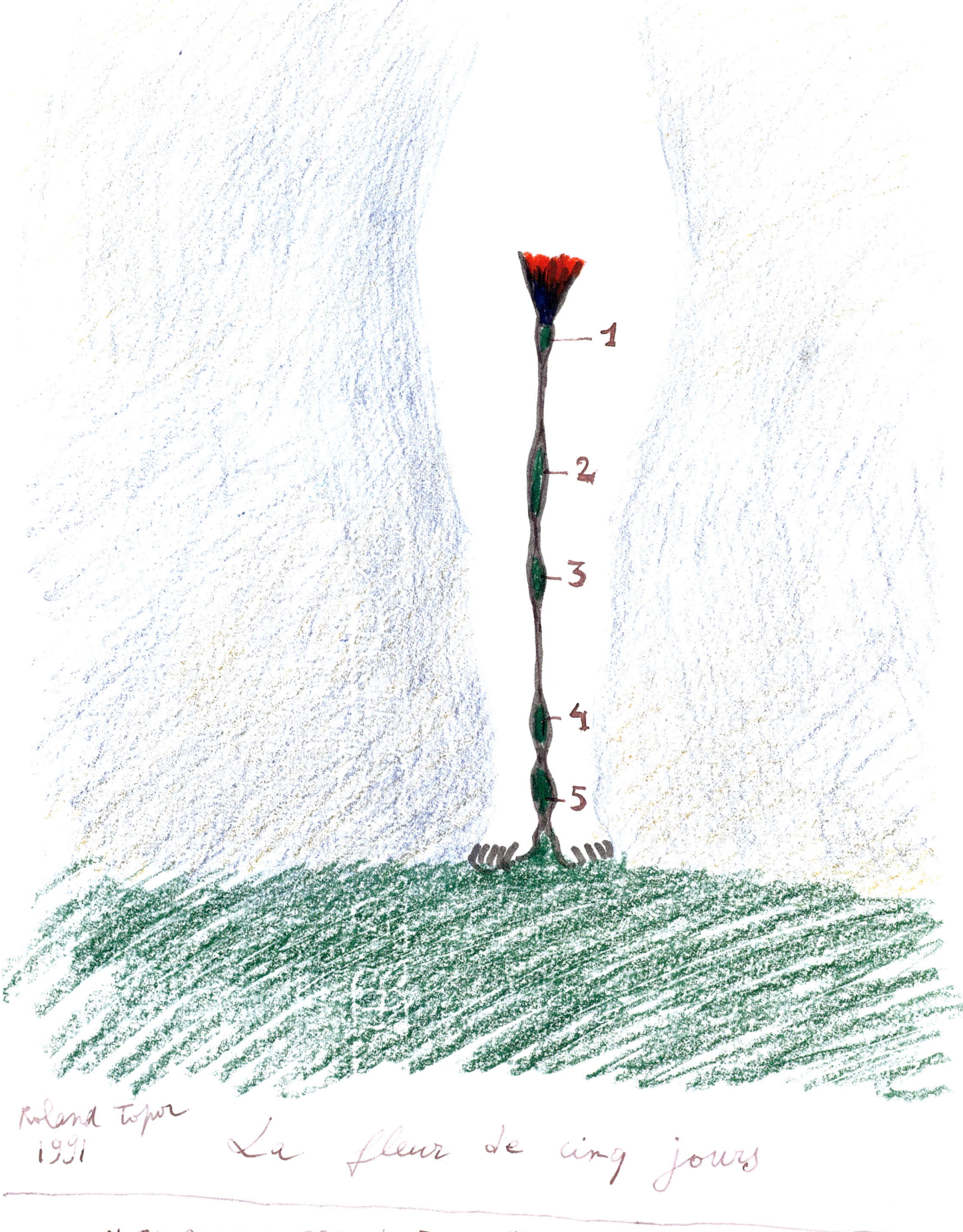

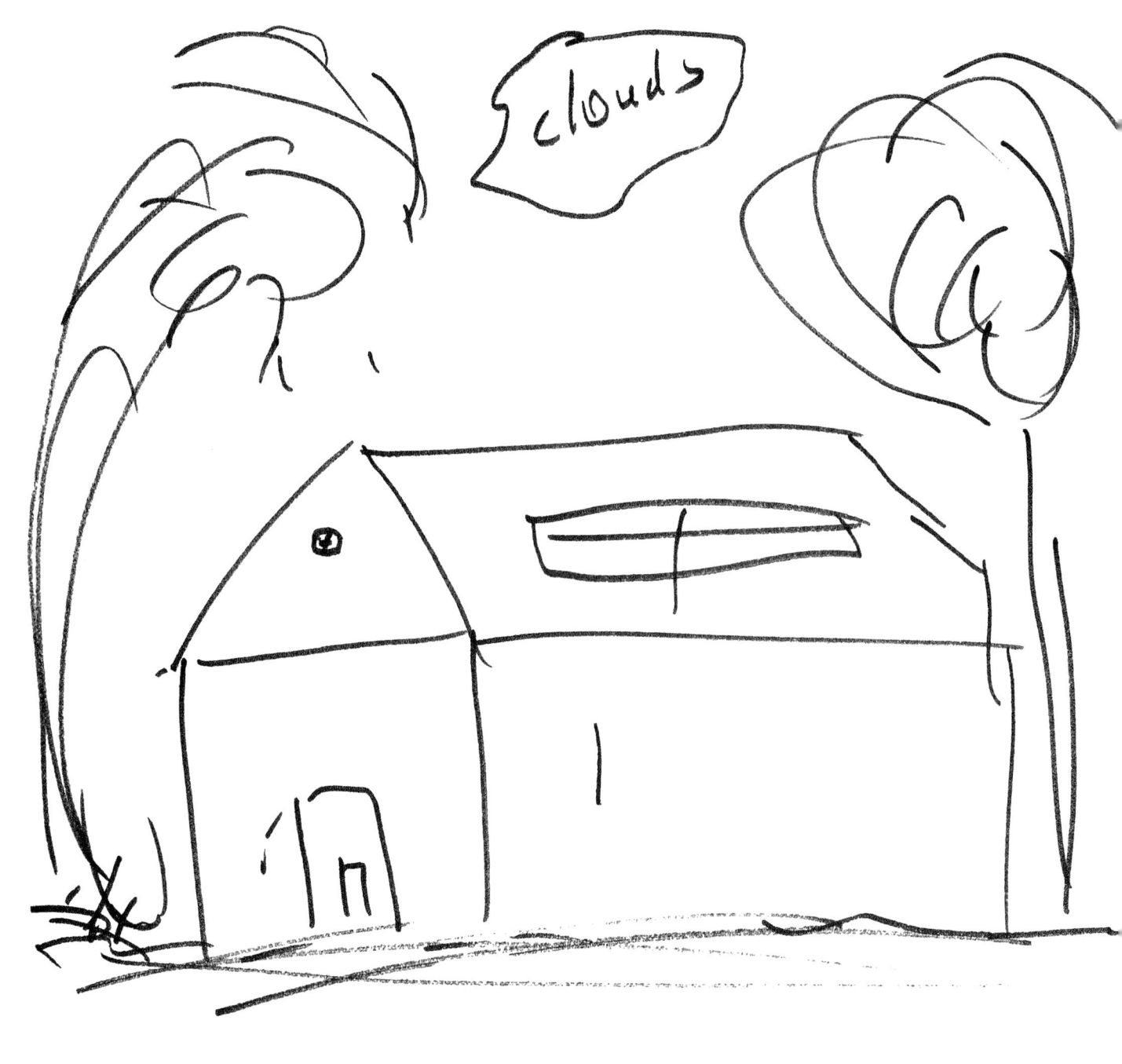

STEVE RUBELL | *1982*
ROLAND TOPOR | *1991 (facing)*

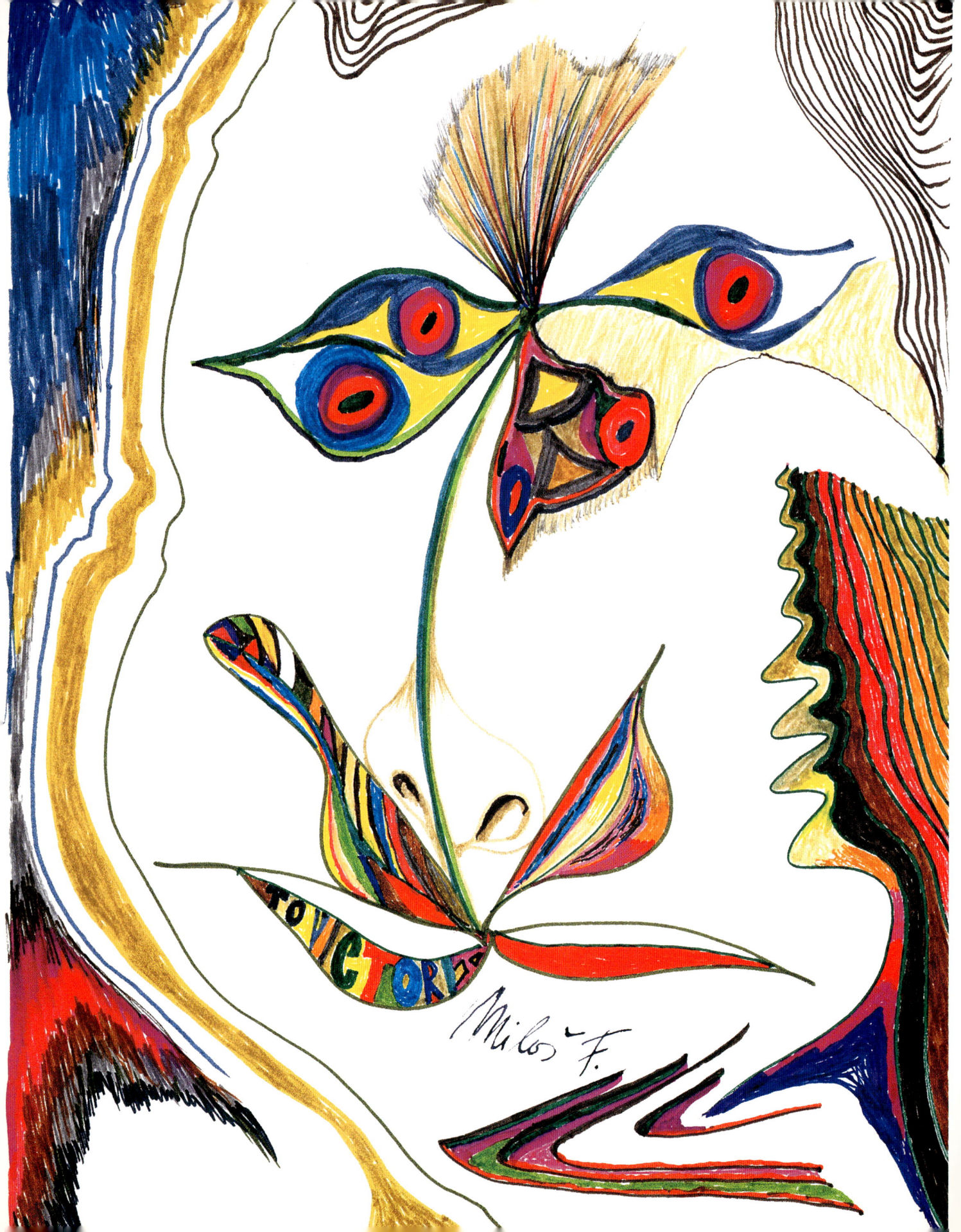

MILOS FORMAN | 1997

Jean Stein, author of *Edie: An American Biography* and editor of the literary journal *Grand Street,* has been a family friend for years. She was introduced to my father by Leonard Bernstein in the 1950s when Dad and Lenny were filming *Bernstein in Israel.* I met Jean and she sort of adopted me for about a year in the mid-1980s.

JEAN INVITED ME to some of the most fascinating parties I've ever attended. At one of these parties I walked in the door, and before I could even get a drink, was introduced to a group of four women in mid-conversation: Diana Ross, Joan Kennedy, Diane Keaton, and Joanne Woodward. This was just too much all at once. I needed to catch my breath, to find someone to talk to—another unknown like me.

THEN I NOTICED an attractive European-looking gentleman with a large plaster cast on his leg sitting in the corner by himself smoking a cigar. I immediately struck up a conversation with him. I had just returned from the Telluride Film Festival with my father where I had seen Mexican filmmaker Paul Leduc's film *Frida.* I went on and on about the movie, the acting, the colors, the direction. We must have been speaking for about two hours. Finally this very patient man looked up at me and said in a thick Czech accent, "My God! You szchlaav movies!" To which I replied, "Yes, I do." We were tipsy.

He asked me, "Vat do you do?"

"I make movies," I replied, feeling very confident that someday I would.

"My God! I schmake movies, too!"

"I'm Victoria Leacock."

"My name's Milos Forman."

AT WHICH POINT I felt like a rock had hit me in the head. I'd seen every film he'd ever made.

I WAS TOO embarrassed to contact Milos for a good year after that. I also stopped drinking. Nevertheless, this chance encounter began a friendship that has spanned a decade and several continents. Milos finally settled down in his farmhouse in Connecticut to draw this floral self-portrait and I must say, I szchlaav it.

JULES FISHER | *1988*
RICHARD AVEDON | *1987 (facing)*

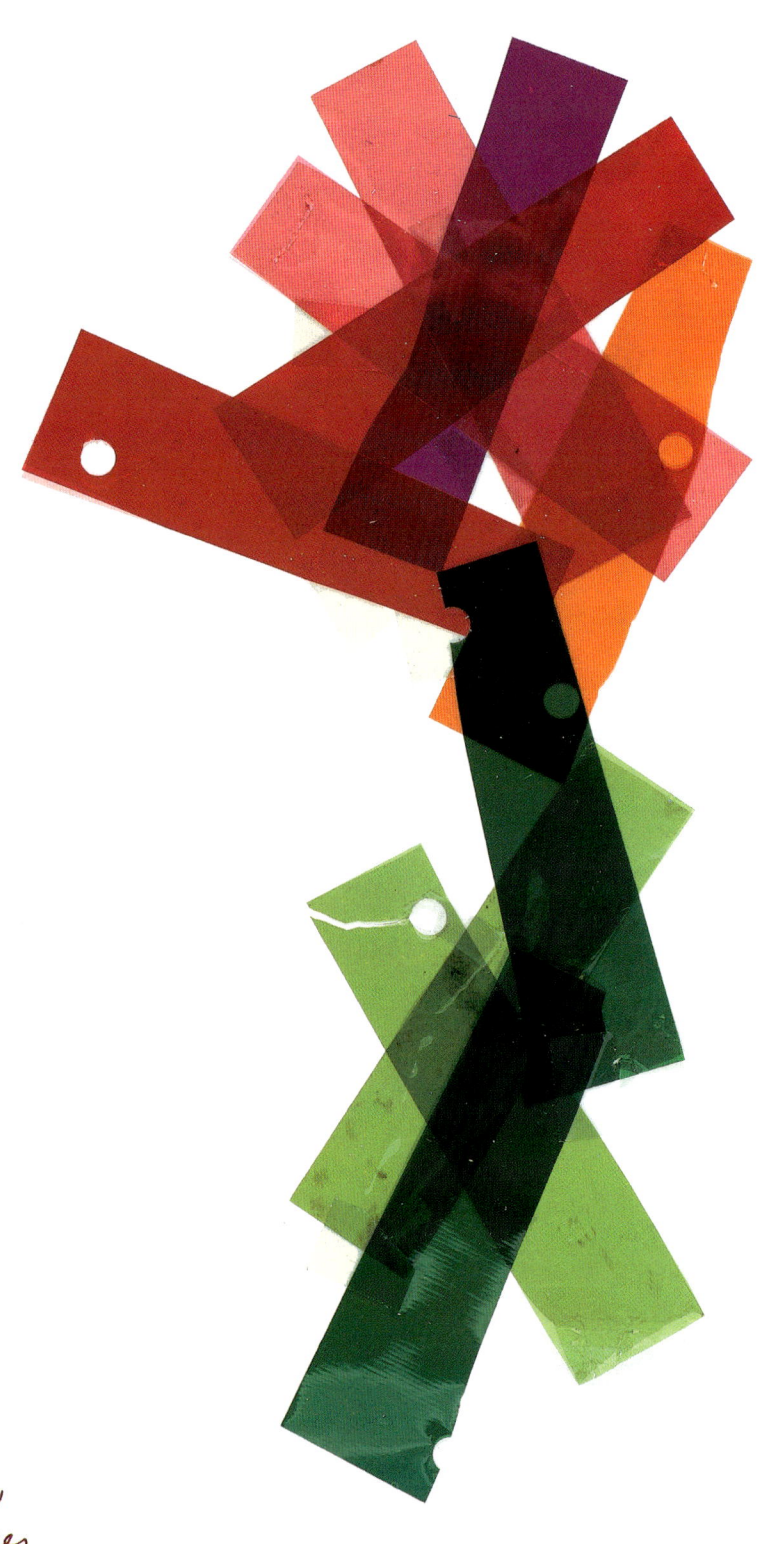

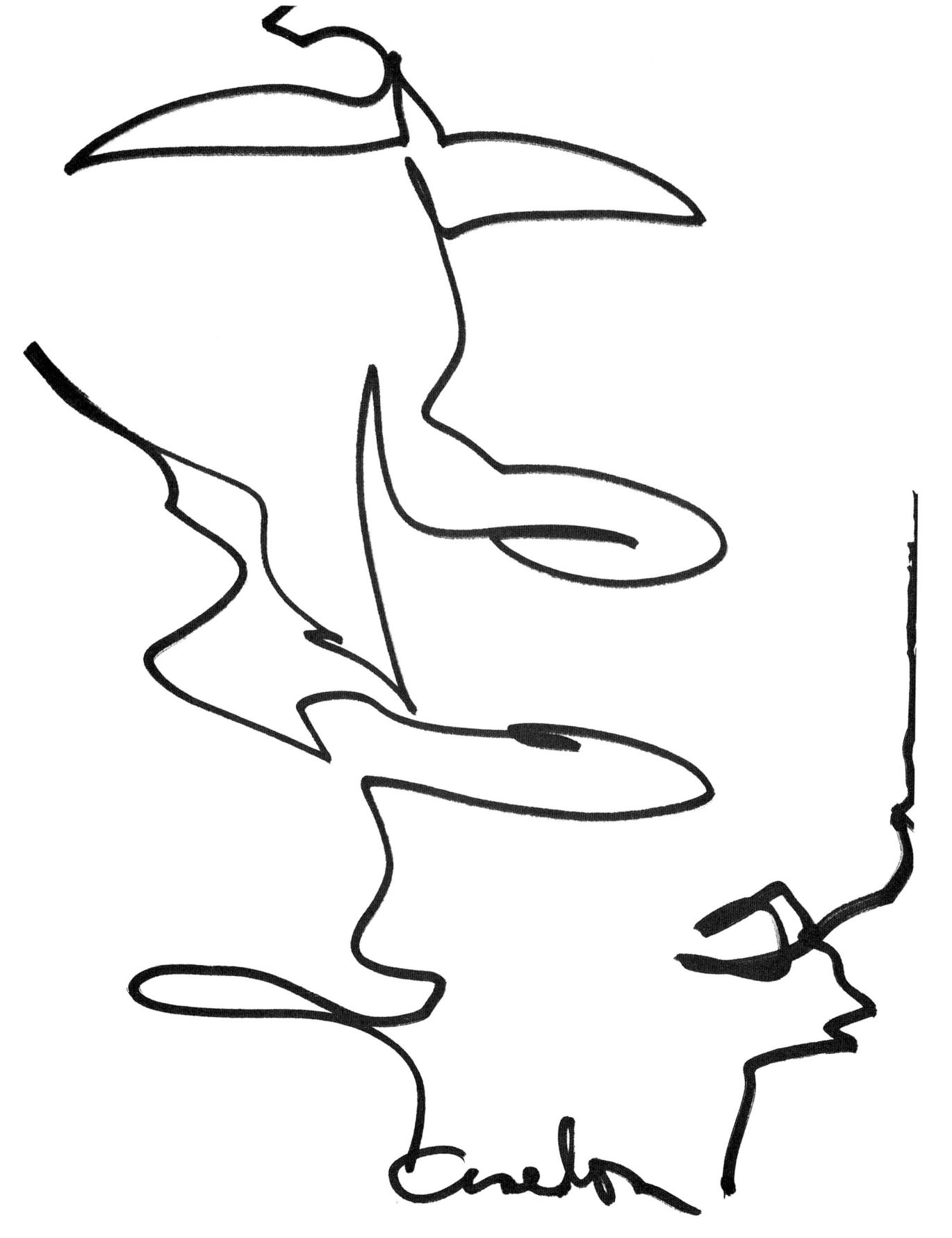

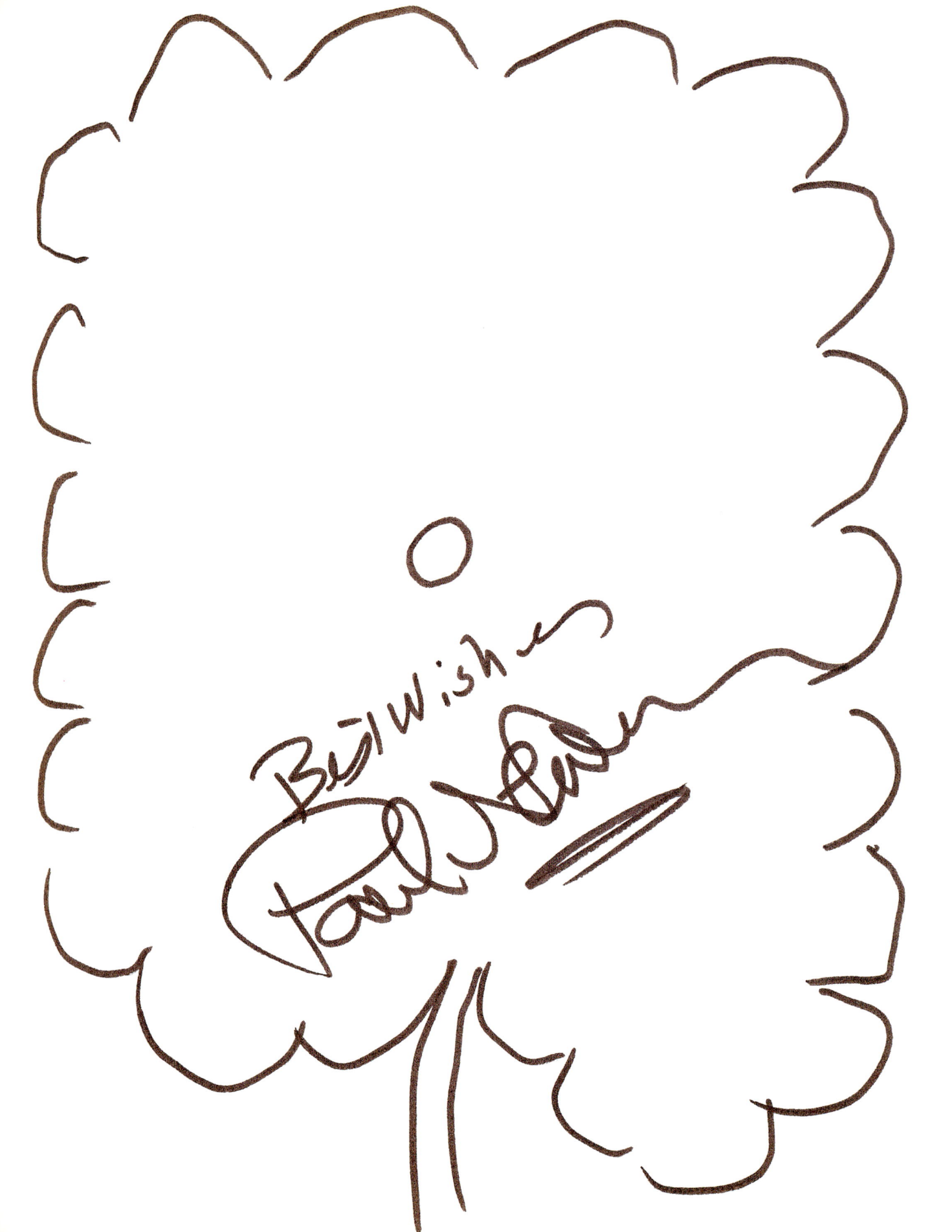

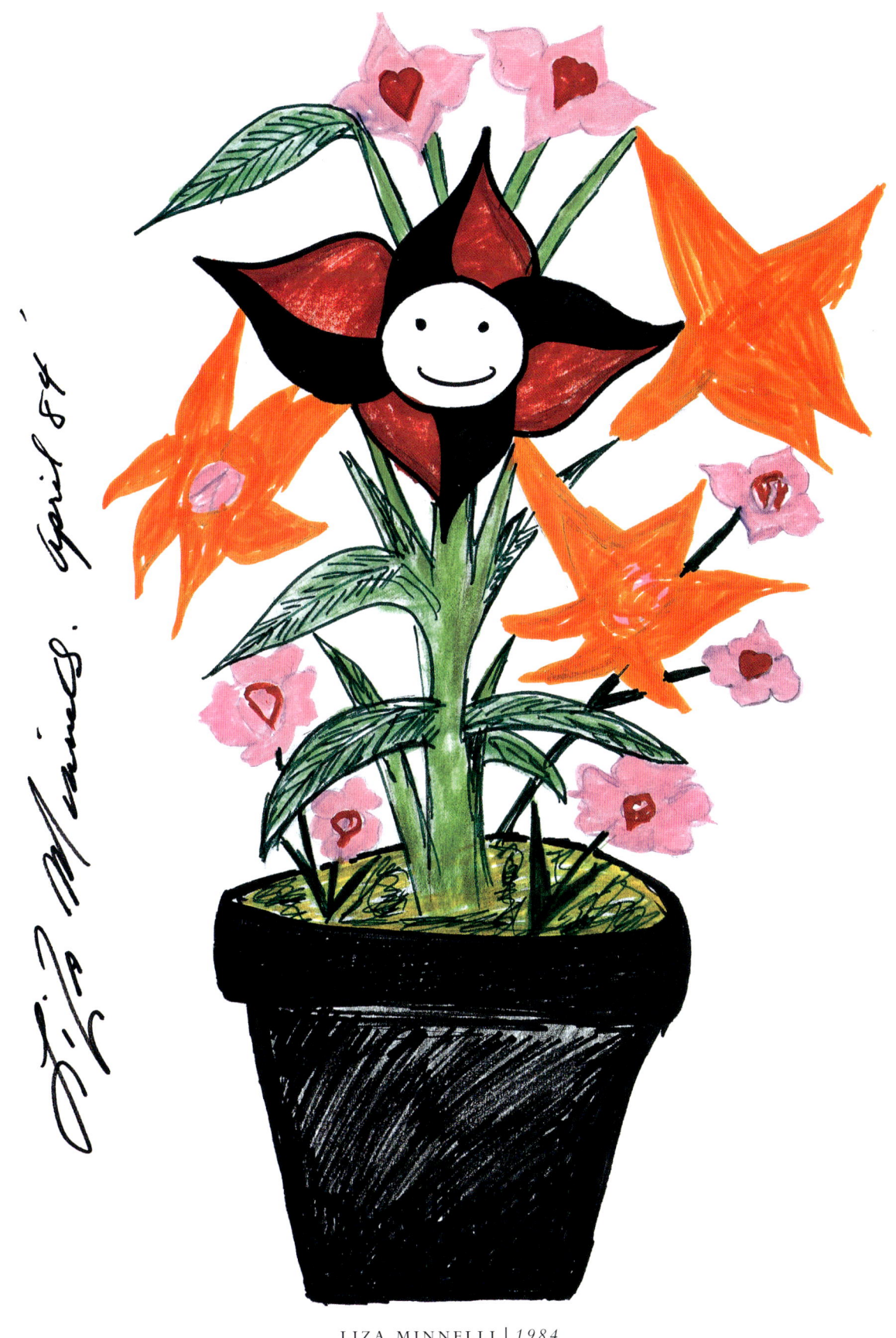

LIZA MINNELLI | *1984*
PAUL NEWMAN | *1980 (facing)*

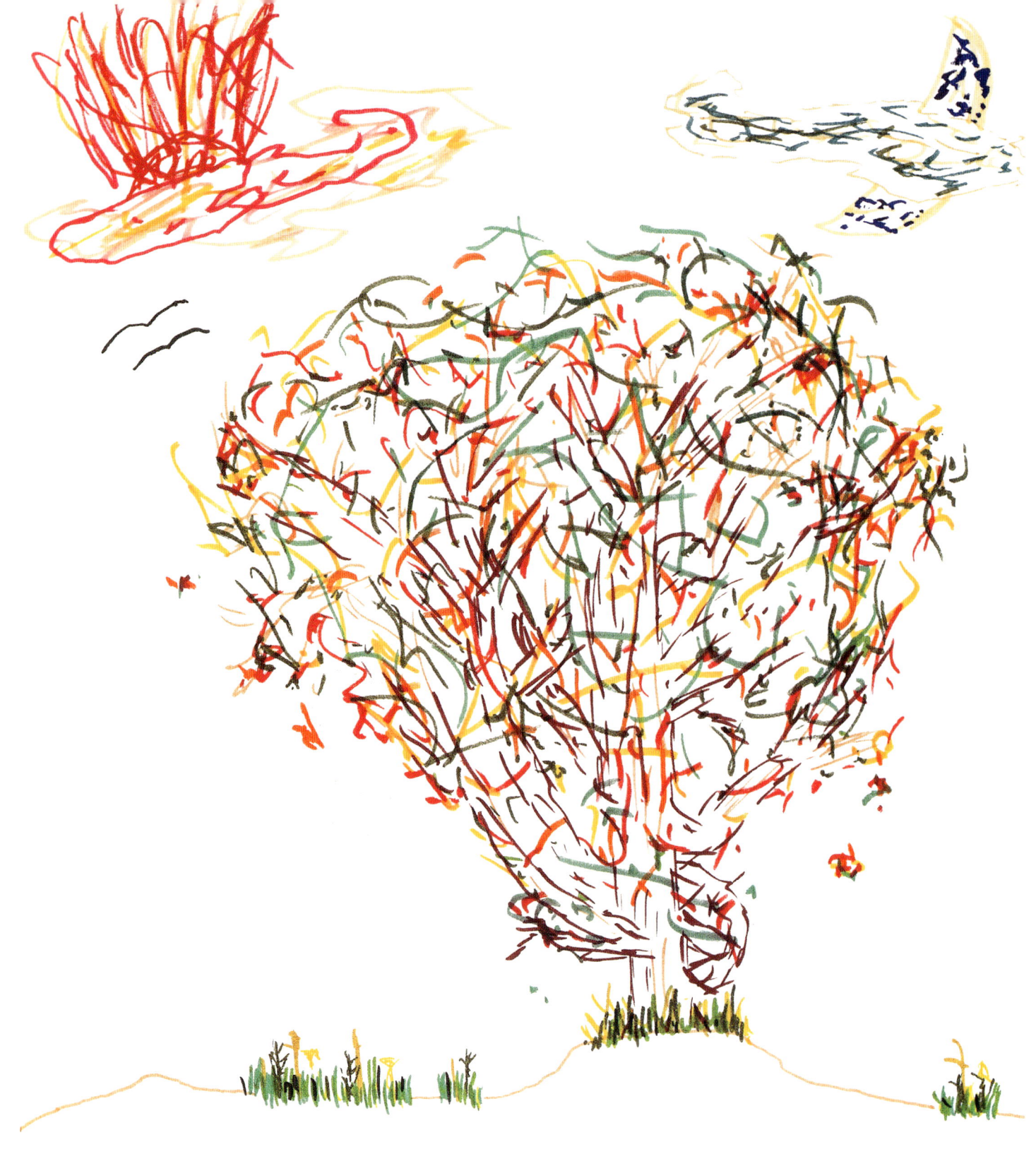

CAMPBELL SCOTT | 1994
GERALDINE PAGE | 1982 (facing)

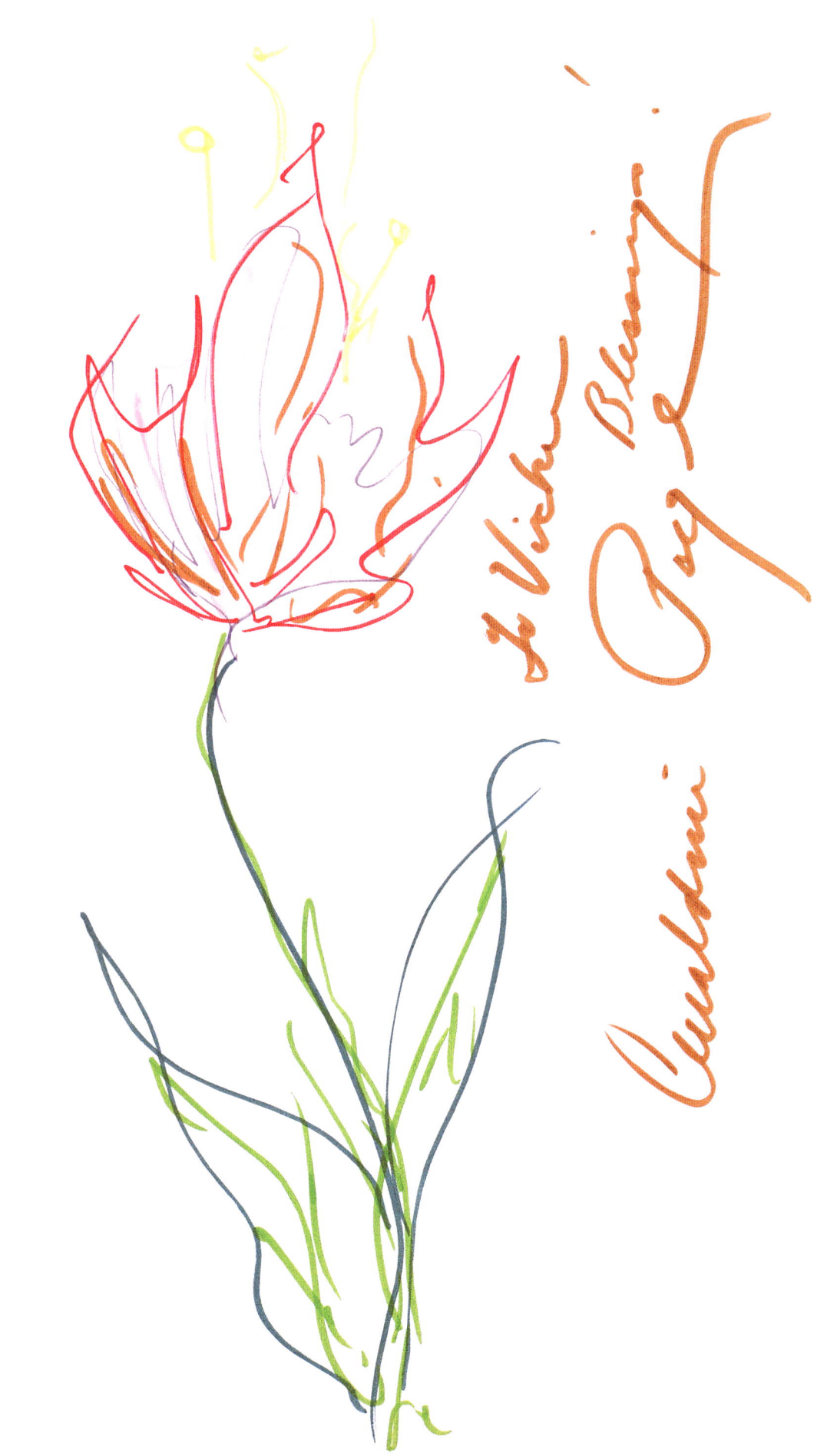

JONATHAN LARSON | *1986*

In 1981 I was a freshman in the acting program at Adelphi University. Working to complete my required "tech hours," I was hanging lights for the upcoming production of *Godspell*. The actors were busy rehearsing on stage. I looked up to see the young actor playing Jesus dangling from the rafters in the crucifixion scene. It was one of those moments—I knew with absolute conviction that he would be my first love. His name was Jonathan Larson.

JONATHAN AND I had a wonderful romance, and when it cooled we settled into an intense and rewarding friendship. I always had faith in Jonathan, working alongside him as he struggled to make a name for himself in the theater. Together we produced several of his works in various locations around New York. I really felt like we were Mickey and Judy from those old MGM musicals. We had nothing but energy and determination, and, come hell or high water, we were going to put on a show.

MY FLOWER BOOKS had become a running joke between Jonathan and me. After he and a few other friends had drawn in one of my books at a party in 1986, I had taken the flowers out because the artists weren't famous enough. Big mistake. Jonathan was furious. I explained to him that it wasn't that I didn't believe he would be successful—I did. It's just that he wasn't ready for the book yet. I knew Jonathan would one day be a huge star, and when that time came I would ask him for his flower. If he wanted to, he could tell me to jump in a lake.

FINALLY WE MADE a deal. On the opening night of *Rent*, the musical he had been working on for seven years, Jonathan would draw his official flower.

IT WAS 1996, and I was in Siberia working on a film with my father when I got word of Jonathan's shocking, unexpected death. He had died of an aortic aneurysm at the age of thirty-five on the first night of *Rent* previews. Shortly thereafter, what we had known all along became clear to everyone—Jonathan was a star. He won the Pulitzer and the Tony, and *Rent* was a smash Broadway musical.

AFTER FIVE HOURS of searching through every box in my storage unit, I found the original flower Jonathan had drawn all those years before. The tears came so fast that I had to throw my head back to keep from destroying it.

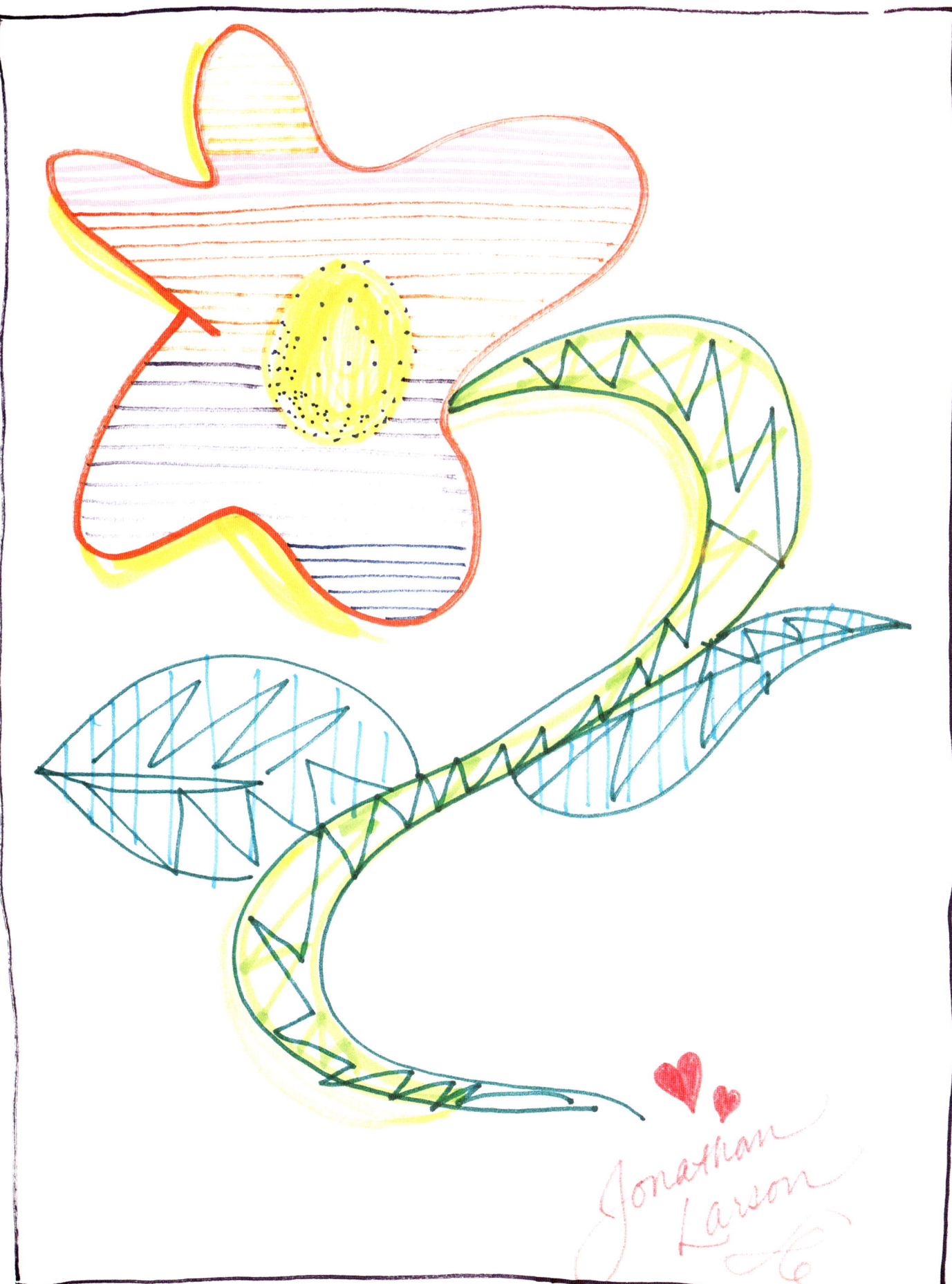

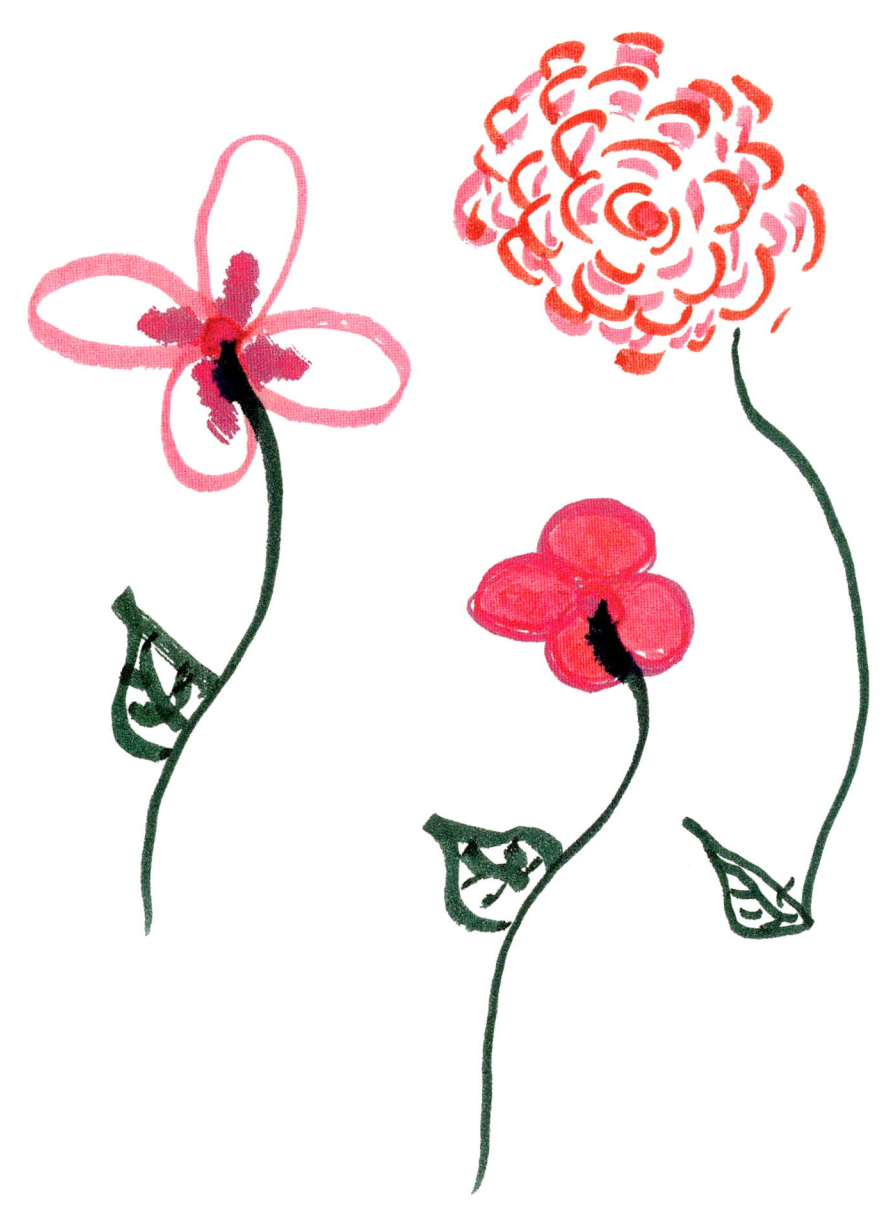

PENELOPE ANN MILLER | 1993

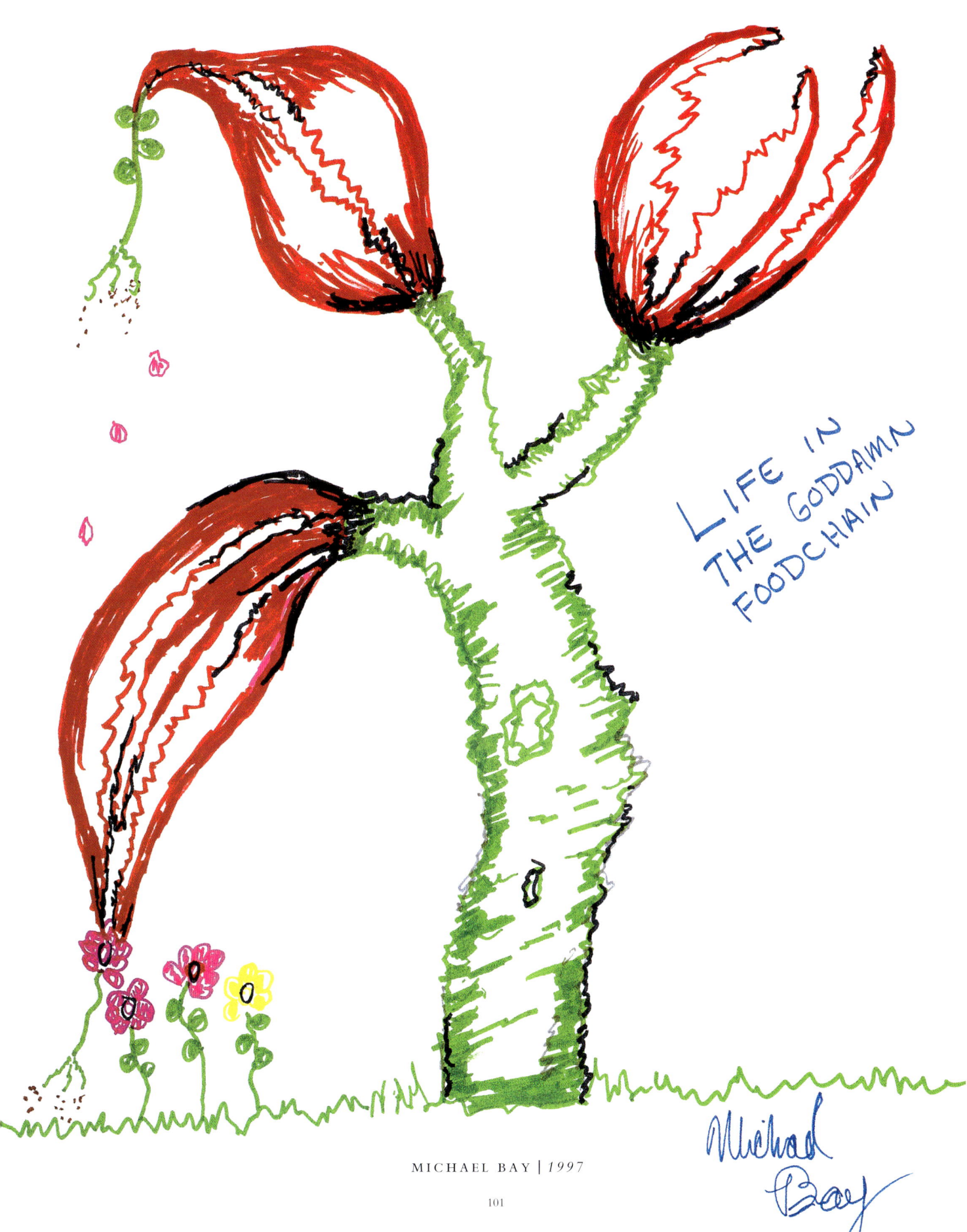

VIVA | *1987*
RICHARD E. GRANT | *1998*
(facing)

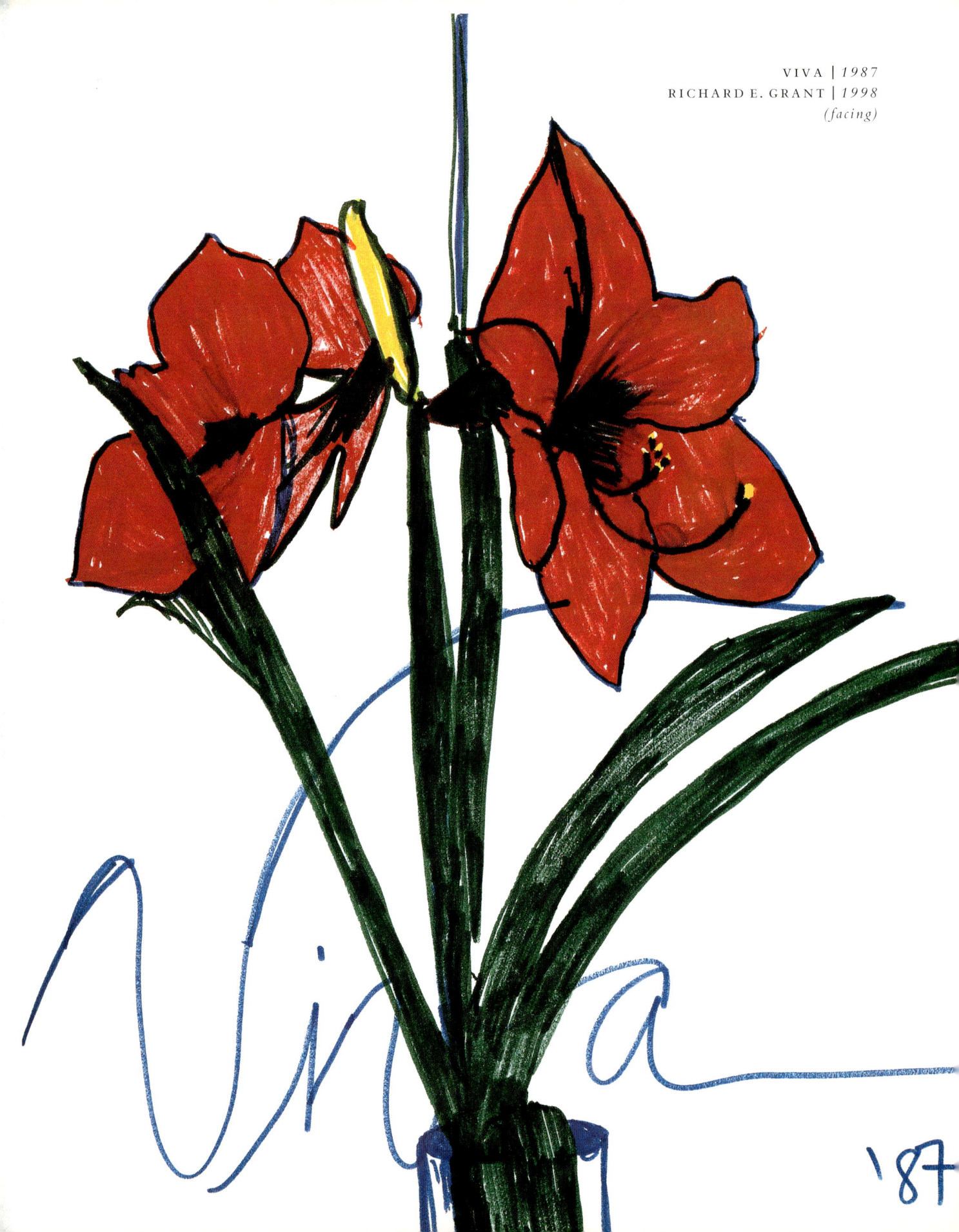

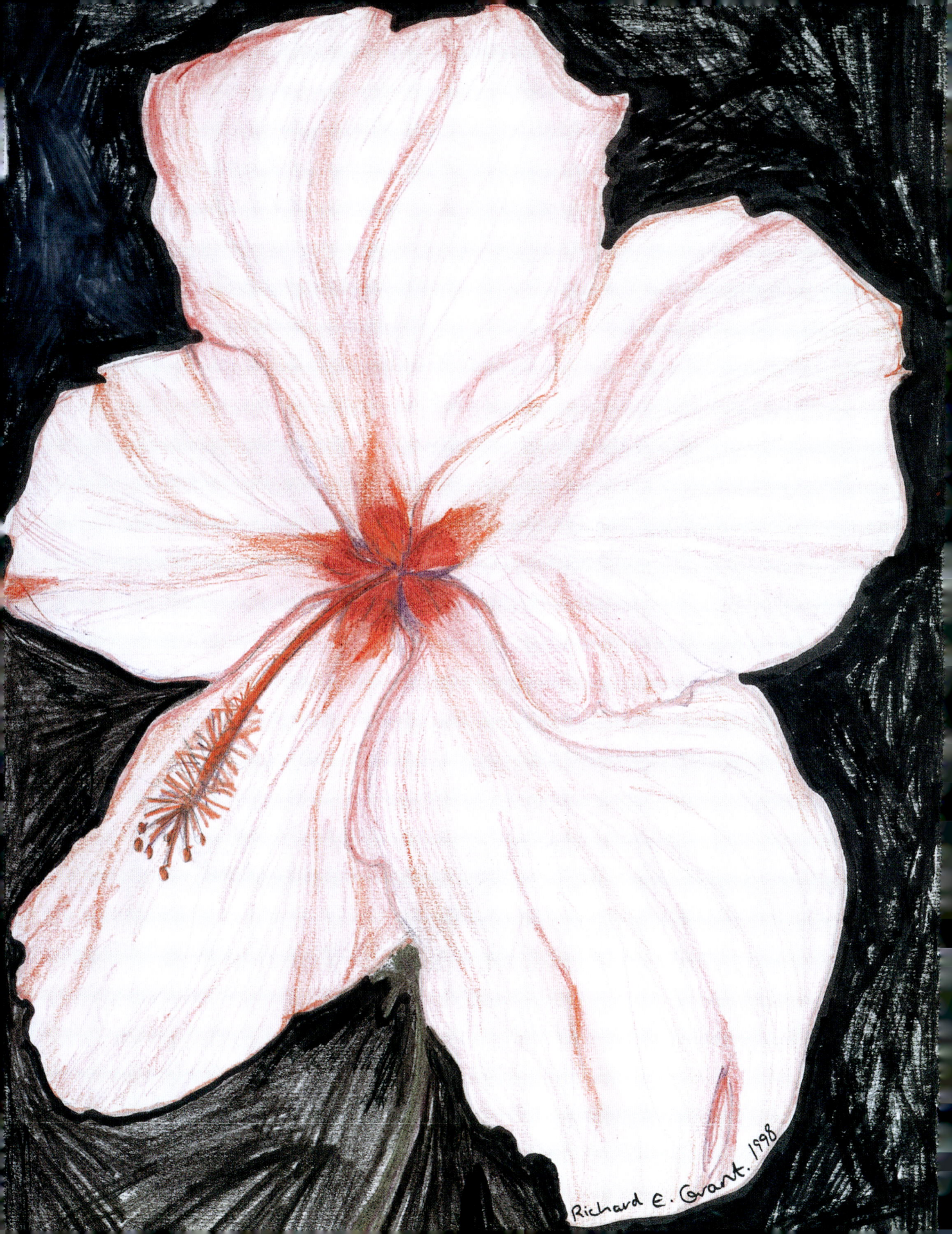

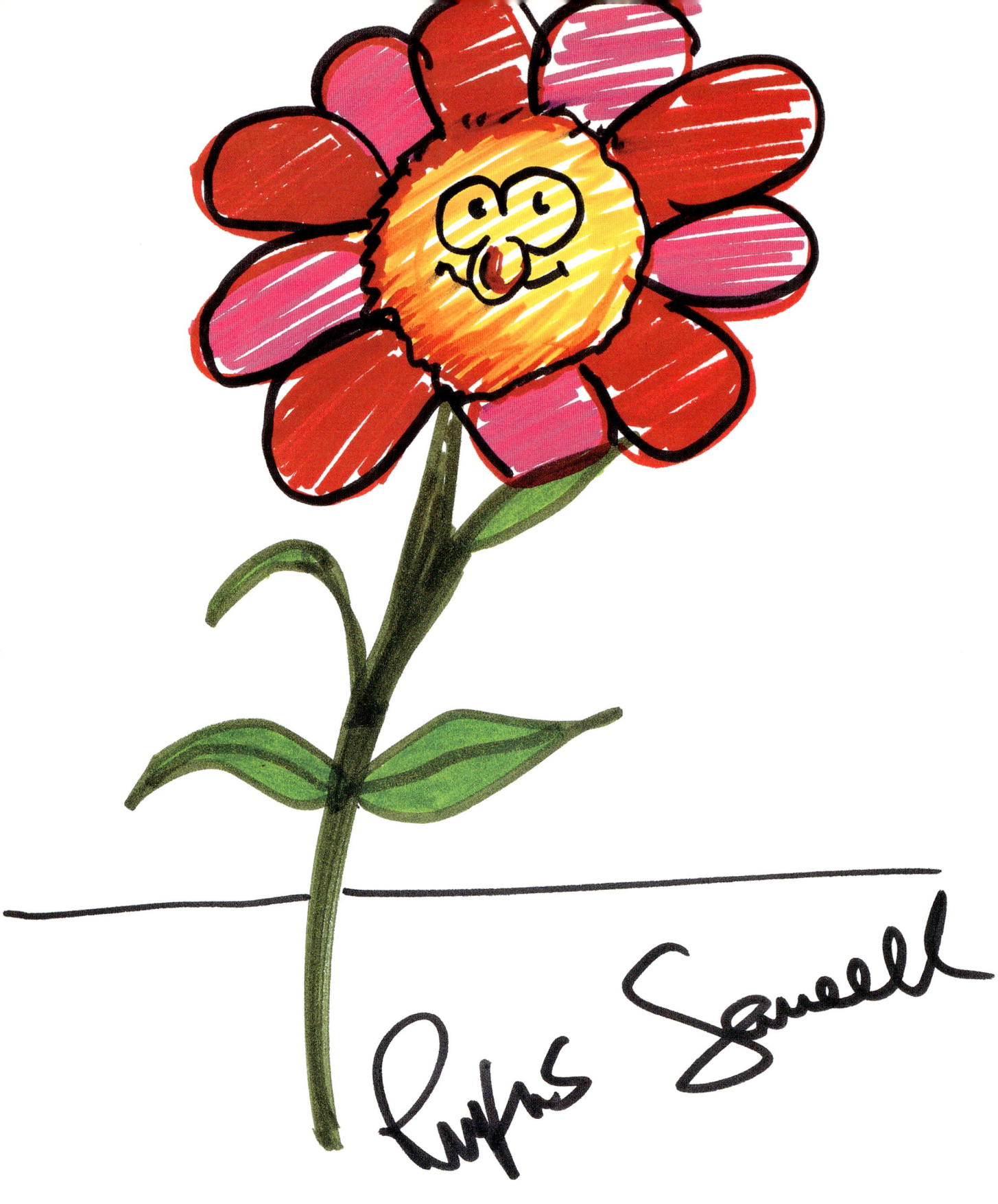

RUFUS SEWELL | 1997

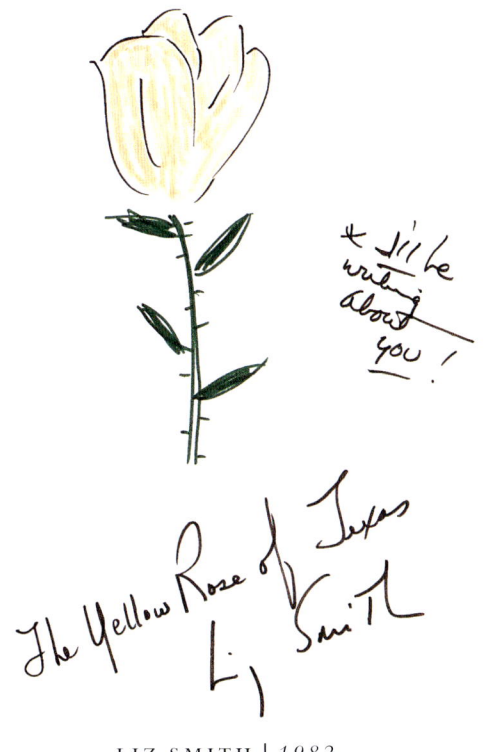

LIZ SMITH | 1982

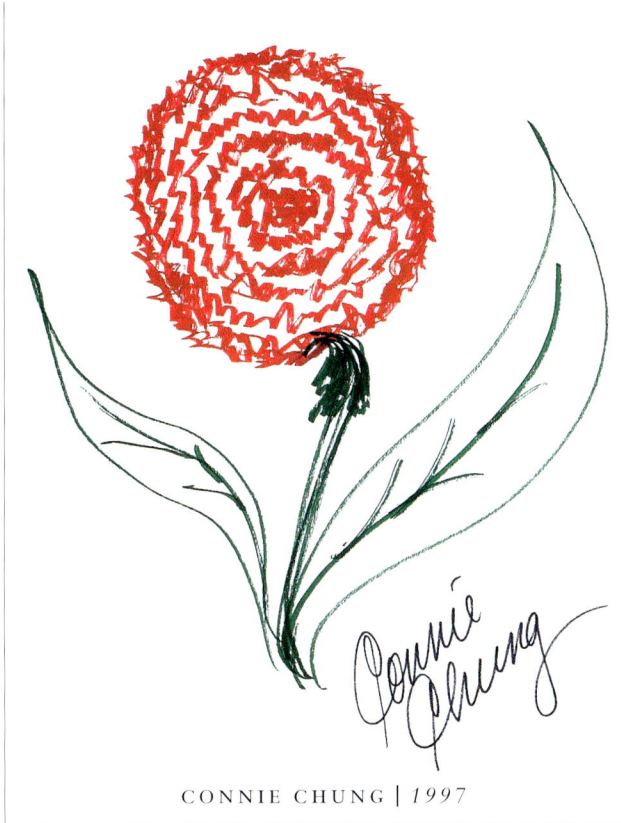

CONNIE CHUNG | 1997

BILL BOGGS | 1980

JOSEPH PAPP | 1981

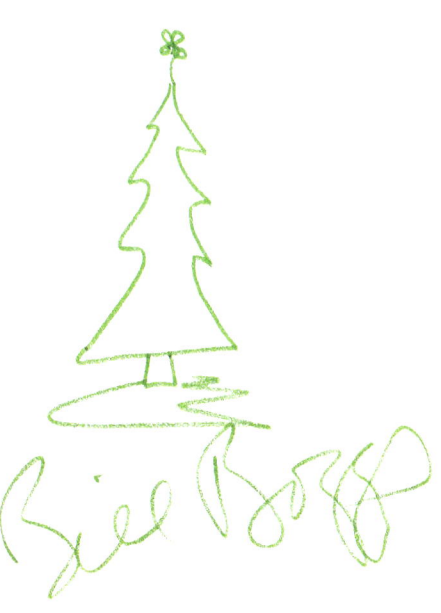

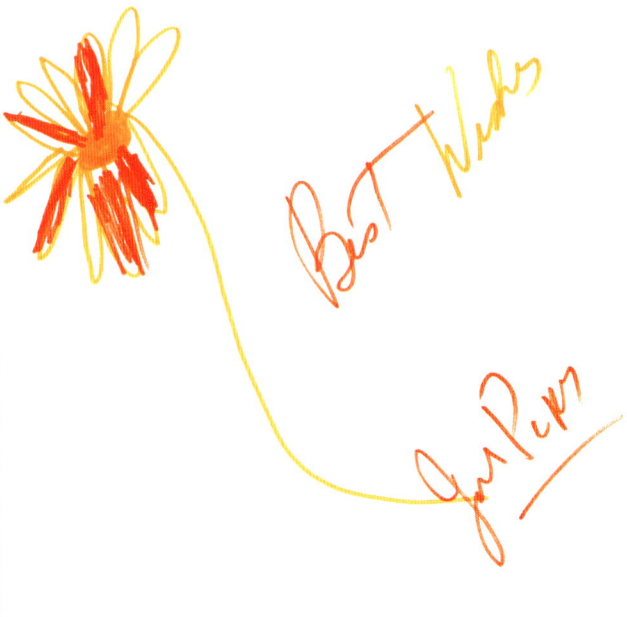

CINDY CRAWFORD | *1997*

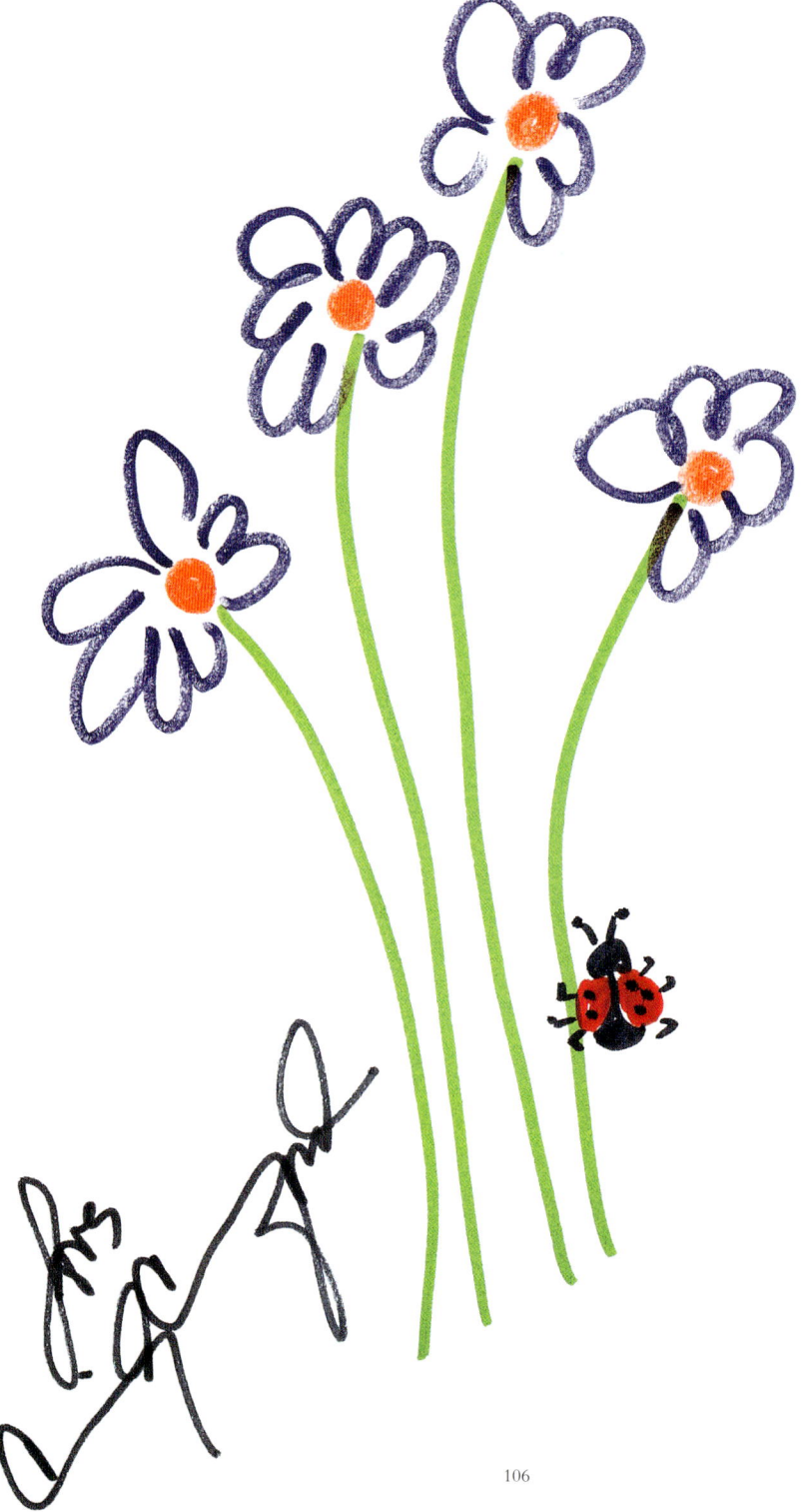

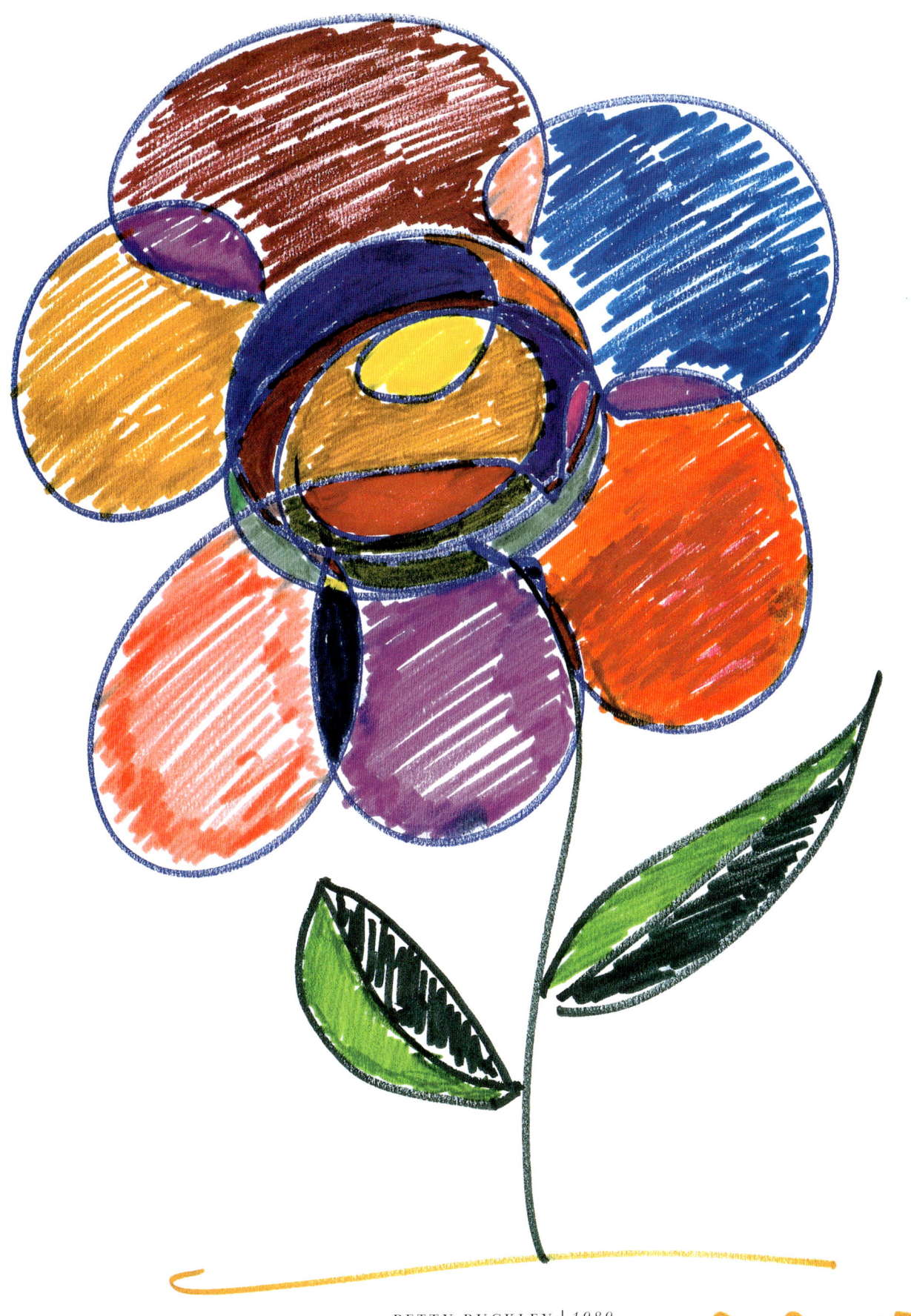

BETTY BUCKLEY | *1989*

LEONARDO DICAPRIO | *1998*

Where was Leonardo DiCaprio on the night *Titanic* won eleven Academy Awards, tying *Ben-Hur* for most awards ever received? The film's young star was watching the ceremony on television at my friend's Soho loft while tracing his shadow to create this flower.

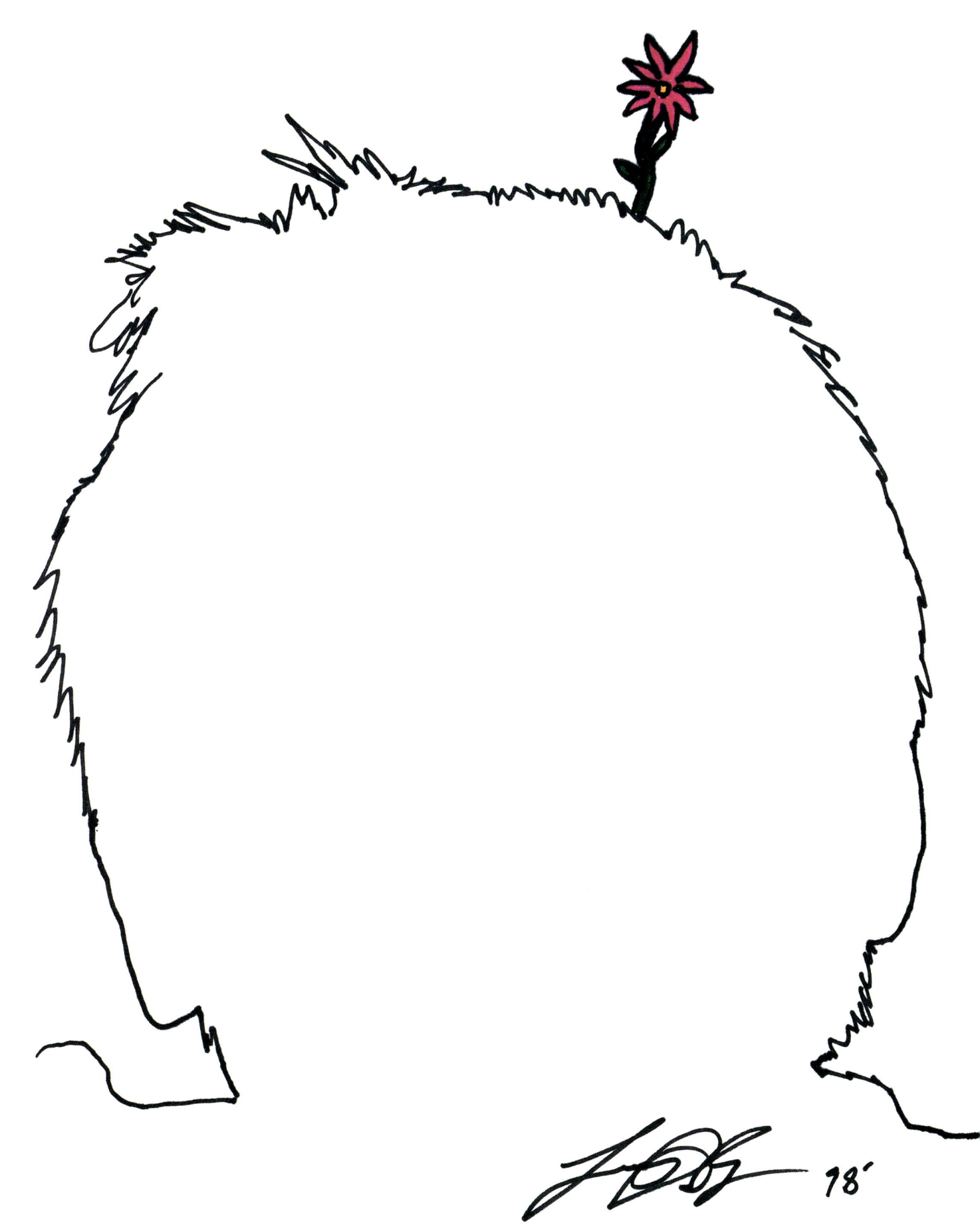

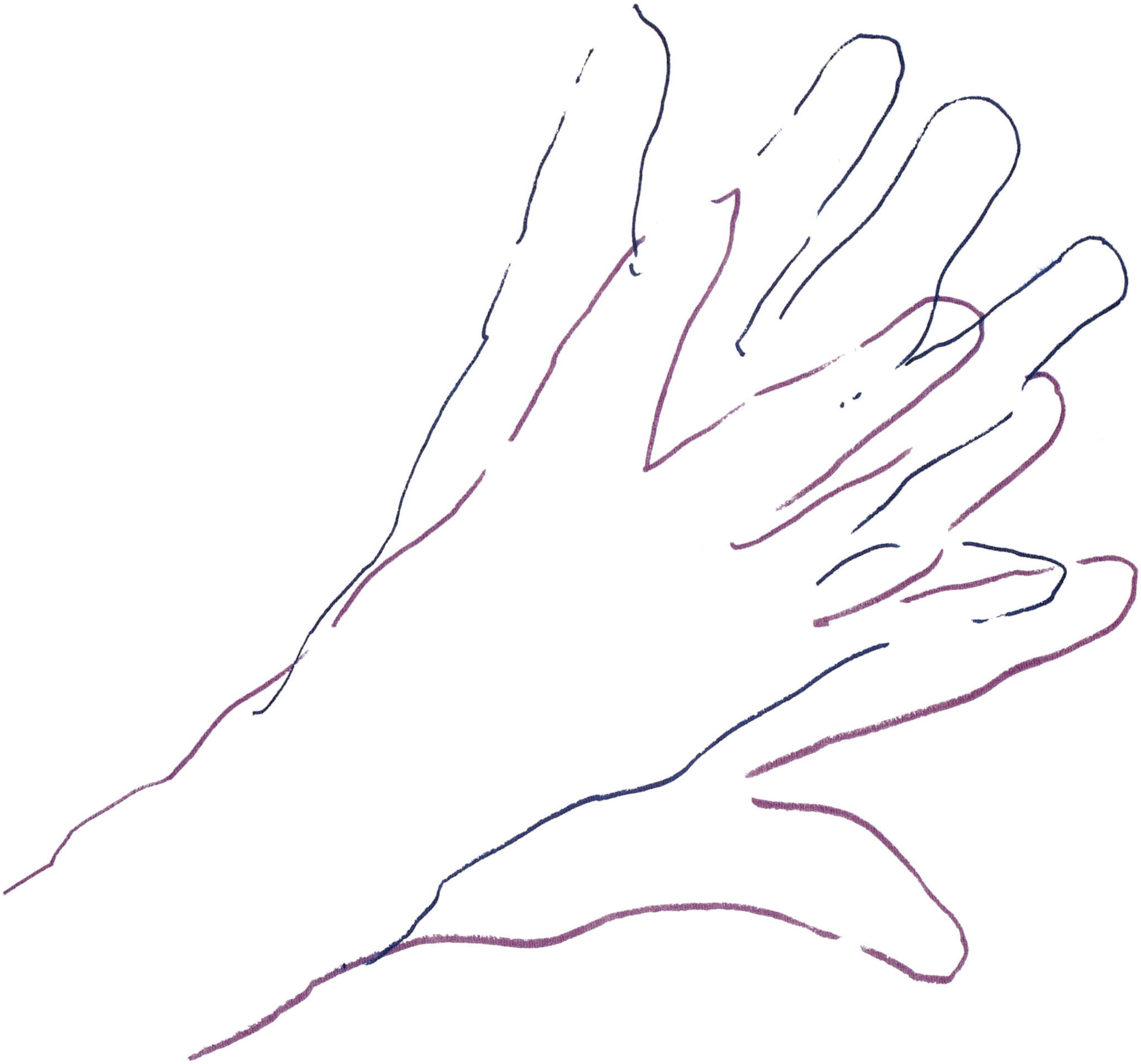

JOHN CAGE | 1991

MERCE CUNNINGHAM | *1991*

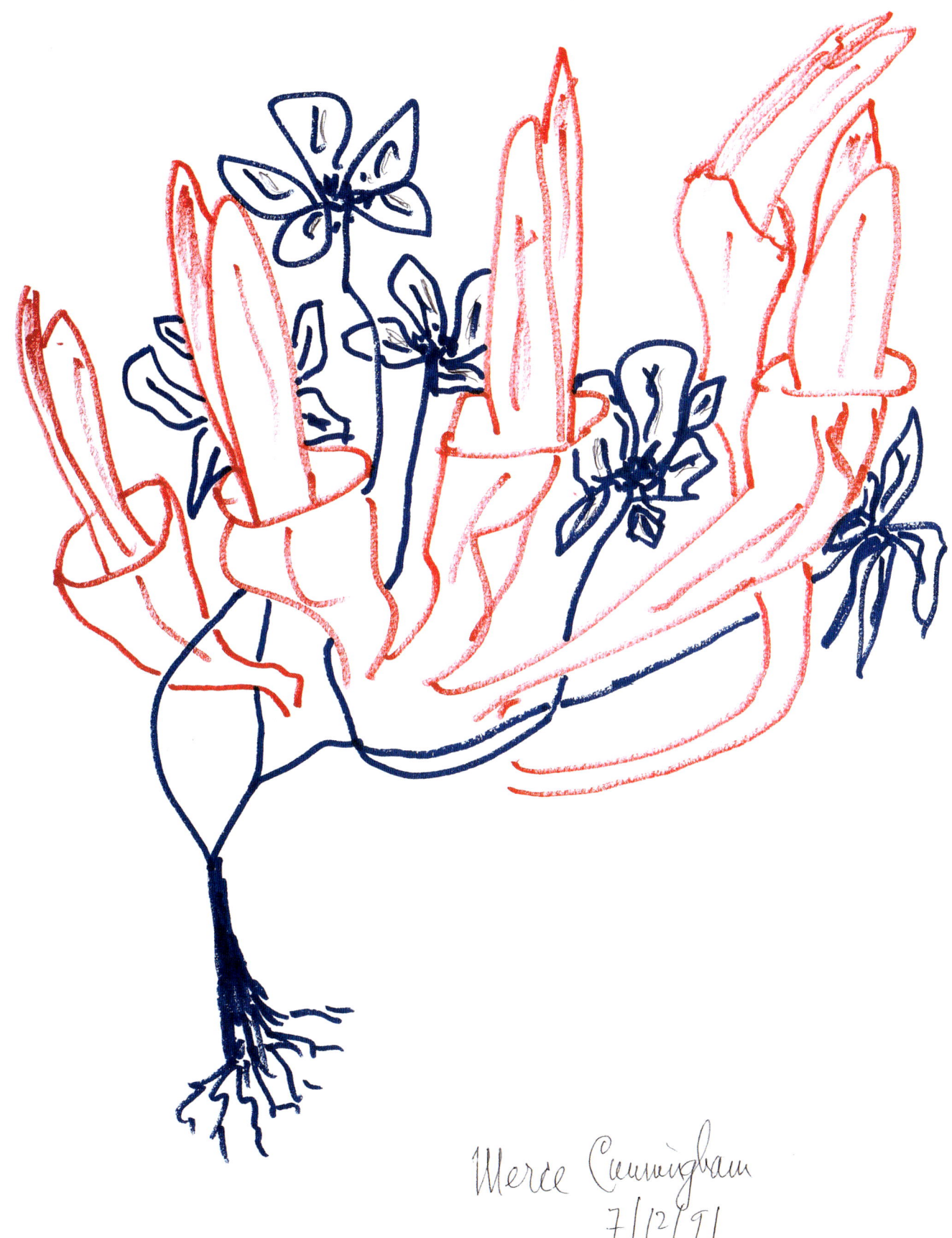

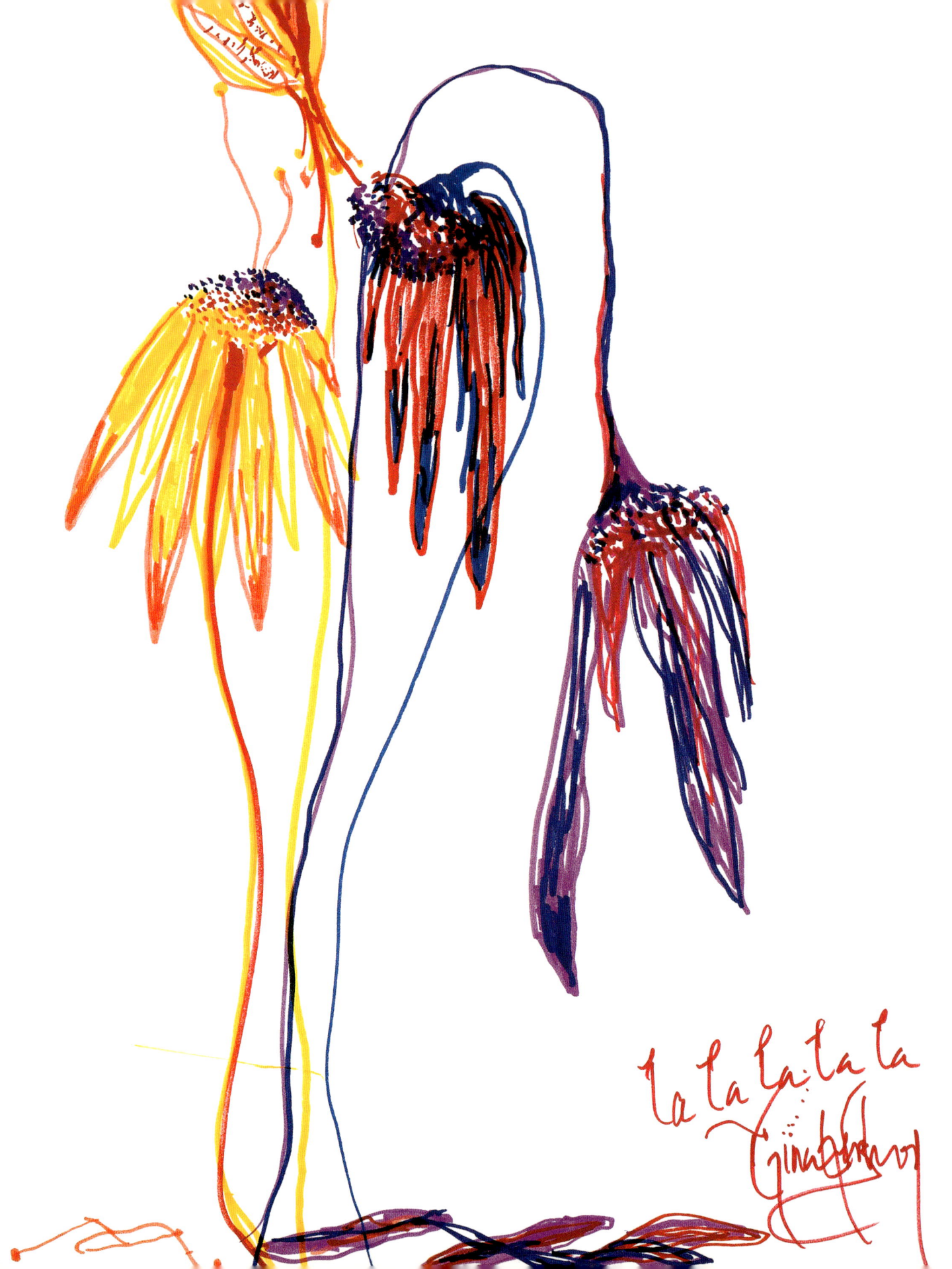

PRINCESS GRACE OF MONACO | *1981*
GINA GERSHON | *1990 (facing)*

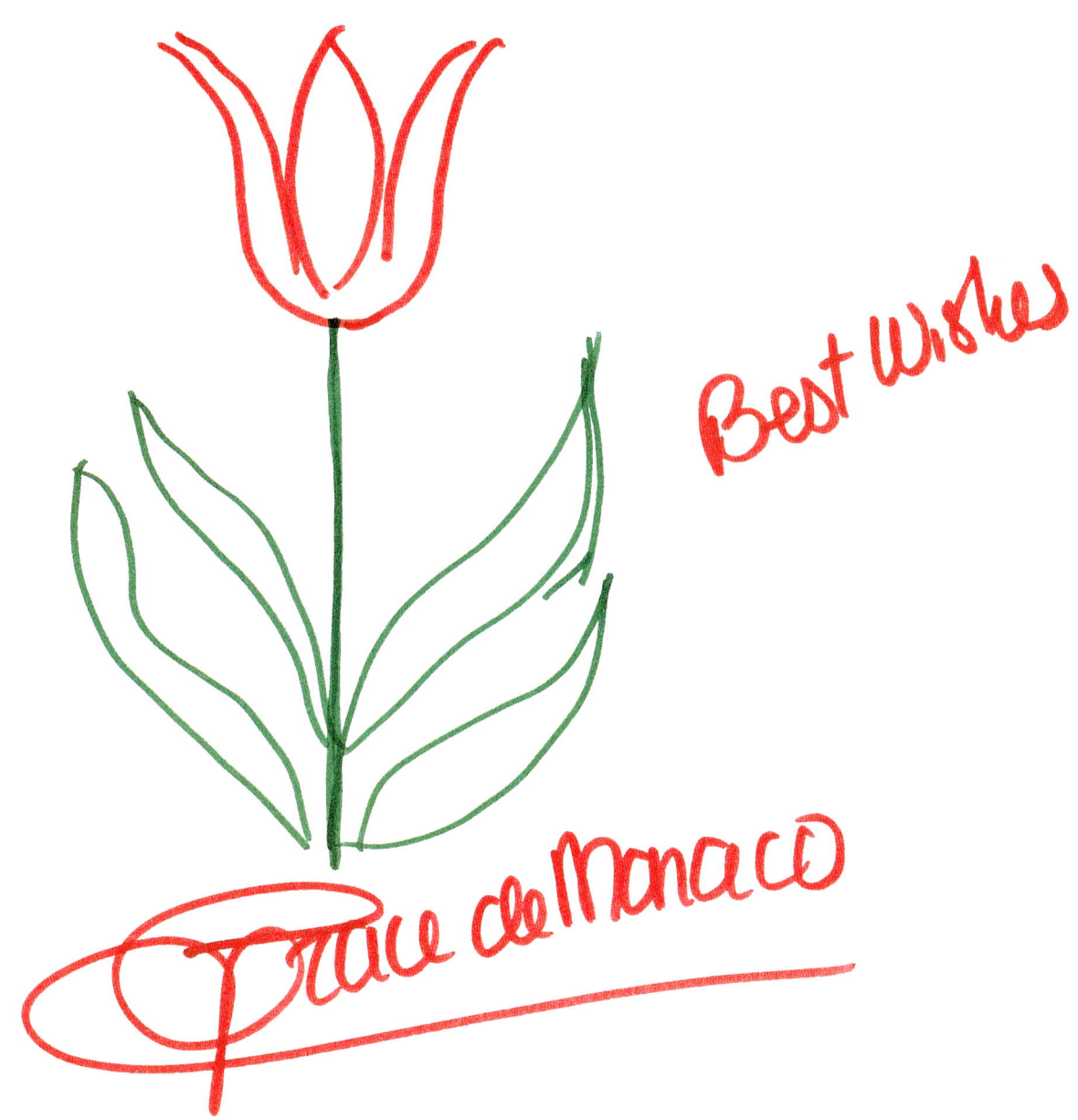

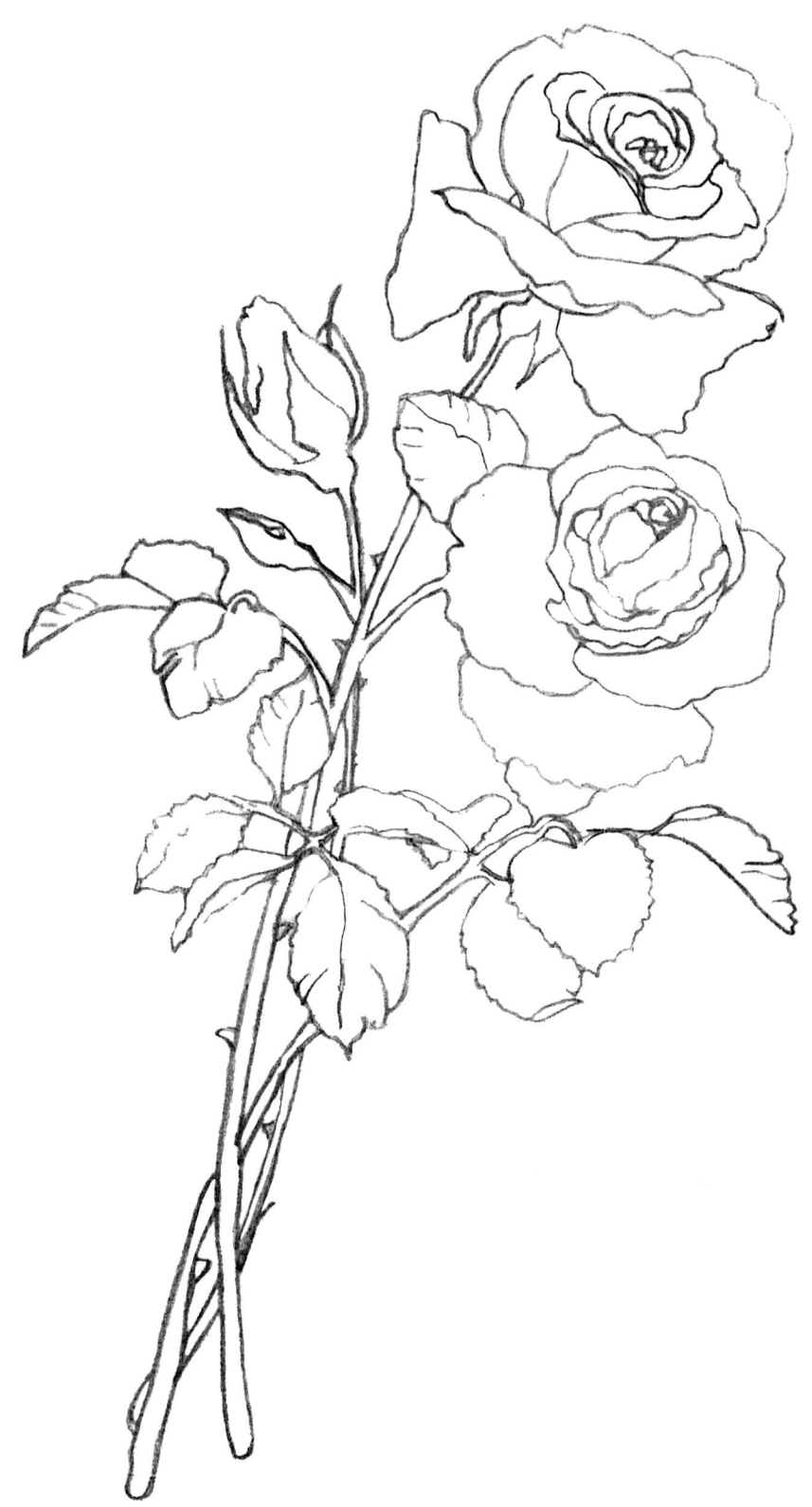

ALISON GERTZ | 1992

Ali Gertz was one of my best friends. We met at Studio 54 in 1983, when she was seventeen and I was nineteen. She was tall with long black hair, and she was beautiful. She was also a talented young artist.

OVER THE YEARS I would see her at parties, and we'd promise to have dinner, "Soon!" But we were young and crazy busy with our lives. Finally, after knowing each other for five years, we went out to dinner. We talked for hours, catching up on my search for true love and the perfect job, and Ali's speculation on when her boyfriend of three years would propose to her. That night Ali cautioned me that I was "too single" and that I needed to be careful because of this thing that was just then being called AIDS. We didn't know much about it, but we did know that you could get it from sex, and that there seemed to be no cure. Ali went home early that night because she didn't feel well and thought she was getting the flu. Ten days later she went into the hospital where she was poked and probed and nearly died. Finally someone decided to run the test for HIV. Ali Gertz was twenty-two when she was diagnosed with full-blown AIDS. In 1988 it was so unusual for a woman to get AIDS from sex that Ali was put on the cover of *People* magazine, *Esquire* named her Woman of the Year, and Barbara Walters introduced the segment of *20/20* that told Ali's story. There was even a movie made about her life called *Something to Live For: The Alison Gertz Story*, starring Molly Ringwald.

ALI DECIDED THAT she would do everything in her power to change the narrow perception of AIDS and who is at risk. She traveled the country speaking to thousands of young people in colleges and high schools. During the last four years of her life, she was radiant. Her capacity to love and be a friend is one of the greatest gifts I have ever received. I asked Ali to draw a flower for my collection, because she was one of the most extraordinary people I'd ever met. She started this delicate rose on tracing paper . . . she was never able to finish it. Ali Gertz died on August 8, 1992, at the age of twenty-six.

Victoria Leacock is donating 30 percent of her royalties from the publication of this book to Love Heals and AmFAR.

Love Heals, the Alison Gertz Foundation for AIDS Education, was co-founded in 1992 by Ali's three best friends, Leacock, Stefani Greenfield, and Dini von Mueffling, in order to continue Ali's crusade to put a personal face on AIDS education. Love Heals' educators have reached tens of thousands of young people with their message of AIDS awareness and prevention. A film entitled *Ali Gertz: In Her Own Words*, directed by Leacock, covers the last four years of Ali's life and is used in Love Heals' educational workshops and distributed to schools and organizations nationwide. For more information about Love Heals, call (212) 371-1335, or write to Love Heals, 345 Park Avenue, New York, NY 10154.

The American Foundation for AIDS Research (AmFAR) is the nation's leading nonprofit organization dedicated to the support of AIDS research (both basic-biomedical and clinical), AIDS prevention, and the advocacy of sound AIDS-related public policy. Since 1985, AmFAR has invested over $144 million in program support, primarily through grants to more than 1,700 research teams. For more information about AmFAR, call (800) 392-6327, or write to AmFAR, 120 Wall Street, 13th Floor, New York, NY 10005-3902.

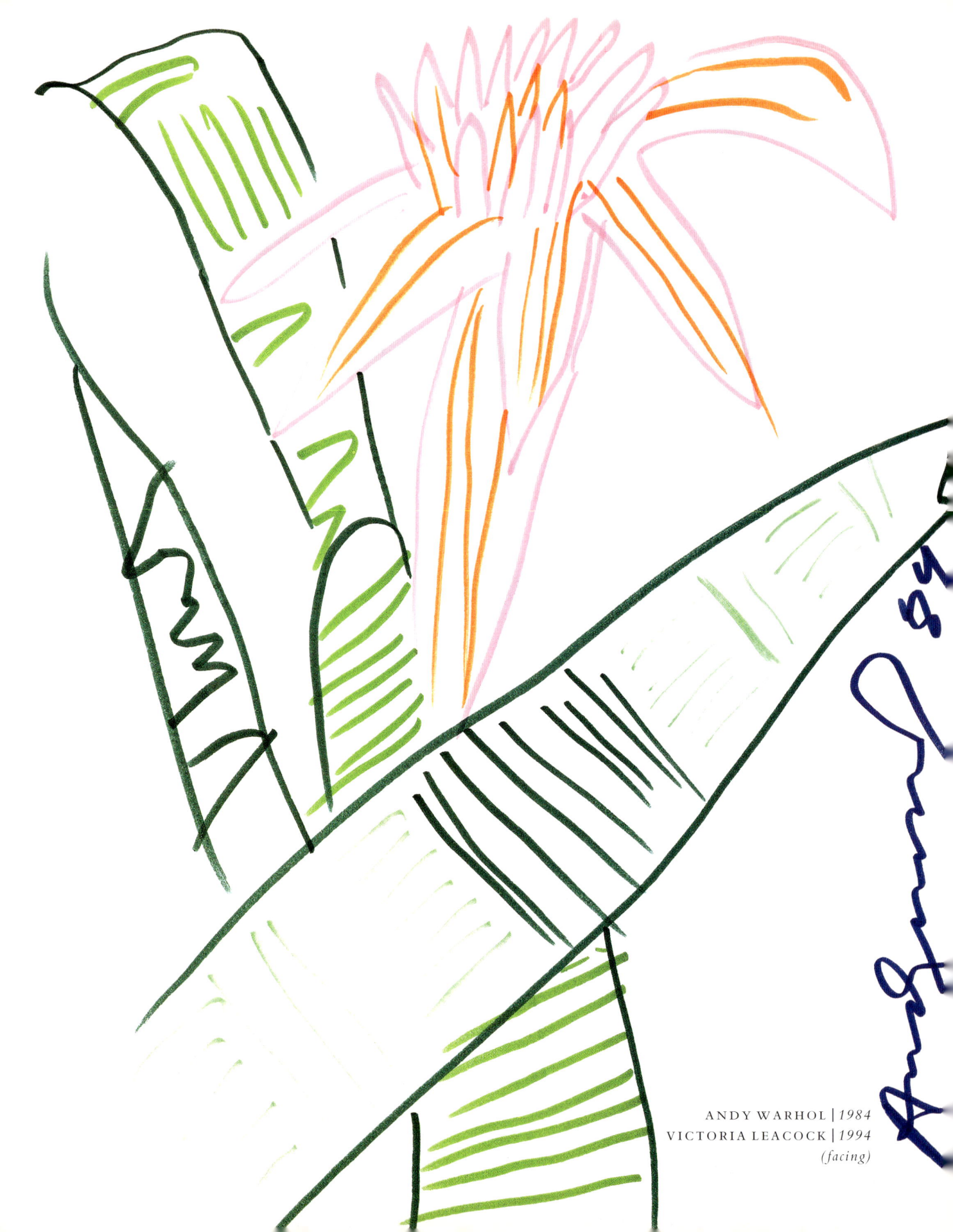

ANDY WARHOL | 1984
VICTORIA LEACOCK | 1994
(facing)

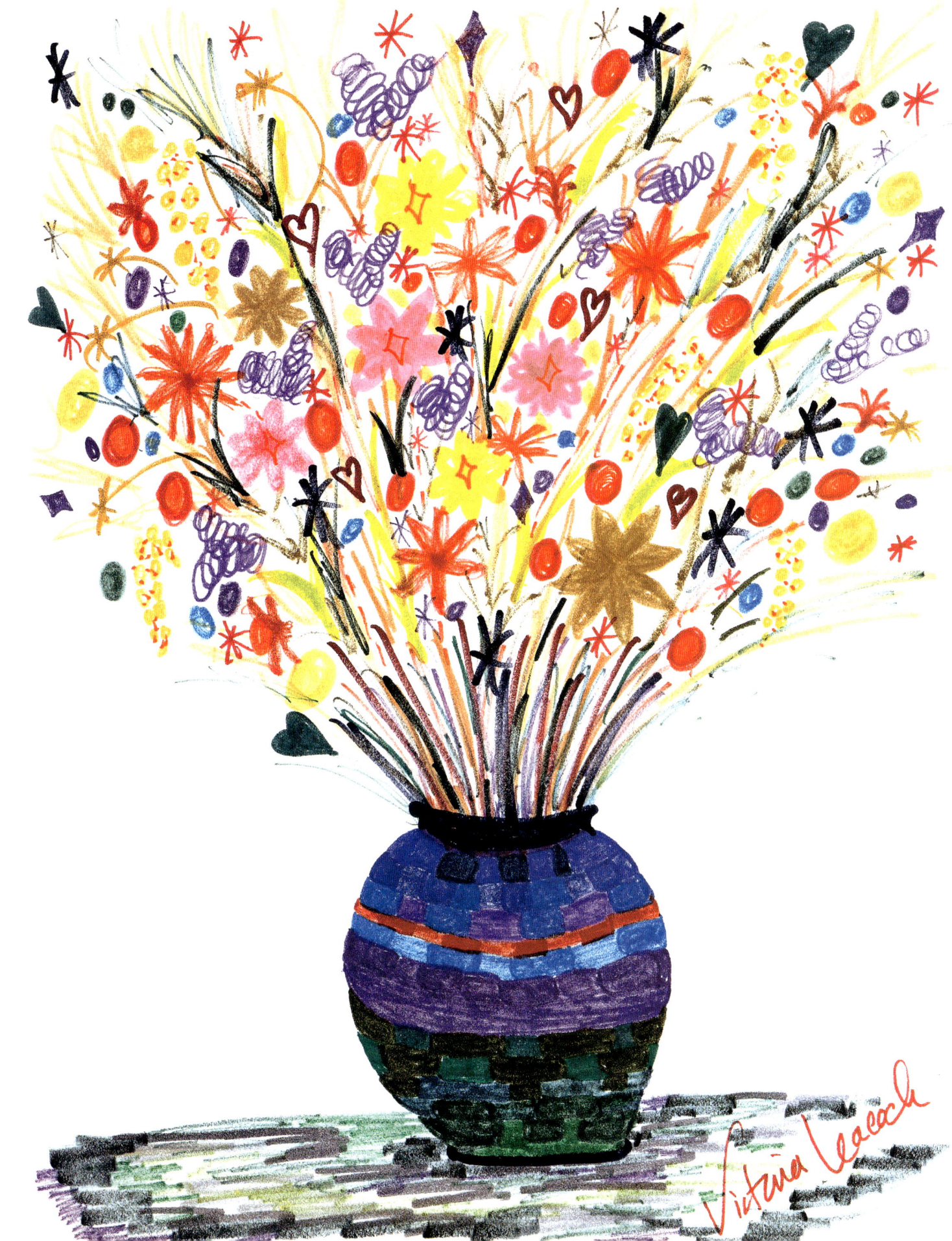

BIOGRAPHIES

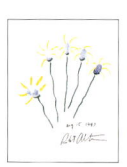
(page 21)

ROBERT ALTMAN

is one of the most prolific and visionary directors to emerge from post-1960s Hollywood. He is a maverick artist whose mystique sometimes threatens to overshadow his many extraordinary films. Although he worked in film and television from the 1940s onward, his breakthrough came with the release of *M★A★S★H* in 1970. Since then he has made such controversial and acclaimed films as *McCabe and Mrs. Miller*, *Nashville*, *The Player*, and *Short Cuts*. He is the first artist to use his fingerprints in a flower autograph.

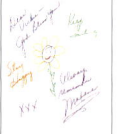
(page 72)

JON ROBIN BAITZ

is one of America's most prominent playwrights. His plays include *Dutch Landscape*, *The Film Society*, *The End of the Day*, and the Pulitzer Prize–nominated *A Fair Country*. He wrote the screenplay for and co-produced the film of his play *The Substance of Fire*, which was released by Miramax. Baitz won an American Academy of Arts and Letters Humanities Award for adapting and directing his play *Three Hotels* for American Playhouse. He drew his flower autograph backstage during the production of Nicole Burdette's *Chelsea Walls* at Naked Angels.

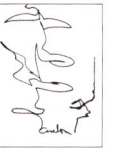
(page 84)

MAXENE ANDREWS

is a World War II entertainment icon. With her sisters Patty and LaVerne, she was one of the singing Andrews Sisters. During the 1940s the Andrews Sisters starred in many Hollywood musicals and recorded such classic songs as "Boogie Woogie Bugle Boy," "Beer Barrel Polka (Roll Out the Barrel)," and "Bei Mir Bist Du Schoen (Means That You're Grand)." At fourteen years of age, Victoria's mother met Maxene after sitting in the front row of an Andrews Sisters show for six consecutive performances. After being introduced backstage, they became close friends, and later Maxene became Victoria's godmother.

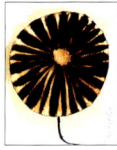
(page 101)

MICHAEL BAY

was one of the most sought-after commercial directors by the age of twenty-six, working with such clients as Nike, Budweiser, Levi's, and Coca-Cola. He has received numerous awards, including the Grand Prix Clio for commercial of the year for his "Got Milk?/Aaron Burr" spot. Bay thrilled audiences with his 1995 feature film debut, *Bad Boys*, and with the blockbuster *The Rock* in 1996. At the premiere of David Fincher's *The Game*, Bay sat in the center of a wild party for almost twenty minutes drawing his posy-eating monsters, with his film *Armageddon* evidently on his mind.

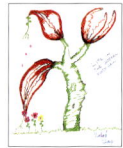
(page 93)

RICHARD AVEDON

grew to fame as a postwar fashion photographer in magazines like *Vogue*, blurring the lines between commercial and art photography. The character of fashion photographer Dick Avery in the film *Funny Face* was based on Avedon, who worked closely with director Stanley Donen and Fred Astaire on the portrayal. Avedon has shown his acclaimed work in museums and galleries internationally and has published several photography books, including *An Autobiography*, *In the American West 1979–1984*, and *Evidence: 1944–1994*.

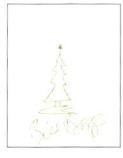
(page 50)

ROSS BLECKNER

has been a pioneer in the revival of American painting since he began to attract attention in the art world in the early 1980s. A major mid-career retrospective of his paintings was held at the Guggenheim Museum in 1995. Bleckner's work shows his quest to express abstract emotional ideas, including those in response to the losses suffered in the AIDS epidemic. When not preparing for his highly anticipated shows, Bleckner has forayed into other media, such as with his cameo appearance in the film *Good Will Hunting*.

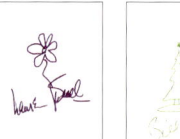
(page 49)

LAUREN BACALL

was a model when her picture on the cover of *Harper's Bazaar* caught the attention of Slim Hawks, then wife of film director Howard Hawks. Her first movie, *To Have and Have Not*, made her an international star. Soon after its release, Bacall married leading man Humphrey Bogart in one of the great Hollywood love stories. Bacall's five-decade film career has included such classics as *The Big Sleep*, *Key Largo*, and *Harper*. At a tribute to John Huston at Lincoln Center, Victoria was surprised to learn that Bacall's voice sounds even lower in person.

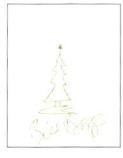
(page 105)

BILL BOGGS

hosted his own daytime talk show, *Midday Live with Bill Boggs*, for thirteen years beginning in 1975. A four-time Emmy winner, he hosts and produces *Bill Boggs Corner Table* on the Food Network and *Historic Traveller* and *Freeze Frame* at the Travel Network. As a teenager, Victoria spent many afternoons in the studio audience of *Midday*, grilling celebrity guests and then running home to see herself on television. Eventually, Boggs began to refer to her as his unofficial co-host. They are still friends.

ERIC BOGOSIAN

has written award-winning plays including *subUrbia* and *Talk Radio*, and his Obie award–winning monologues include *Drinking in America*, *Sex, Drugs, and Rock & Roll*, and *Pounding Nails in the Floor with My Forehead*. The films he has made of his work include *Talk Radio*, directed by Oliver Stone and starring Bogosian, and *subUrbia*, directed by Richard Linklater. He has acted in films as disparate as Steven Seagal's *Under Seige 2: Dark Territory* and Woody Allen's *Deconstructing Harry*. For his flower, he made this collage from things he pulled from his pockets.

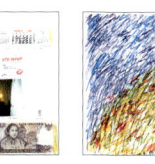
(page 23)

LESLIE CARON

was cast opposite Gene Kelly in Vincente Minnelli's masterpiece *An American in Paris* and her long, illustrious career in film was launched. At a time when postwar America was obsessed with everything French, Caron was the archetypal Parisian gamine and went on to star in such Hollywood musicals as *Daddy Long Legs* and *Gigi*. Her dramatic performance in *The L-Shaped Room* garnered her a British Academy Award and her second Oscar nomination. Victoria is forever grateful for the help Caron once provided in the face of an exploding coffeepot.

(page 62)

JUSTIN BOND

is best known for his collaboration with keyboardist Kenny Mellman as the deranged show-biz duo Kiki & Herb that has been taking New York and San Francisco by storm since 1992. Justin has appeared in the national tour of transsexual playwright Kate Bornstein's groundbreaking *Hidden: A Gender*, Theatre Couture's production of *Charlie—They're No Angels*, and as Clytemnestra in Tiny Mythic's *Elektra Fugues* as well as at numerous nightclubs in New York. *Kiki & Herb: Total Eclipse of the Heart* (directed by Victoria Leacock) won Best Music Video at the USA Film Festival in Dallas.

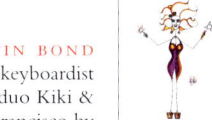
(page 44)

MARTIN CHARNIN

began his career in the theater playing Big Deal in *West Side Story*. The lyricist and director became a big deal himself when he brought the smash hit musical *Annie* to Broadway. *Annie* became one of the longest-running musicals in history and spawned a sequel, film, and twentieth-anniversary revival. He has won Emmys, Grammys, and a Tony. Charnin has contributed to numerous theatrical productions, including *I Remember Mama*, *Lena Horne: The Lady and Her Music*, and *Laughing Matters*. Victoria met him backstage at *Annie* when she was fourteen years old and has known him ever since.

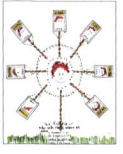
(page 64)

BETTY BUCKLEY

is often recognized for her portrayal of the gym teacher who befriends Carrie White in the classic horror film *Carrie*, and as the stepmother in the 1970s television series *Eight Is Enough*. However, the singer and actress will doubtless be best remembered for originating the role of Grizabella in the smash Broadway show *Cats* (for which she won a Tony Award for best featured actress in a musical), and for playing Norma Desmond in the American stage production of *Sunset Boulevard*. She stepped off the dance floor to draw her bodacious flower at the 1983 Tony Awards ball.

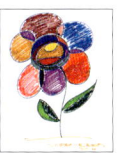
(page 107)

CONNIE CHUNG

is a outstanding journalist whose direct and incisive style is her trademark. She began her career in journalism in her native Washington, D.C., and has worked for NBC in New York anchoring *NBC News at Sunrise*, the *Saturday Nightly News*, and various specials. She won two Emmy Awards for her CBS news magazine *Eye to Eye with Connie Chung*, one for a 1987 report entitled "Shot in Hollywood" and the other for her powerful 1989 interview with Marlon Brando. In 1993 she became co-anchor with Dan Rather of the *CBS Evening News*. She is currently a correspondent for ABC news magazines.

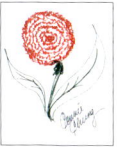
(page 105)

JOHN CAGE

produced a revolutionary body of work in modern musical composition and performance. His radical works challenge even the most basic assumptions of classical music tradition. In his legendary piece *4′33″*, for instance, Cage sat in perfect silence at his piano for the entire four minutes and thirty-three seconds, forcing the audience to reconsider their musical expectations. His collaboration with the choreographer and dancer Merce Cunningham is legendary. Cage's exuberant exploration of what constitutes music is a legacy that lives on for composers today.

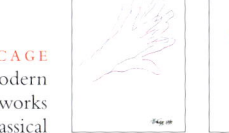
(page 110)

DICK CLARK

has been immortalized as the oldest living teenager in America. Best known for hosting the long-running television shows *American Bandstand* and *TV's Censored Bloopers*, Clark has also become a holiday fixture, annually ringing in the new year with *Dick Clark's New Year's Rockin' Eve*. Dick Clark Productions is one of the most successful companies in the television industry. His daughter, Cindy Clark, also a producer, included two of Victoria's films in *The Doomsday Plan* for TBS.

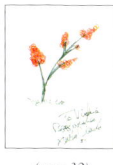
(page 32)

BIOGRAPHIES

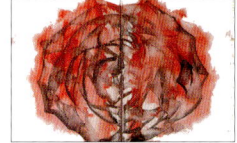
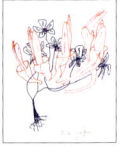

FRANCESCO CLEMENTE
was born in Naples, Italy. He briefly studied architecture in Rome before becoming an internationally recognized painter. Throughout the 1970s he lived and exhibited in Rome and traveled across the Indian subcontinent. In 1981 he moved to New York, where he lives with his glamorous wife Alba and their children. He has published collaborative works with poets such as Gregory Corso, Allen Ginsberg, and Rene Ricard. Clemente was responsible for the ravishing paintings in the 1998 film *Great Expectations*. He continues to show in galleries and museums worldwide.

(back endpaper)

MERCE CUNNINGHAM
was a soloist in the dance company of Martha Graham before founding the Merce Cunningham Dance Company in 1953. Since then he has choreographed more than 150 works including *The Seasons* for the New York City Ballet, *Duets* for the American Ballet Theatre, and *Points in Space*, which has been presented on television and on stage. His profound influence on modern dance is rooted in his innovative approach to sound and movement without reliance on linear elements like storyline. His work has been explored on film and in books, and his compositions are performed all over the world.

(page 111)

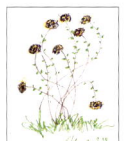
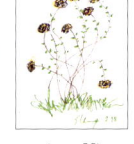
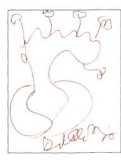

SHAWN COLVIN
acquired a devoted following with the release of her albums *Steady On* in 1989 and *Fat City* in 1992. She has toured constantly to appreciative audiences who welcome her intelligent and honest music. Colvin's platinum-selling 1996 album *A Few Small Repairs* included the hit single "Sunny Came Home" which garnered the singer two Grammys at the awards given in 1998. She drew her flower at the rehearsal for the Grammys while crews dismantled the lights around her, and she finished by the glow of a lighter.

(page 55)

ROBERT DE NIRO
is considered to be one of the greatest screen actors of his generation. He has worked with such directors as Elia Kazan, Brian DePalma, and Francis Ford Coppola. He is best known, however, for his collaborations with Martin Scorsese. In *Mean Streets, Taxi Driver, New York, New York, Goodfellas*, and *Raging Bull* (for which he won one of his Academy Awards), he created a group of characters that will forever be etched in the American psyche. He made his feature film directorial debut with *A Bronx Tale* in 1993. His father was an artist; Victoria thinks he is one, too.

(page 18)

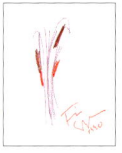
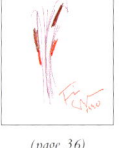
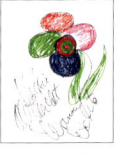

FRANCIS FORD COPPOLA
became a superstar with the release of the cinematic classic *The Godfather* in 1972. Since then he has garnered practically every major honor a director can receive, including numerous Academy Awards and Golden Globes. His films include cult classics like *The Conversation*, artistic triumphs like *Apocalypse Now*, and popular successes like *Peggy Sue Got Married*. Coppola drew this flower at the end of a week of filming a climactic scene from *The Godfather Part III* on location in front of Victoria's apartment building on Elizabeth Street in New York.

(page 36)

DANNY DEVITO
is renowned for an unforgettable presence that is belied by his diminutive stature. His 1970s work includes memorable supporting roles in such notable pictures as *Lady Liberty*, *One Flew Over the Cuckoo's Nest*, and *The Van*. He became a household name as Louie, the obnoxious dispatcher in the mega-hit television series *Taxi*. In the 1980s and '90s he continued his film career with starring roles in *Romancing the Stone*, *Get Shorty*, and *L.A. Confidential*. Behind the camera, he directed *Throw Momma from the Train*, *The War of the Roses*, and *Hoffa*.

(page 46)

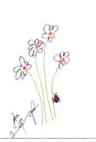
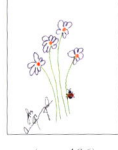
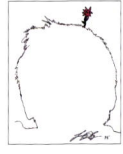

CINDY CRAWFORD
rose to modeling fame in the 1980s, breaking the hold of the petite blond look that was then in vogue. Crawford has become a successful spokeswoman for Revlon Cosmetics, host of MTV's *House of Style*, and author of the best-selling book *Cindy Crawford's Basic Face*. Victoria met Cindy in 1988 when Cindy was on her second date with Richard Gere. Ten years later, Cindy drew this flower in Los Angeles at a benefit for St. Jude Children's Research Hospital.

(page 106)

LEONARDO DICAPRIO
has portrayed characters who have been slapped, beaten, stabbed, and sexually violated. In his rise to stardom, he has played an abused child, a retarded teenager, a drug addict, a bisexual poet, and a doomed lover. His films include *This Boy's Life*, *What's Eating Gilbert Grape?* (for which he received an Oscar nomination), *The Basketball Diaries*, *The Quick and the Dead*, *William Shakespeare's Romeo and Juliet*, and *Marvin's Room*. With the release of *Titanic*, every teenage girl in America has discovered what some have known for years—Leo is dreamy.

(page 109)

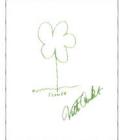
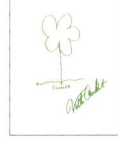
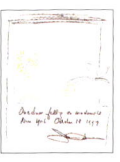

WALTER CRONKITE
was the voice and face of American journalism for almost two decades, announcing to the nation the news of such landmark events as the assassination of John F. Kennedy, the first man to walk on the moon, and the resignation of Richard Nixon. Cronkite, who began his career as a campus correspondent, went to work for CBS News in Washington, D.C., in 1950. In 1962 he assumed his duties behind the *Evening News* desk, where he remained for the next nineteen years. His many awards include the Presidential Medal of Freedom, presented by Jimmy Carter in 1981.

(page 32)

JOAN DIDION
is an essayist, novelist, journalist, and screenwriter whose style is at once as spare and rich as her native Northern California landscape. Her books include the collections of essays *Slouching Towards Bethlehem* and *The White Album*, the political reports *Salvador* and *Miami*, and novels *Play It As It Lays*, *A Book of Common Prayer*, *Democracy*, and *The Last Thing He Wanted*. With her husband, John Gregory Dunne, she penned the screenplays for *The Panic in Needle Park*, *True Confessions*, and *Up Close & Personal*. The windowsill pictured is in the New York City apartment where she writes.

(page 72)

BIOGRAPHIES

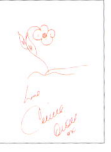

CELINE DION

began as a Canadian nightclub singer in her teens and has become one of the top-selling recording artists in history. She has made a career of singing love songs and won her first Academy Award for singing the theme from Disney's animated hit *Beauty and the Beast* with Peabo Bryson. In 1996 she performed at the opening ceremonies for the U.S. Olympic Games in Atlanta. Dion sang the theme song to *Titanic*, which won best original song at the 1997 Academy Awards.

(page 65)

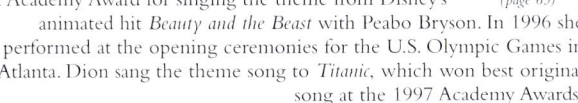

GINA GERSHON

has a look, whether it's her eyes or the curve of her lips, that brings a sexual edge to her films. She's worked her magic in Robert Altman's *The Player*, John Sayles's *City of Hope*, and John Woo's *Face/Off*. Her portrayal of Cristal, the Las Vegas superdiva, has turned Paul Verhoeven's sex epic *Showgirls* into an underground cult film. Gershon's film *Bound*, with Jennifer Tilly, found her cast as a gorgeous lesbian ex-con-turned-handywoman and made her a star. She drew her flower backstage during the 1990 production of *Chelsea Walls* at Naked Angels.

(page 112)

BRET EASTON ELLIS

was described by his hero, Joan Didion, in *Vanity Fair* as "the sweetest, most sensitive person." He is also the person who introduced an entire generation of readers to the porn genre known as "snuff films" in his first novel, *Less Than Zero*. Ellis became a twenty-one-year-old literary star with the publication of that work; six years later the icy violence of his third novel, *American Psycho*, generated a lot of controversy. He continues to write, splitting his time between New York and Los Angeles. He drew his flower at one of his legendary Christmas parties.

(page 72)

ALISON GERTZ

was diagnosed with AIDS in 1988 after having contracted the virus through a single sexual encounter when she was sixteen. She brought her story to the public in an effort to help others and soon became an internationally recognized spokesperson for AIDS awareness and prevention. Addressing young people across the country, she became one of the first credible voices of her generation to alert her peers to the reality that anyone can get AIDS. Her story was featured in numerous magazine and newspaper articles, and in an ABC made-for-television movie.

(page 114)

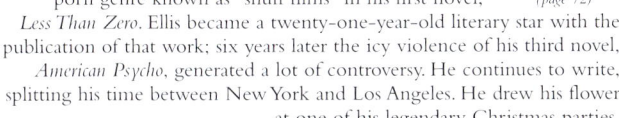

JULES FISHER

has won more Tony Awards than any other lighting designer. He began his career on Broadway working with director/choreographer Bob Fosse on *Pippin*; their collaboration continued with *Dancin'* and *Big Deal*. Fisher has brought his dazzling and innovative light to the productions of such notable directors as Arthur Laurents, Tommy Tune, and George C. Wolfe. His recent creations include *Jelly's Last Jam*, *Bring in 'Da Noise, Bring in 'Da Funk*, and the smash hit *Ragtime*. Appropriately, his flower is an intricate collage of lighting gels.

(page 92)

CYNTHIA GIBB

began her career at the age of fifteen when Woody Allen cast her in *Stardust Memories*. By the age of seventeen she was working as a regular on such series as *Search for Tomorrow* and *Fame*. Gibb has starred in numerous television and cable movies, most notably the title roles in *The Karen Carpenter Story* and *Gypsy*, earning a Golden Globe nomination for the latter. Her feature credits include *Youngblood*, *Short Circuit II*, Oliver Stone's *Salvador*, and *Death Warrant*. Cynthia and Victoria have been friends for seventeen years.

(page 22)

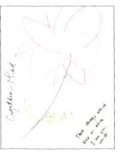

MILOS FORMAN

was born in Czechoslovakia. As a film director he established an international reputation with the release of *Loves of a Blonde* in 1965 and *The Fireman's Ball* in 1967. Eventually Forman left his homeland, seeking greater freedom of artistic expression. After moving to the United States he directed such monumental films as *One Flew Over the Cuckoo's Nest*, *Hair*, *Ragtime*, *Amadeus*, and *The People vs. Larry Flynt*. Victoria is most impressed by the fact that the Academy Award–winning director still answers his own phone.

(page 90)

ELLIOTT GOULD

became a star on Broadway playing the lead in *I Can Get It for You Wholesale*. He fell in love with co-star Barbra Streisand, they married and left for Hollywood, where Gould quickly became known as a nontraditional leading man. Nominated for an Academy Award for his work in *Bob & Carol & Ted & Alice*, he became an international star in Robert Altman's *The Long Goodbye* and *M★A★S★H*. Victoria met Elliott at a dinner party, got his crayon flower, and has been crazy about him ever since.

(page 80)

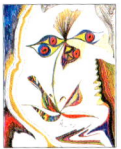 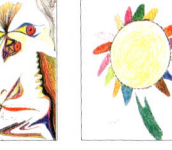

RICHARD GERE

made a splash early in his career playing a piece of rough trade brought home by Diane Keaton in *Looking for Mr. Goodbar*. Soon afterward he became a star in such memorable films as *Bloodbrothers*, *American Gigolo*, *An Officer and a Gentleman*, and *Pretty Woman*. Politically, Gere is an outspoken humanitarian who has devoted time and energy to the causes of Tibetan Buddhism and independence. He is more than willing to donate his friends' time, too. Victoria has organized three benefits for Tibet to date.

(page 27)

PRINCESS GRACE OF MONACO

began her life as Grace Kelly, one of Hollywood's most glamorous actresses of the 1950s. She starred in classics ranging from *High Noon* to *High Society* and won an Academy Award for her performance in *The Country Girl*. Some of her greatest achievements on film were as the leading lady in Alfred Hitchcock's timeless thrillers *Dial M for Murder*, *Rear Window*, and *To Catch a Thief*. The latter was filmed partially on location in Monaco, where she met her future husband Prince Rainier. They were married in 1956.

(page 113)

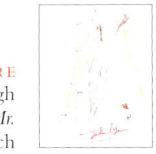 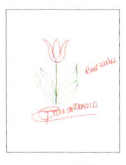

BIOGRAPHIES

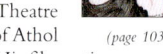

RICHARD E. GRANT
(page 103)

was born in Mbabane, Swaziland. He studied literature and theater at University of Capetown in South Africa, where he co-founded the multiracial Troupe Theatre Company with former classmates and members of Athol Fugard and Yvonne Bryceland's Space Theatre. His film acting successes include *Withnail & I*, *Henry & June*, *Bram Stoker's Dracula*, and *The Age of Innocence*. Richard drew this Caribbean hibiscus after Victoria met him in Barbados at a New Year's Eve party.

JIM HAYGOOD
(page 48)

has cut, jumped, dissolved, and faded for the last fifteen years as one of Hollywood's busiest film editors. Having cut close to a "zillion" commercials for the likes of Levi's, AT&T, and Budweiser and music videos for Madonna, The Rolling Stones, and Counting Crows, his innovative, visceral style led to a close association with video directing czar David Fincher and their collaboration on the film *The Game* starring Michael Douglas. He has also edited some amazing Nike spots for director Robert Leacock, Victoria's older brother.

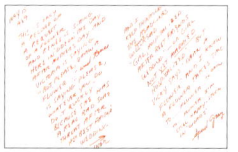
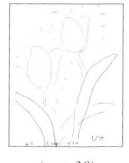

SPALDING GRAY
(page 66)

is a performance artist, actor, and writer. He began his career as an actor at the Alley Theater in Houston before moving to New York in 1969. Most famous for his solo performance monologues, he has written and performed such pieces as *Swimming to Cambodia*, *Monster in a Box* (both of which have been made into feature films), and *Gray's Anatomy* throughout the world. In 1988 he made his Broadway debut playing the Stage Manager in a critically acclaimed revival of Thornton Wilder's *Our Town*.

DAVID HOCKNEY
(page 30)

is internationally celebrated as a consummate painter, draftsman, photographer, and stage designer. His first solo exhibition was held in late 1963, and since then he has had numerous one-man shows and retrospectives at museums and galleries worldwide. After relocating from England to the United States in the mid-1960s, his work began to reflect the landscapes of his newly adopted Southern Californian surroundings. In recent years, Hockney has revolutionized photography with his epic cut-and-paste, cubism-influenced panoramas. He drew this flower at the opening of an exhibit without missing a hello or good-bye.

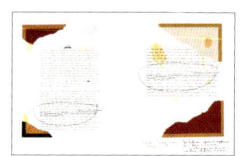
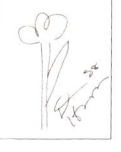

PETER GREENAWAY
(page 52)

is a filmmaker whose inspiration comes not so much from storytelling as from experimentation with visual and intellectual concepts. He has challenged audiences with such films as *The Draughtman's Contract*, *A Zed & Two Noughts*, *The Cook, The Thief, His Wife & Her Lover*, and *Prospero's Books*. Greenaway is also a painter and novelist. The "flower" he designed for Victoria is a collage of manuscript pages. Lacking glue, Greenaway stuck the sheets down with wild Australian honey.

DENNIS HOPPER
(page 17)

became a counterculture icon in 1969 with the release of *Easy Rider*, which he co-wrote and starred in with Peter Fonda. He had been a successful actor since the fifties when he appeared with James Dean in *Rebel Without a Cause* and *Giant*. He has maintained the rebel tradition throughout his career, which includes such films as *Blue Velvet*, *Rumble Fish*, *The Texas Chainsaw Massacre 2*, and *Speed*. He was nominated for a supporting actor Oscar for his moving performance as an alcoholic in *Hoosiers* in 1986.

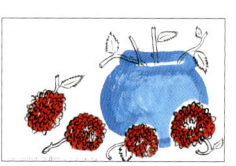
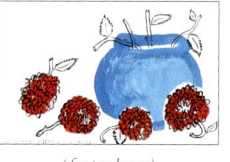
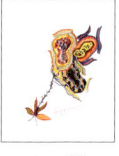

KEITH HARING
(front endpaper) *(page 59)*

arrived in New York in 1978. A voracious student of popular culture, he submerged himself in the multicultural hodge-podge that was the East Village. He was inspired by the graffiti he saw in the subways, admiring the calligraphic quality of the graffiti artists' "tags." In 1980 his work received widespread attention when he began to make drawings in subway stations. Seemingly overnight Keith Haring became an art star whose work still travels the world and whose popularity, even posthumously, continues to grow.

LENA HORNE
(page 83)

began her career as a dancer in Harlem's famed Cotton Club in the 1930s. Before long she found herself in Hollywood, where she starred in *Cabin in the Sky* and *Stormy Weather*, which also became her signature song. Her beauty and talent led to an international career as a nightclub entertainer. Through her success and fame, she made a major contribution toward breaking down color barriers in the fight for civil rights. She won a Tony Award for her appearance on Broadway in *Lena Horne: The Lady and Her Music*. Her flower blossomed in her dressing room, backstage in London.

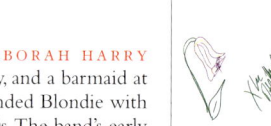
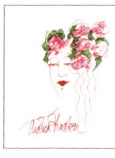

DEBORAH HARRY
(page 49)

worked as a beautician, a Playboy bunny, and a barmaid at Max's Kansas City before she founded Blondie with guitarist Chris Stein in the 1970s. The band's early momentum peaked with their third album *Parallel Lines* (1978) which went platinum. Memorable hits from the group include "Heart of Glass," "Call Me," "The Tide Is High," and "Rapture." Harry's solo career has included the critically acclaimed album *Rockbird*, and a Blondie reunion album is planned. The rock and roll goddess has appeared in several films including *Union City*, *Videodrome*, *Hairspray*, and *Heavy*.

ANJELICA HUSTON
(page 61)

had her first film lead in 1969 in her father John Huston's medieval romance *A Walk with Love and Death*. After this experience she only flirted with film until she appeared as the unforgettable Mae Rose in *Prizzi's Honor*, again directed by her father. The performance brought her an Oscar nomination and made her a star, and since then she has created memorable characters in *The Dead*, *Crimes and Misdemeanors*, and *The Grifters*. She made her directorial debut with the critically acclaimed *Bastard Out of Carolina*.

BIOGRAPHIES

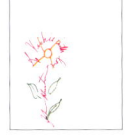

JOHN HUSTON
(page 60)

began his career as a screenwriter on such memorable films as *Jezebel* and *High Sierra*. He went on to become one of the most successful directors in motion picture history, creating the classics *The Maltese Falcon*, *The Treasure of the Sierra Madre*, *The African Queen*, and *Prizzi's Honor*. Though he occasionally acted, like his father, Walter, and daughter Anjelica, it is for his vivid range of work that he will be remembered, from *Moby Dick* to *Casino Royale*, and from *Annie* to his last film, *The Dead*.

ANGELA LANSBURY
(page 49)

made her film debut in 1944 in the classic *Gaslight*. Never fully recognized as a leading lady in Hollywood, she nevertheless spent the next few decades stealing scenes in films including *The Picture of Dorian Gray*, *The Manchurian Candidate*, and *Bedknobs and Broomsticks*. She has received Tonys for best actress in the musicals *Mame*, *Dear World*, *Gypsy*, and for her celebrated role as Mrs. Lovett in *Sweeney Todd*. For the role of Jessica Fletcher on television's immensely popular *Murder, She Wrote*, Lansbury won four Golden Globe Awards and thirteen Emmy nominations.

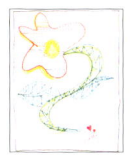

JEAN PIERRE JEUNET
(page 86)

created *Delicatessen*, a popular French independent film, along with co-writer and director Marc Caro. They followed with *City of Lost Children*, a terrifying story that mixed stunning special effects with a fantastical story about an evil despot who steals the dreams of children because he cannot dream himself. Jeunet made his breakthrough into the mainstream by directing Sigourney Weaver and Wynona Ryder in the Hollywood blockbuster *Alien Resurrection*. On assignment for *Paper* magazine, Victoria's efforts at interviewing Jeunet were quite humorous as she spoke little French and he spoke no English.

JONATHAN LARSON
(page 99)

was a lyricist, playwright, and composer. With his Pulitzer Prize–winning stage phenomenon *Rent*, Larson restored belief to performers everywhere that Broadway, and more specifically the musical, could be vital and relevant. Tragically, on the eve of the show's opening, Larson died suddenly of an aortic aneurysm and never got to witness this success himself. The Jonathan Larson Foundation for the Performing Arts was established in his memory to give grants and encouragement to young artists who, as he did, refuse to settle for anything less than their best.

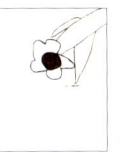 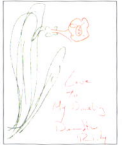

DIANE KEATON
(page 51)

appeared with Woody Allen in memorable 1970s films including *Play It Again, Sam*, *Sleeper*, *Love and Death*, and *Annie Hall*, for which Keaton won an Academy Award. Her extensive film credits also include *The Godfather*, and an Academy Award–nominated performance in *Reds*. In 1987 she made her directorial debut with *Heaven*. Recently, Keaton has engaged cinemagoers in the popular *The First Wives Club* and with her Oscar-nominated performance in *Marvin's Room*. Personally as eclectic as the characters she portrays, Keaton drew this flower in her kitchen while a gospel choir rehearsed in her living room.

RICHARD LEACOCK
(page 42)

is one of the most influential filmmakers of the cinema verité movement. He was born in England but moved to the U.S. in his teens. Leacock and Robert Drew began making television films for Time-Life using newly created equipment that permitted discreet coverage of events. *Primary* covered the battle for the Wisconsin primary between Senators Humphrey and Kennedy, and *The Chair* showed the ordeal of a man sentenced to death. Victoria's father is currently working in digital video in locations as varied as Siberia, France, and Cuba.

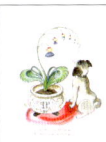 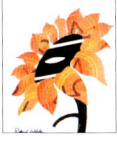

HILARY KNIGHT
(page 82)

is an illustrator and author who grew up in New York City. In the early fifties, Knight met Kay Thompson, who had invented the character of an irrepressible six-year-old moppet named Eloise. Their first book, *Eloise*, became a best-seller and was soon followed by *Eloise in Paris* and *Eloise in Moscow*. Knight has illustrated over fifty books, nine of which he wrote himself. Since 1997 he has been a staff artist for *Vanity Fair*, and his work includes album covers, fashion advertising, and the Neiman Marcus catalog.

RICHARD LINKLATER
(page 31)

brought Generation X to the mainstream with his low-budget first film *Slacker*. Hollywood took notice. Linklater introduced film idol Matthew McConaughey and indie princess Parker Posey in his follow-up film *Dazed and Confused*. His third work, *Before Sunrise*, starred Ethan Hawke. Linklater seems comfortable working with a core group of actors including Hawke and McConaughey, who also appeared in his most recent film *The Newton Boys*, and Posey, who appeared in his screen adaptation of Eric Bogosian's *subUrbia*.

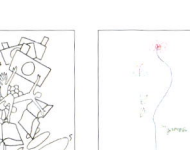 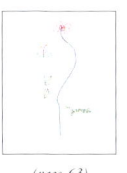

MARK KOSTABI
(page 38)

is a painter and sculptor who has generated tremendous controversy by employing assistants to paint work he eventually signs. The flower in this book is a Kostabi original. In fact, there is videotaped footage, shot by Victoria's brother Robert at a gallery opening, of the artist himself not only drawing in the book but continuing the work off the page and onto Victoria's décolletage before discarding the used pen down the front of her dress and walking away.

MADONNA
(page 63)

is perhaps the greatest diva in pop history. She transformed her way to superstardom first as a Boy Toy and then as the glamorous Material Girl. The role model for legions of teen Madonna wanna-bes in the 1980s, she has become high priestess of a generation of health-conscious, twenty-something gay men by exploring a post-AIDS spirituality in the 1990s. Part of her appeal lies in her ability to reduce complicated emotional concepts into catchy slogans like "express yourself" and "open your heart."

BIOGRAPHIES

NORMAN MAILER

is a novelist, journalist, giant-sized personality, and pointed observer whose prose is considered by some to be unequaled since James and Faulkner. He reigned especially large in America during the twenty-year period from 1959 to 1979, between the publication of *Advertisements for Myself* and *The Executioner's Song*, when his writings reflected the rebellious undercurrent of the time. His other works include *The Naked and the Dead* and *Tough Guys Don't Dance*. His most recent book is an anthology of his work titled *The Time of Our Time*.

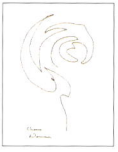

(page 73)

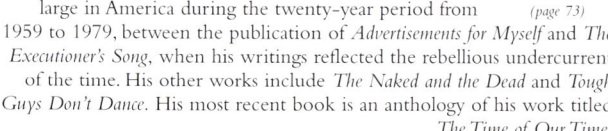

(page 100)

PENELOPE ANN MILLER

has played the leading lady opposite such varied and distinguished men as Pee-Wee Herman in *Big Top Pee-Wee*, Marlon Brando in *The Freshman*, Robert De Niro in *Awakenings*, and Arnold Schwarzenegger in *Kindergarten Cop*. Her career began on Broadway playing the ingenue Daisy in Neil Simon's *Biloxi Blues*, a role she later reprised on screen with Matthew Broderick. She received a Tony nomination for her portrayal of Emily in the 1988 revival of *Our Town*, and in 1993 a Golden Globe nomination for her performance in *Carlito's Way* opposite Al Pacino.

MARY MCCORMACK

is a glamorous movie and television star who sends Victoria into fits of laughter with her hysterically funny impromptu monologues and imitations. Her acting talents have been put to good use by John Hughes in his 1994 remake of *Miracle on 34th Street*, in *Private Parts* as Mrs. Howard Stern, and as the only woman astronaut trying to save the planet in *Deep Impact*. She has also been praised for her work in Steven Bochco's television series *Murder One*.

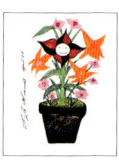

(page 29)

(page 95)

LIZA MINNELLI

is the daughter of director Vincente Minnelli and Judy Garland. It seems as if it were her destiny to become one of the biggest musical-comedy stars of her era. Minnelli became the youngest performer to win a Tony Award for her Broadway debut in *Flora, the Red Menace*, in 1965. She went on to become an international star with her Academy Award–winning performance in *Cabaret*, and starring roles in Scorsese's *New York, New York* and the hit comedy *Arthur*. Minnelli currently performs in sell-out concerts throughout the world. Victoria was thirteen when she first met Liza and still gets tongue-tied in her presence.

JAY MCINERNEY

has become something of a symbol for his times. In the 1980s his rebellious first novel *Bright Lights, Big City* chronicled the club-going hedonism and confusion of an entire generation. The movie rights for his book were optioned, and McInerney became a prominent member of the fast-paced, highly visible social scene in New York City. He went on to document the boom and subsequent collapse of the 1980s with *Brightness Falls* and *The Story of My Life*. His most recent books are *The Last of the Savages* and *Model Behavior*.

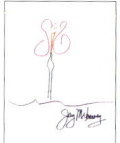

(page 72)

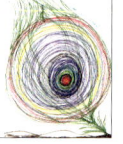

(page 45)

MIKE NEWELL

has been a successful film director for more than thirty years. His career took off in 1976 with *The Man in the Iron Mask*, starring Richard Chamberlain. In the 1980s, the British native directed the Cannes prizewinner *Dance with a Stranger* and *The Good Father*, which won the Prix Italia. In 1991 *Enchanted April* was nominated for three Academy Awards and won two Golden Globes. His most popular film was the hugely successful *Four Weddings and a Funeral*, followed by *Donnie Brasco*, which received an Oscar nomination for best picture.

SARAH MCLACHLAN

comes from a long legacy of Canadian singer-songwriters. Over the course of a career born with the release of her debut album *Touch* in 1988, her songs of love and loss have developed from youthful, Kate Bush–inspired compositions to mature roots-driven rock songs and ballads. Her multi-platinum albums *Fumbling Towards Ecstasy* and *Surfacing* made her an international star. In 1997 she organized the first Lilith Fair, an all-woman line-up of popular singers, which became the top concert draw of that year. One dollar from each ticket sold for the Lilith Fair goes to local and national charities.

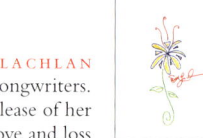

(page 40)

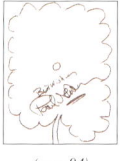

(page 94)

PAUL NEWMAN

is known for the blue eyes that still cause fans to swoon, whether they are gazing from the screen, racetrack, or grocery shelves. He began his career on Broadway, appearing in such plays as *Picnic*, where he met his second wife and collaborator Joanne Woodward. His hit movies include *The Long Hot Summer*, *The Hustler*, *Hud*, *Cool Hand Luke*, *Butch Cassidy and the Sundance Kid*, and *The Color of Money*, for which he won an Academy Award. Victoria was thrilled that Newman made an exception in his firm no-autograph policy when she asked him to draw a flower and speechless when he telephoned to give his permission to be in this book.

BETTE MIDLER

rose to stardom in the 1970s as a camp icon at New York's Continental Baths. The Hawaiian native has sold millions of records since then, sells concerts out worldwide, and is an internationally known film star. Midler earned an Academy Award nomination for best actress in her debut film *The Rose*, a thinly veiled biography of rock legend Janis Joplin. She has gone on to have hits with such films as *Down and Out in Beverly Hills*, *Ruthless People*, *Beaches*, and *The First Wives Club*.

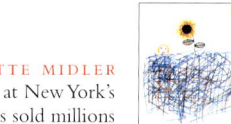

(page 47)

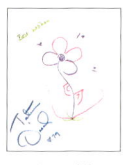

(page 49)

TATUM O'NEAL

became the youngest recipient of an Academy Award at age ten. She won best supporting actress in 1973 for *Paper Moon* in which she played a streetwise cigarette-smoking schemer opposite her father Ryan O'Neal. Her subsequent films—*Nickelodeon*, *The Bad News Bears*, *International Velvet*, and *Little Darlings*—left their mark on a generation of young people who grew up in the 1970s and early '80s. Most recently, O'Neal appeared in *Basquiat*. She was the second person to draw a flower for Victoria, on the set of *Circle of Two* with Richard Burton in 1979.

BIOGRAPHIES

GERALDINE PAGE

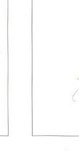
(page 97)

was an actress who moved easily from the stage to film and was rewarded with both Academy and Tony awards. One of the greatest interpreters of the works of playwright Tennessee Williams, she appeared in both the stage and film adaptations of *Summer and Smoke* and *Sweet Bird of Youth*. Late in her life she won a Tony for her performance in *Agnes of God* and an Oscar for best actress as the widow in *A Trip to Bountiful*. Victoria's father met Geraldine in the 1950s when he came to the assistance of his neighbor and extinguished her flaming frying pan.

REX REED

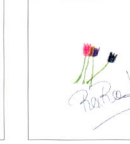
(page 32)

has been called the "Rhinestone Cowboy of Journalism." His nonfiction books include *Do You Sleep in the Nude?*, *Valentines and Vitriol*, and *Travolta to Keaton*. In the latter, Reed recounts his experience in a New York recording studio in 1978, watching Liza Minnelli record the album for her Broadway show *The Act*. One track was troublesome, but after several attempts, Minnelli was singing what seemed to be the perfect take. That is, until a girl with a ponytail opened the door. The guilty intruder was fifteen-year-old Victoria.

JOSEPH PAPP

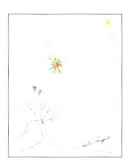
(page 105)

was one of the most influential figures in American theater. He was a defender of the First Amendment and an early advocate of multiculturalism. As founder of the New York Shakespeare Festival, he brought free Shakespeare to Central Park in New York City. With the Public Theater, he created one of the nation's most important showcases for emerging directors like Michael Bennett and George C. Wolf, and actors like Kevin Kline and Meryl Streep. Papp was also responsible for such seminal musicals as *A Chorus Line* and *Hair*.

PETER RIEGERT

(page 28)

worked as an English teacher, social worker, and aide-de-camp to Congresswoman Bella Abzug before turning to acting. His extensive theater work includes David Mamet's *The Old Neighborhood* and *Sexual Perversity in Chicago* and Wendy Wasserstein's *An American Daughter* and *Isn't It Romantic*. He made his film debut in *National Lampoon's Animal House*, and starred in *Local Hero*, *Crossing Delancey*, and *The Mask*. On television, he portrayed Herbie in *Gypsy*, was nominated for an Emmy for *Barbarians at the Gate*, and played the president of NBC on the final episode of *Seinfeld*.

GEORGE PLIMPTON

(page 74)

is the author or co-editor of many best-selling books, including *American Journey: The Times of Robert F. Kennedy*, *Edie: An American Biography*, and *D.V.*, a biography of Diana Vreeland. Founding editor of *The Paris Review*, Plimpton has edited nine volumes of interviews with famous literary figures entitled *Writers at Work*. He is known for extraordinary forays into participatory journalism, including playing quarterback for the Detroit Tigers and flying on trapeze in a circus. His most recent book is *Truman Capote*.

MOLLY RINGWALD

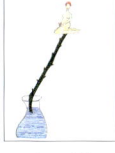
(page 41)

began performing at age four with her father Bob Ringwald's Fulton Street Jazz Band. Nominated for a Golden Globe Award at age thirteen for her film debut in Paul Mazursky's *Tempest*, she became a star with her portrayal of world-weary innocents in the films *Sixteen Candles*, *The Breakfast Club*, and *Pretty in Pink*. She has worked with such varied directors as Jean-Luc Godard, John Hughes, and Cindy Sherman. Off Broadway, she received a Theater World Award nomination for her debut in *Lily Dale* and recently returned in the Pulitzer Prize–winning *How I Learned to Drive*. Victoria believes in the sun, the moon, and Molly.

BILL PLYMPTON

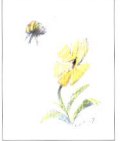
(page 85)

is an animator whose films begin with our world and then turn it upside down and inside out. His award-winning shorts and "Microtoons" are a popular MTV offering. His shorts, including *How to Kiss*, *25 Ways to Quit Smoking*, and *One of Those Days*, have been seen around the country, highlighting many animation festivals. His first full-length animated movie, *The Tune*, received rave reviews and was followed by the two live-action films *J. Lyle* and *Guns on the Clackamas*. His latest extravaganza is *I Married a Strange Person*.

GINGER ROGERS

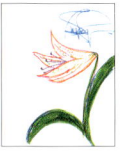
(page 57)

was touring in vaudeville as a teenager and had made nineteen films before she was partnered with Fred Astaire. Together they became of one of the greatest screen teams in Hollywood history. In such depression-era musicals as *The Gay Divorcee*, *Swing Time*, and *Top Hat*, she warmed his sophistication and he provided her with cool. Rogers went on to become a leading lady in her own right and won an Academy Award for her leading role in *Kitty Foyle* in 1940. She drew her glamorous flower backstage at Radio City Music Hall.

RAMONES

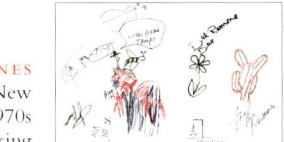
(page 24)

The Ramones shaped the sound of the New York punk rock scene in the mid-1970s with their hard, fast, loud songs featuring deadpan lyrics and an impenetrable wall of guitar chords. After releasing their self-titled debut album, the band traveled to England where they influenced the nascent London punk movement with such songs as "Beat on the Brat" and "Blitzkrieg Bop." In 1979 they were immortalized in Roger Corman's classic *Rock 'n' Roll High School*, which featured one of their signature songs, "I Want to Be Sedated."

MARK ROMANEK

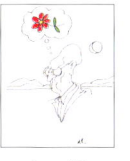
(page 81)

has directed music videos for artists including Michael and Janet Jackson, R.E.M., Madonna, Nine Inch Nails, David Bowie, and En Vogue. His music videos have received over a dozen MTV awards, a Grammy, three Clios, and three Billboard Music Awards, among others. Two of Romanek's music videos (for Nine Inch Nails' "Closer" and Madonna's "Bedtime Story") have become part of the Museum of Modern Art's permanent collection. In 1985, Romanek directed the critically acclaimed independent feature film *Static* starring Amanda Plummer and Keith Gordon.

BIOGRAPHIES

ALEXANDER STERLING CALDER ROWER

is one of artist Alexander Calder's grandchildren and has devoted his life to studying and supporting Calder's work. Rower is the director of The Alexander and Louisa Calder Foundation and co-founder of The Calder Foundation, which has amassed an archive of thousands of documents, photographs, books, and films on Calder. He provides invaluable assistance to curators, including the restoration of Calder sculptures. Victoria and Sandy, as he is known, attended grade school together. He drew this amazing flower with a ballpoint pen.

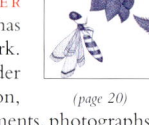
(page 20)

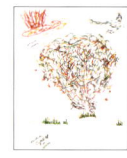
(page 96)

CAMPBELL SCOTT

is the son of actors George C. Scott and Colleen Dewhurst. His first role in a feature film was as Willy in the groundbreaking *Longtime Companion*, about the AIDS epidemic. He also appeared in *Dead Again* and *Dying Young*. In spite of a certain theme in his movies, his career has flourished. Some of his more upbeat films include *Singles*, *Mrs. Parker and the Vicious Circle*, *The Daytrippers*, *Big Night*, and David Mamet's *The Spanish Prisoner*. Although he is married, he retains his status as the thinking woman's sex symbol.

STEVE RUBELL

and partner Ian Schrager co-owned the fabled discothèque Studio 54. They kicked off the age of one-name celebrity—Cher, Andy, Bianca, Liza, and Halston—and rode a miraculous wave of power and pleasure until allegations of tax evasion were made. When they bid farewell on the eve of serving their prison terms, the greatest club of all time had not even been open for three years. When Rubell and Schrager returned to New York City, they opened the wildly successful nightclub The Palladium, and expanded into hotels, including Morgans, the Royalton, and the Paramount. Steve Rubell died in 1989, but his legend lives on.

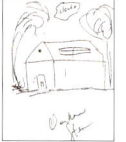
(page 89)

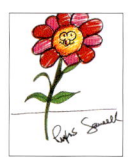
(page 104)

RUFUS SEWELL

has found his niche as a curly-locked and chiseled leading man in such period films as *Cold Comfort Farm*, *Carrington*, and *Dangerous Beauty*. His latest film is the film noir–inspired *Dark City*, directed by Alex Proyas (*The Crow*). He was featured on the cover of *Vanity Fair* magazine in 1998 as an up-and-coming Hollywood talent. Besides seeing him in movies and on magazine covers, Victoria has run into the London native numerous times in New York coffee shops.

RUPAUL

burst on to the 1990s music scene with the release of "Supermodel (You Better Work)," which was a hit on the dance charts and on MTV. RuPaul quickly became a fixture on the television talk-show circuit, propagating a philosophy that combined self-help assertiveness and a good-natured challenge to convention. He recorded an updated version of "Don't Go Breakin' My Heart" with Elton John, but has become best known for his expanding career as the host of *The RuPaul Show* on VH-1 and for his contract with MAC cosmetics. Victoria met Ru at a New York Restoration Project benefit organized by Bette Midler.

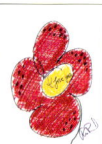
(page 56)

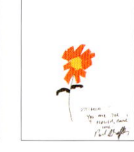
(page 54)

PAUL SHAFFER

is the legendary musical director of *The Late Show with David Letterman*. He first became known as a member of the original band on *Saturday Night Live*. On Broadway, he was musical director for Gilda Radner's hit one-woman show, *Gilda Live*. In the late 1970s he was musical director for two hit Blues Brothers albums and most recently added his creative genius to the soundtrack of the film *The Blues Brothers 2000*. Shaffer is also musical producer of the annual Rock and Roll Hall of Fame induction ceremonies.

SUSAN SAINT JAMES

started her career as a model, but has made her mark as a television star. She won an Emmy for her work on *The Name of the Game*, but she became a household name during her five-year stint with Rock Hudson and Nancy Walker in the popular crime series *McMillan and Wife*. In the 1980s she was one half of the sitcom duo *Kate & Allie* with Jane Curtin. Her film work includes the disco-era vampire hit *Love at First Bite* with George Hamilton and the comedy *Carbon Copy*.

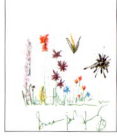
(page 70)

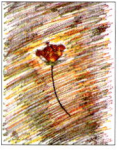
(page 16)

JOHN SHEA

is an actor perhaps best known today for playing the devilish Lex Luther on the international television hit *Lois and Clark: The New Adventures of Superman*. He made his Broadway debut in *Yentl*, which garnered him a Theater World Award, and also played in *The End of the World* and *How I Learned to Drive*. On film he has appeared in Constantin Costa-Gavras's *Missing* as well as in *Windy City* and *A Weekend in the Country*. He won an Emmy award for the television production *Baby M*. In 1998 Shea made his directorial debut with the film *Southies*. His flower actually contains a real rose.

MARTIN SCORSESE

is a director who has created some of the best films of the last twenty-five years. Scorsese first made his mark with the release of the critically acclaimed *Mean Streets* in 1973. He followed this artistic success with the commercially successful releases *Alice Doesn't Live Here Anymore* and *Taxi Driver*. Scorsese's career continues to flourish and has included an astonishing range of movies, from *Raging Bull* to *The Age of Innocence*, from *Cape Fear* to *Kundun*.

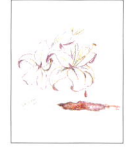
(page 76)

(page 78)

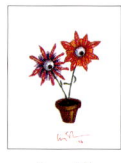
(page 19)

CINDY SHERMAN

is a photographer and filmmaker and one of today's most important visual artists. Her hallmark series *Untitled Film Stills*, a collection of photographs that capture the artist in various guises resembling scenes from B pictures, was purchased by the Museum of Modern Art for a reported $1 million. She was awarded a MacArthur Foundation fellowship grant to continue her work in 1996. In 1997 she released her first feature film, *Office Killers*, a horror movie in which she directed Carol Kane, Molly Ringwald, and Jean Tripplehorn. Her ghoulish flower was started on the set of *Office Killers*.

BIOGRAPHIES

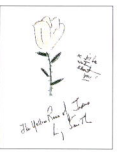

(page 105)

LIZ SMITH

has earned a living as a legal typist, hearing-aid salesperson, bank secretary, press agent, radio and television producer, movie magazine editor, society columnist, film critic, book reviewer, and sports writer. Today she is a gossip columnist whose syndicated writings are read by forty million Americans. Smith wrote a nonfiction book entitled *The Mother Book*. The Texas native drew that state's flower, a yellow rose, and signed it, "I'll be writing about you." We'll see....

(page 71)

ALEX TAVOULARIS

is a Hollywood production designer for some of the decade's edgiest films, including William Friedkin's *Jade*, Abel Ferrara's *Dangerous Games* and *King of New York*, and Paul Bartel's *Scenes from the Class Struggle in Beverly Hills*. Switching gears, he was production designer for *Beethoven* and art director on the Disney remake *The Parent Trap*. His original story boards for *Star Wars* appear in the book *The Art of Star Wars*, and Francis Ford Coppola had him paint the dramatic portrait for the poster for the re-release of the classic *Napoleon*.

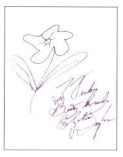

(page 34)

REX SMITH

became a teen heartthrob in the late 1970s with the release of his pop album *Sooner or Later* and the television movie of the same name. In addition to his recording career, he has appeared on Broadway in *Grease*, *The Pirates of Penzance*, and *Grand Hotel*. On television he starred as the host of the syndicated music review *Solid Gold*. Smith has also appeared in the made-for-TV movie *Perry Mason: The Case of the Silenced Singer* and the 1994 film *A Passion to Kill*.

(page 39)

ELIZABETH TAYLOR

has maintained undeniable star stature for more than forty years. Her personality and legend are so immense that sometimes the brilliance of her best onscreen work is overlooked. Some of her memorable films include *National Velvet*, *A Place in the Sun*, *Cat on a Hot Tin Roof*, and *Cleopatra*, and she won Oscars for her performances in *Butterfield 8* and *Who's Afraid of Virginia Woolf?* More recently Taylor has used her indomitable grit and determination, along with the power of her celebrity, in the battle against AIDS.

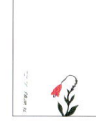

(page 37)

STEPHEN SPROUSE

is a fashion designer known for outlandish outfits that have been worn by rock stars and those unafraid to make a statement. His first runway collection, in 1983, featured all Day-Glo and post-psychedelic Pop art tailorings inspired by the work of Andy Warhol. Sprouse continues to make an impact in the fashion world with his use of Warhol imagery, wild colors, and hi-tech fabrics. His flower is a perfect example of his work—beautiful and striking.

(page 68)

LILI TAYLOR

has turned in memorable performances in several Hollywood movies, including *Born on the Fourth of July* and *Ransom*. However, this queen of the indie film has truly shone in such arthouse films as *Arizona Dream* and *I Shot Andy Warhol*, in which she played Valerie Solanas. Originally a stage actress, Lili is a founding member of the New York–based theater company Naked Angels. One night at a party in L.A. she sat in a dark booth and drew this flower.

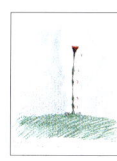

(page 69)

PATRICK STEWART

is known throughout the world as Captain Jean-Luc Picard of the *Starship Enterprise* in the wildly popular *Star Trek: The Next Generation*. However, he is also a highly respected British stage actor. He began touring with the London Old Vic Theatre Company alongside legendary actress Vivien Leigh in productions of Alexandre Dumas's *Lady of the Camellias* and Shakespeare's *Twelfth Night*. He later joined the prestigious Royal Shakespeare Company where he remained for over two decades. Stewart remains active in theater and television, and has appeared recently in the films *Jeffrey*, *Masterminds*, and *Conspiracy Theory*.

(page 88)

ROLAND TOPOR

was a major artist of the twentieth century, who put his ferocious humor into his painting, writing, acting, designing, and directing. His many novels include *Le Locataire Chimerique*, which was later filmed as *The Tenant* by Roman Polanski. In 1973, he was celebrated at the Cannes Film Festival for the characters he drew and built for the full-length animated feature *La Planete Sauvage*. Topor was awarded the prestigious Grand Prix National des Arts Graphiques. Victoria was delighted to receive an offer to visit Topor's Paris studio after she met him on a boat on the Seine.

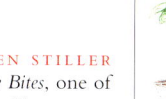

(page 87)

BEN STILLER

made his film directing debut with *Reality Bites*, one of the first films really to capture the Gen-X moment. Several of the film's actors, including Wynona Ryder, Janeane Garofalo, and Ethan Hawke, went on to become majors stars, and the soundtrack was a huge success. After a season on *Saturday Night Live*, he starred in the *Ben Stiller Show* which earned him an Emmy. Stiller's acting credits include the films *If Lucy Fell*, *Happy Gilmore*, *Flirting with Disaster*, and *Zero Effect*. In 1996 he directed the darkly funny *Cable Guy* starring Jim Carrey.

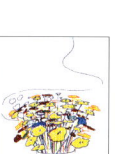

(page 33)

GUS VAN SANT

is a textbook example of an independent film auteur making it in Hollywood. He is famous for pulling the performance of a lifetime out of the actors he directs, including Matt Dillon in *Drugstore Cowboy*, River Phoenix in *My Own Private Idaho*, and Nicole Kidman in *To Die For*. Perhaps the greatest example of this strength to date is the movie *Good Will Hunting*, which turned both Matt Damon and Ben Affleck into household names and gave four-time Academy Award nominee Robin Williams his first win.

BIOGRAPHIES

VIVA

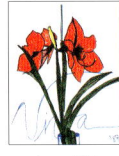
(page 102)

was the vamp with high cheekbones featured in many of Andy Warhol's underground movies of the 1960s. Along with Edie Sedgwick, Ultra Violet, and Joe Dallesandro, she made up Andy's legendary stable of Superstars. Viva lived in the Chelsea Hotel for thirty-two years and it was there that she began to develop her skills as a writer and painter. With her friend Jane Lancelotti she co-authored a book entitled *Gaby at the Chelsea*, casting her daughter Gaby Hoffman as a modern-day Eloise. Viva drew the amaryllis that author Jean Stein sent to her on the death of Andy Warhol.

ANDY WARHOL

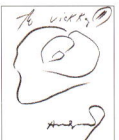
(page 15) *(page 116)*

was a modern genius who could look at a can of soup and see instead an image that would revolutionize the world's concept of art. His life was the ultimate celebration of celebrity—a continuous round of parties, galas, interviews, art openings, and evenings spent at glamorous restaurants and clubs. He had dozens of museum shows, was a filmmaker, author, and the founder of *Interview* magazine. His protégés include Keith Haring and Jean-Michel Basquiat. There would be no flower book without him.

BARBARA WALTERS

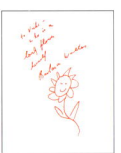
(page 32)

is America's first lady of television journalism. She rose to stardom as co-anchor of NBC's *Today* show in the mid-1960s. In 1976 she made headlines when she moved to ABC to become the first network anchorwoman and one of the highest-paid journalists in the world. *The Barbara Walters Special* has set the standard for celebrity interviews for over twenty years and has become a tradition for preshow Oscar viewers. In 1985 she became co-host of the popular news magazine *20/20*.

JANN WENNER

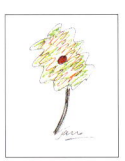
(page 26)

began a quirky, rock music–oriented biweekly called *Rolling Stone* in 1967 and changed American culture. Treating the interests of America's increasingly vocal youth with a seriousness unknown before, *Rolling Stone* spoke to and for an entire generation. Today the magazine continues to reign at the forefront of American journalism, and Wenner is also the publisher of *US: The Entertainment Magazine* and *Men's Journal*. Victoria edited Jann's home movies for almost a decade, and commissioned Jonathan Larson to compose original songs for Wenner's three sons, Alexander, Theo, and Gus.

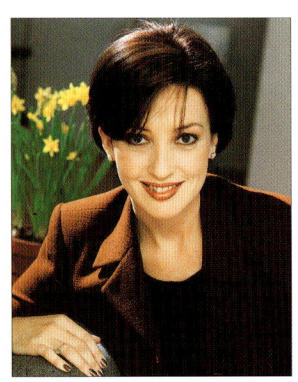

VICTORIA LEACOCK

is a filmmaker, writer, and theatrical producer. Her award-winning films include *The Dead Speak*, based on Douglas Coupland's *Generation X* and *Life After God*, which commemorated the fiftieth anniversary of the bombing of Hiroshima, and the musical extravaganza *Kiki and Herb: Total Eclipse of the Heart*. She spent a year chronicling the daily drama in a doctor's office in Juan Botas's AIDS documentary *One Foot on a Banana Peel, the Other Foot in the Grave* produced by Jonathan Demme, and she has toured with the Ramones and Blondie for MTV News. Her articles have appeared in *Interview*, *Paper*, and the *New York Post*, and she illustrated Christina Oxenberg's book *Taxi*. For more than a decade she worked exclusively on productions with Jonathan Larson, including early development of his musical *Rent*. Since 1992 she has lectured to thousands of young people on AIDS awareness and prevention through Love Heals, the Alison Gertz Foundation for AIDS Education, which she co-founded. *Signature Flowers* is her first book.

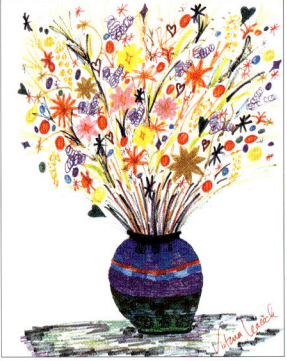

ACKNOWLEDGMENTS

This book would not be what it is without the love, support, and participation of Molly Ringwald and Justin Bond. I can never thank you enough for helping me finish this project of almost twenty years. I love you both. I am also grateful to Diana Barrows, who invited me to so many wonderful parties and events when I was a teenager and whose friendship means a great deal to me. I thank Bill Boggs for giving me total access backstage at his talk show *Midday Live* in the early 1980s, which helped me meet many of the wonderful artists in this book. I appreciate the many friends who became involved with helping me reach people, especially Brad Boles, Anthony Ciccone and Merrie Lawson, Dana Giacchetto, Bob Guccione, Jr., Christina Oxenberg, Susan Povich, and Lynda Wells. Valery Lameignère and Ingrid Sischy, I am grateful for your contributions. And special thanks to Gillian Sowell for working so hard on the book and to Charlie Melcher for his enthusiasm: you both helped me realize my dream. Thanks to Sandy Rower for helping me find John Klotnia and Pentagram, who made my book look like my book. Also thanks to Broadway Books for believing in my flowers and giving me the opportunity to share them with everyone. I thank my friends and family, especially Louise and Peter Rogers, and Valerie Lalonde and my dad, for their love and support.

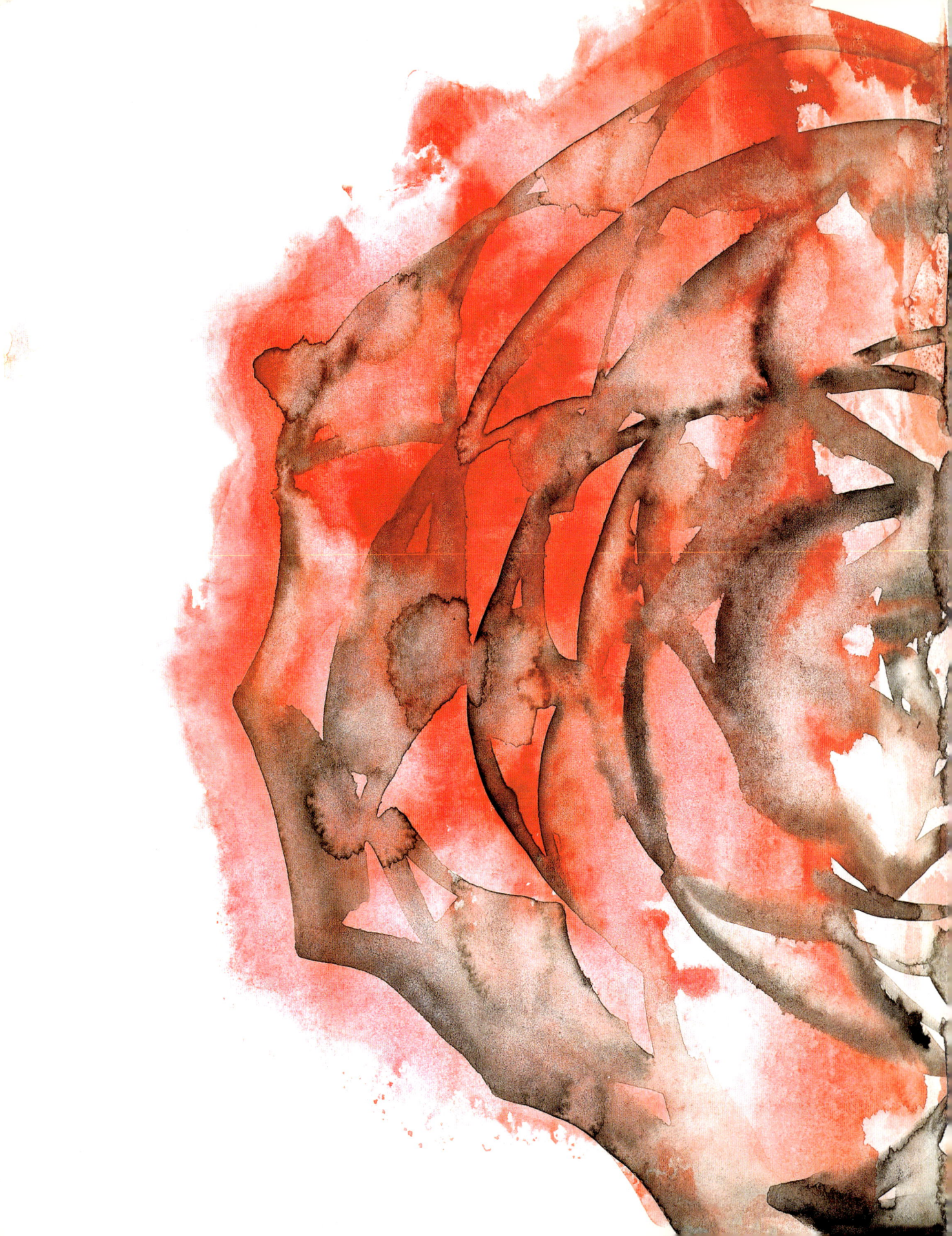